*Gods in
Everyman*

OTHER BOOKS BY JEAN SHINODA BOLEN

The Tao of Psychology

Goddesses in Everywoman

Gods in Everyman

A New Psychology of Men's Lives and Loves

Jean Shinoda Bolen, M.D.

1817

Harper & Row, Publishers, San Francisco

New York, Cambridge, Philadelphia, St. Louis
London, Singapore, Sydney, Tokyo

FIRST EDITION

Library of Congress Cataloging-in-Publication Data

Bolen, Jean Shinoda.
   Gods in everyman.

   Bibliography: p.
   Includes index.
   1. Men—Psychology. 2. Archetype (Psychology)
3. Gods, Greek—Psychology. 4. Mythology, Greek—
Religious aspects. I. Title.
BF692.5.B64 1989   155.6′32   88-45663
ISBN 0-06-250098-8

89 90 91 92 93 WAK 10 9 8 7 6 5 4 3 2 1

Contents

Preface

As the author of *Goddesses in Everywoman,* I've often been asked about the gods in men. Men who have heard me lecture on the goddesses have repeatedly asked, "What about *us?*" *Gods in Everyman* is thus a natural sequel to my previous book; but my profession, the historical time, and (paradoxically) being a woman also have prompted me to write this book about the archetypes in men.

In writing this book, I'm a woman doing what women traditionally have done for men. Women have served as interpreters of the inner lives of their men, because men often share with women what they do not usually share with each other. Many men, for example, choose women psychiatrists because they feel safer and find it easier to talk with a woman. Some men say that they want to avoid the competitive feelings and consequences that they fear might arise in themselves or in a male therapist.

And sometimes a significant woman may play an important role as "dream carrier" in the life of a successful man, as psychologist Daniel Levinson noted in his book *The Seasons of a Man's Life:* This is also a role in which a woman Jungian analyst is sometimes cast. In psychoanalysis, men share their inner lives, and find their vulnerabilities and their strengths. As they gain insight into themselves, they teach me. I see who the man is under the surface, and come to know the archetypes in him, and the difficulties he may have in being himself and feeling authentic. Levinson wrote,

> The special woman is like the true mentor: her special quality lies in her connection to the young man's Dream. She helps animate the part of the self that contains the Dream. She facilitates his entry into the adult world and his pursuit of the Dream. She does this partly through her own actual efforts as teacher, guide, host, critic, sponsor. At a deeper psychological level she enables him to project onto her his own internal feminine figure—the 'anima,' as

Jung has depicted it—who generates and supports his heroic strivings.[1]

For many reasons, many men often do feel more understood by women than by other men, and reveal more of themselves to women than they do to each other. As the *McGill Report on Male Intimacy* testifies,

> One man in ten has a male friend with whom he discusses work, money, marriage; only one in more than twenty has a friendship where he discloses his feelings about himself or his sexual feelings. . . . The most common male friendship pattern is for a man to have many "friends," each of whom knows something of the man's public self and therefore a little about him, but not one of whom knows more than a small piece of the whole.[2]

McGill found that if a man reveals himself at all it is likely to be to a woman, sometimes to his wife or to another woman. As most women suspect, men are much more likely to tell their feelings, thoughts, and dreams to them, than to each other.

Also, as Jean Baker Miller noted in *Toward a New Psychology of Women,* whenever there is a superior and inferior group (male, female; white, black; rich employers, poor servants), the less empowered group out of necessity studies the other and knows more about them than vice versa. Because of this, as well as the people-oriented nature of most women, women have forever been attentive observers of men.[3]

Gods in Everyman is thus a psychology of men as seen by a woman who is doing what women have done over the ages for men they have cared about: reflecting back what she sees, and being aware of the need for sensitivity as she describes men's flaws and problems and of the importance of appreciating their positive qualities. The perspective of this book is that of a compassionate observer, a perspective that I've gained through professional and personal experience.

I am a psychiatrist and Jungian analyst and a clinical professor of psychiatry at the University of California, San Francisco. I have men as well as women as clients in my private practice and I'm a woman in a male profession with male mentors, friends, and colleagues. In turn, I have mentored and taught men as well as women.

In addition, I was an affirmed "father's daughter," a "Daddy's little girl," whose father took pride in my accomplishments. As a consequence, I found it easier than many women to find validation in this patriarchal culture. I was also a wife for nineteen years in a marriage that had both traditional and egalitarian roots, separated for three years and then divorced. And I am the mother of a son and a daughter, both born at the beginning of the seventies, the decade of the women's movement, when issues of stereotypes—of nurture over nature—were most strongly voiced.

A BINOCULAR VISION OF PSYCHOLOGY

Gods in Everyman provides a "binocular vision" of psychology, a depth perspective that takes both powerful inner archetypes and conformity-demanding stereotypes into consideration in an effort to understand where our conflicts lie and how we might better achieve wholeness.

This perspective has grown out of my professional training and personal experience. My practice has developed my awareness of what goes on inside men and women's hearts and heads, of the joy that comes from having a sense of wholeness and integration when what we do is consistent with who we are. Conversely, our bodies and dreams and symptoms express conflict and pain when what is archetypally true is consciously denied and repressed. What these archetypes are, and how they are expressed in individual lives, becomes clearer only after years of in-depth work in psychology.

Also essential is an understanding of what the women's movement called "consciousness raising." In the past two decades, we have learned how stereotypes can distort and limit human potential—specifically, women's. In this period, many women became aware of the how living in a patriarchal culture affects them personally. Everyone's values and beliefs are shaped by culture, which is reflected in our laws and customs, affects how power is distributed and how worth and status are determined. In a patriarchal society, women do not fare well. But male stereotypes also hold power over men, limiting who they can comfortably be by rewarding some qualities and rejecting others.

GODS AND GODDESSES IN EVERYPERSON

When I speak about gods in Everyman, I discover that women often find that a particular *god* exists in them as well, just as I found that when I spoke about goddesses men could identify a part of themselves with a specific *goddess*. Gods and goddesses represent different qualities in the human psyche. The pantheon of Greek deities together, male and female, exist as archetypes in us all, although the gods are usually the strongest and most influential determinants of a man's personality, as the goddesses are for women.

Every archetype is associated with particular "god-given" or "goddess-given" gifts and potential problems. Appreciating that this is so makes either arrogance or self-blame less likely. And because whatever we do that arises out of our archetypal depths has meaning for us, a man who knows which god or gods are active in him may be able to make choices knowing which options or directions are likely to be personally more satisfying.

Reading about the gods sometimes turns out to be a means of "re-membering" cut-off (dismembered) parts of ourselves. This process may be also aided by dreams, memories, and myths that tap into our unconscious.

Learning about the different Gods in Everyman is also important to women, many of whom put a great deal of effort into trying to understand men (usually one particular man at a time). Psychologically minded women sometimes realize that they repeatedly get involved with a particular type of man, and they sense that they really need to know "who" attracts them. The Gods in Everyman can tell them they have been drawn to a particular god or archetype in a series of men, and this "god" is not compatible with their expectations, which explains why their relationships repeatedly have unhappy endings.

Insight into the "gods" provides parents of boys (especially single mothers) with a means of seeing and appreciating "who" their sons are. The net result is a parent who feels more competent because she (or he) understands what it's like to be her particular son, how the world is likely to treat him, what his strengths and difficulties may be, and where he can use some help.

Both men and women also need to see their fathers clearly, often in order to forgive them, as much as to understand them. Understanding the gods and their myths may provide an objective picture of the father.

And because there are "gods" in women too, women can gain self-knowledge from knowing the gods. The "Aha!" of recognition may be particularly appreciated by a woman who is already familiar with the "goddesses," and who now finds that a particular god explains part of her own behavior. She can grasp the satisfaction that we all feel when a jigsaw puzzle piece fits just so—especially when it is the missing piece, the one that completes the picture and makes sense of a life.

There are gods and goddesses in every person. Through them, you glean that moment of insight when something you intuitively know about yourself connects with a clear image and articulate words. Like looking into a mirror and seeing our own features for the first time, this flash can reveal what others react to in you, and show you to yourself more clearly.

I wrote this book for anyone who wants to understand boys and men better, or know about male archetypes in both men and women, or discover something about themselves and their relationships. I wrote it especially for men who want to discover the gods within, for those men who asked me "what about the gods in Every*man*? What about *us*?"

Acknowledgments

Every chapter in this book has many unnamed contributors—patients, friends, colleagues, relatives, every significant man or boy in my life—who by being himself exemplified aspects of a god archetype, or helped me to understand what it's like to be a boy or man in this patriarchal culture. Over the years, women have told me about the men they were close to, sometimes seeming to know them—especially the unreflective men—better than the men knew themselves. Major contributions were made by men who delved deeply with me in Jungian analysis to discover feelings, history, and parts of themselves that they themselves did not initially know, and were cut off from.

Most descriptions are therefore composites of many men, whom I knew under many circumstances; especially through my twenty-five years of psychiatric practice. My work is done within a *temenos* (greek for "sanctuary") of trust, safety, and confidentiality. Here, what was unconscious or unremembered is revealed over time. Each man who has trusted me with his psyche, has taught me more about the psychology of other men and women, including myself. Thank you.

Throughout the book, I have used historical figures, celebrities, and fictional characters to describe a particular facet of a god. I have drawn from the public image of the person and how he has been quoted, not from personal or professional knowledge. Real people usually turn out to be more than and less than their larger-than-life images.

Both this book and *Goddesses in Everywoman* grow out of the discoveries and theories of C. G. Jung. His work on the archetypes of the collective unconscious and on psychological types laid the foundation for my work. Sigmund Freud's description of the Oedipus complex suggested the link between Greek myths and the psyche, which Jungian writers then have developed much further. Much of what has been written about archetypal psychology since Jung has been published through Spring Publications, and much of this has been under the editorship of James Hillman. Many of these publications are listed in the chapter notes and bibliography; Murray Stein's work has been especially important to me.

The growing awareness of the patriarchal culture in which we live—and how it has shaped values, perceptions, and ultimately each one of us—is a major theme in this book, for which there is a whole generation of activists, writers, and scholars to thank, mostly women. For my particular education, I am especially indebted to Gloria Steinem and the Ms. Foundation for Women board and staff; to Jean Baker Miller, M.D., and Alexandra Symonds, M.D., and to women who were members of the Task Force and Committees on Women of the American Psychiatric Association. Anthea Francine, with whom I have co-led numerous workshops, deepened my sensitivity to the effect of family and culture on the child, especially on those whose archetypes are not valued. Alice Miller's writings provided a new perspective in psychoanalytic thinking, which confirmed what I already knew about children and the effect of being damaged by damaged parents.

This book has had a very easy labor and delivery, because it was allowed to emerge in its own time, taking the seasons of my life into consideration instead of the initial contract date. I thank my publisher and editor at Harper & Row, Clayton Carlson, for the gifts of understanding and time, and for assigning Tom Grady to work with me. Tom's sensitive editorial hand has been just right. John Brockman and Katinka Matson, my literary agents, by looking after what they do so well, help me be an author.

My father, Joseph Shinoda, gave me his support to do things in the world. I inherited his intensity, partisanship, literary and historical bent, and ability to write and speak. He died in the first year of my psychiatric residency, and so never knew my children and books. I miss him, and know that although our time together was shorter than I would have liked, I have been fortunate to be my particular father's daughter. This book has warmth and insight partly because I had a successful Zeus father whom I could oppose and struggle against when what mattered to me and what he wanted of me differed.

Mill Valley, California
November 1988

PART I

Gods in Everyman

1.

There Are Gods In Everyman

This book is about the gods in Everyman, the innate patterns—or archetypes—that lie deep within the psyche, shaping
men from within. These gods are powerful, invisible predispositions that affect personality, work, and relationships. The gods
have to do with emotional intensity or distance, preferences for
mental acuity, physical exertion, or esthetic sensibility, yearning
for ecstatic merger or panoramic understanding, sense of time,
and much more. Different archetypes are responsible for the
diversity among, and complexity within, men and have much to
do with the ease or difficulty with which men (and boys) can
conform to expectations and at what cost to their deepest and
most authentic selves.

To feel authentic means to be free to develop traits and
potentials that are innate predispositions. When we are accepted
and allowed to be genuine, it's possible to have self-esteem and
authenticity together. This develops only if we are encouraged
rather than disheartened by the reactions of significant others
to us, when we are spontaneous and truthful, or when we are
absorbed in whatever gives us joy. From childhood on, first our
family and then our culture are the mirrors in which we see
ourselves as acceptable or not. When we need to conform in
order to be acceptable, we may end up wearing a false face and
playing an empty role if who we are inside and what is expected
of us are far apart.

CONFORMITY AS A PROCRUSTEAN BED

The conformity demanded of men in our patriarchal culture is like Procrustes' bed in Greek mythology. Travelers on their way to Athens were placed on this bed. If they were too short, they were stretched to fit, as on a medieval torture rack; if they were too tall, they were merely cut down to size.

Some men fit the Procrustean bed exactly, just as there are men for whom stereotype (or the expectations from outside) and archetype (or the inner patterns) match well. They find ease and pleasure at succeeding. However, conformity to the stereotype is often an agonizing process for a man whose archetypal patterns differ from "what he should be." He may appear to fit, but in truth he has managed at great cost to look the part, by cutting off important aspects of himself. Or he may have stretched one dimension of his personality to fit expectations but lacks depth and complexity, which often make his outer success inwardly meaningless.

Travelers who passed through the Procrustean ordeal to reach Athens may have wondered whether it had been worthwhile—as contemporary men often do after they "arrive." William Broyles, Jr., writing in *Esquire*, wearily described how empty success can be:

> Each morning I struggled into my suit, picked up my briefcase, went to my glamorous job, and died a little. I was the editor in chief of *Newsweek*, a position that in the eyes of others had everything; only it had nothing to do with me. I took little pleasure in running a large institution. I wanted personal achievement, not power. For me, success was more dangerous than failure; failure would have forced me to decide what I really wanted.
>
> The only way out was to quit, but I hadn't quit anything since I abandoned the track team in high school. I had also been a Marine in Vietnam, and Marines are trained to keep on charging up the hill, no matter what. But I had got up the hill; I just hated being there. I had climbed the wrong mountain, and the only thing to do was go down and climb another one. It was not easy: my writing went more slowly than I had expected, and my marriage fell apart.
>
> I needed something, but I wasn't sure what. I knew I wanted to be tested, mentally and physically. I wanted to succeed, but by standards that were clear and concrete, and not dependent on the

4

opinion of others. I wanted the intensity and camaraderie of a dangerous enterprise. In an earlier time, I might have gone west or to sea, but I had two children and a web of responsibilities.

This man had power and prestige, goals that take the better part of a man's life to achieve and that relatively few actually succeed in reaching. But, he suffered from the major ailment I see in many men in midlife: a pervasive low-grade depression. When you are cut off from your own sources of vitality and joy, life feels flat and meaningless.

In this culture, men have the upper hand and seem to have the better roles. Certainly they have the more powerful or remunerative ones. Yet many men suffer from depression masked by alcohol, or by excessive work, or hours of television, all of which are numbing. And many more are angry and resentful, their hostility and rage touched off by anything from the way someone else drives in traffic to the irritating behavior of a child. They suffer a shorter life expectancy, too. The women's movement clearly articulated the problems women have living in a patriarchy; but judging from how unhappy many men are, living in a patriarchy seems to be bad for them, too.

THE INNER WORLD OF ARCHETYPES

When life feels meaningless and stale, or when something feels fundamentally wrong about how you are living and what you are doing, you can help yourself by becoming aware of discrepancies between the archetypes within you and your visible roles. Men are often caught between the inner world of archetypes and the outer world of stereotypes. Archetypes are powerful predispositions; garbed in the image and mythology of Greek gods, as I have described them in this book, each has characteristic drives, emotions, and needs that shape personality. When you enact a role that is connected to an active archetype within you, energy is generated through the depth and meaning that the role has for you.

If, for example, you are like Hephaestus the Craftsman and Inventor, God of the Forge, who made beautiful armor and jewelry, then you can spend solitary hours in your workshop, studio or laboratory intensely absorbed in what you are doing, and doing it to meet the highest standards. But if you are innately like Hermes, the Messenger God, then you are naturally a man on the move. Whether a traveling salesman or an international negotiator, you love what you do, and what you do takes a nimble mind, especially when you find yourself as you are prone to, in gray ethical areas. If you are like either one of these gods, and had to do the other's job, work would cease being an absorbing pleasure. For work is a source of satisfaction only when it coincides with your particular archetypal nature and talents.

Differences in personal life are shaped by archetypes as well. A man who resembles Dionysus, the Ecstatic God, can be totally absorbed in the sensuality of the moment, when nothing is more important than being the spontaneous lover. He contrasts with the man who, like Apollo, God of the Sun, works at mastering skills and becoming an expert in technique of all kinds, which might include making love.

As archetypes, the "gods" exist as patterns governing emotions and behavior; they are powerful forces that demand their due, recognized or not. Consciously recognized (though not necessarily named) and honored by the man (or woman) in whom they exist, these gods help the man really be himself, motivating him to lead a deeply meaningful life because what he does is connected to the archetypal layer of his psyche. Dishonored and denied gods nonetheless also have an influence, which is usually disruptive, as they exert an unconscious claim on the man. Distorted identification can also harm you; sometimes, for example, a man may so identify with one god that he loses his own individuality, becoming "possessed."

WHAT AN ARCHETYPE IS

C. G. Jung introduced the concept of archetypes into psychology. Archetypes are preexistent, or latent, internally determined patterns of being and behaving, of perceiving and responding. These patterns are contained in a collective unconscious—that part of the unconscious that is not individual, but universal or shared. These patterns can be described in a personalized way, as gods and goddesses; their myths are archetypal stories. They evoke feelings and images, and touch on themes that are universal and part of our human inheritance. They ring true to our shared human experience; so they seem vaguely familiar even when heard for the first time. And when you interpret a myth about a god, or grasp its meaning intellectually or intuitively as bearing on your own life, it can have the impact of a personal dream that illuminates a situation and your own character, or the character of someone you know.

As archetypal figures, the gods are like anything generic: they describe the basic structure of this part of a man (or of a woman, for god archetypes are often active women's psyches as well). This basic structure is "clothed" or "fleshed out" or "detailed" by the individual man, whose uniqueness is shaped by family, class, nationality, religion, life experiences, and the time in which he lives, his physical appearance, and intelligence. Yet you can still recognize him as following a particular archetypal pattern, as resembling a particular god.

Because archetypal images are part of our collective human inheritance; they are "familiar." Myths from Greece that go back over 3,000 years stay alive, are told and retold, because the gods and goddesses speak to us truths about human nature. Learning about these Greek gods can help men understand better who or what is acting deep within their psyches. And women can learn to know men better by knowing which gods are acting in the significant men in their lives as well as by finding that a particular "god" may be part of their own psyches. Myths provide the possibility of an "Aha!" insight: something rings true and we intuitively grasp the nature of a human situation more deeply.

The resemblance to Zeus, for example, is strikingly obvious in men who can be ruthless, who take risks in order to accumulate power and wealth, and who want to be highly visible once they achieve status. The stories about Zeus also often fit the men who are identified with him. For example, their marital and sexual lives may resemble Zeus's philandering. The eagle, associated with Zeus, symbolizes characteristics of the archetype: from his lofty position, he has an overview perspective, an eye for detail, and the ability to act swiftly to grasp what he wants with his talons.

Hermes, the Messenger God, was the communicator, trickster, guide of souls to the underworld, and the god of roads and boundaries. A man who embodies this archetype will find settling down difficult, because he responds to the lure of the open road and the next opportunity. Like quicksilver or mercury (his Roman name is Mercury), this man slips through the fingers of people who want to grasp or hold on to him.

Zeus and Hermes are very different patterns, and the men who resemble each god differ from each other. But since all the archetypes are potentially present in every man, both the Zeus and Hermes archetypes can also be active in the same man. With these two acting within him in a balanced way he may be able to establish himself, which is a Zeus priority, with the aid of Hermes' communication skills and innovative ideas. Or he may find himself in psychic conflict, seesawing between the Zeus in him who seeks power, which takes time and commitment, and Hermes' need for freedom. These are just two of the god archetypes that are positively valued in a patriarchal culture.

The gods that were denigrated—the rejected ones, whose attributes were not valued then and are not now—are also still active in men's psyches, as they were in Greek mythology. There was prejudice against them as gods; Western culture has a similar negative bias against them as archetypes in human psyches—the sensuality and passion of Dionysus, the frenzy of Ares on the battlefield that might under other circumstances have as easily gone into dance, the emotionality of Poseidon, the withdrawn intense creativity of a Hephaestus, the introspective focus of Hades. This continuing bias affects the psychology of individual men, who may repress these aspects in themselves in an effort to conform to cultural values that reward emotional distance and coolness and the acquisition of power.

Whether working, making war, or making love, when you are just conforming to what is expected of you, and no archetypal energy inspires you, you will expend too much energy and effort. Your effort may have its rewards, but will not be deeply satisfying. In contrast, doing what you love affirms you inwardly and gives you pleasure; it is consistent with who you are. You are indeed fortunate if what you do is also rewarded and recognized in the outer world.

ACTIVATING THE GODS

All the gods are potential patterns in the psyches of all men, yet in each individual man some of these patterns are activated (energized or developed) and others are not. Jung used the formation of crystals as an analogy to help explain the difference between *archetypal patterns* (which are universal) and *activated archetypes* (which are functioning in us). An archetype is like the invisible pattern that determines what shape and structure a crystal will take when it does form. Once the crystal actually forms, the now recognizable pattern is analogous to an activated archetype.

Archetypes might also be compared to the "blueprints" contained in seeds. Growth from seeds depends on soil and climate conditions, the presence or absence of certain nutrients, loving care or neglect on the part of gardeners, the size and depth of the container, and the hardiness of the variety itself. A seed may not grow at all, or not survive after it has sent out its first shoots. If it does, it may grow magnificently or be stunted, perhaps due to conditions that are far from optimal. Circumstance will affect the particular appearance of what grows from the seed, but the basic form or identity of the plant—like an archetype—will still be recognizable.

Archetypes are basic human patterns, some of which are innately stronger in some people than in others, as are such human qualities as musical aptitude, an innate sense of time, psychic ability, physical coordination, or intellect. As humans, we all have some musical potential, for example, but some individuals (like Mozart) are child prodigies, and others (like me) have trouble repeating a simple tune. So it is with archetypal patterns. Some men seem to embody a particular archetype from Day One and stay pretty much on this course throughout their lives; or an archetype may emerge in another man in the middle years of his life, for example, if he precipitously falls in love and suddenly knows Dionysus.

INHERENT PREDISPOSITION AND FAMILY EXPECTATIONS

Babies are born with personality traits—they are energetic, willful, placid, curious, able to spend time alone, or wanting the company of others. Physical activity, energy, and attitude differs from boy to boy: a newborn whose lusty cry has an unmistakable power to demand what he wants right now, and who by age two physically hurls himself into every activity is a very different child from the sunny, agreeable toddler who seems to be the soul of reasonableness even at his young age. They are as different as intense instinctively physical Ares and even-tempered, friendly Hermes.

As an infant, as a boy, and finally as a man, actions and attitudes that begin as inherent predispositions or archetypal patterns are judged and reacted to through the approval, disapproval, anxiety, pride, and shame of others. The expectations of a child's family support some archetypes and devalue others, and hence those qualities in their sons, or the very nature of that boy himself. The ambitious two-career upwardly mobile couple who learned that "It's a boy" from the amniocentesis, may await the birth of their son, whom they anticipate as a Harvard freshman. They expect a personable son who can focus his intellectual efforts on a far-distant target. A son who is archetypally like Apollo or Zeus will fit the bill nicely, please his parents, and do well in the world. But if the child who comes is archetypally someone else, disappointment and anger at his inability to meet their expectations are likely. An emotional Poseidon, or Dionysus with his here-and-now sense of time, will have problems conforming to the program his parents have for him. And this mismatch will probabably adversely affect his self-esteem.

Often one child in a family doesn't "fit" into the family assumptions or style. A child who values solitude, like Hades, or emotional distance, like Apollo, is not only intruded on all the time, but also may be considered weird by his extraverted*, expressive family. The Poseidon or Ares boy, who would be at home in this kind of family, is odd man out in a coolly rational, physically undemonstrative family, his needs for contact disapproved of and left unfilled.

In some families, there are expectations that a boy be like his father and follow his footsteps. In others, where the father

---

*The psychological concept of extraversion (*extra* in Latin means "outside") and introversion, and the words *extravert* and *introvert* were introduced by C. G. Jung. Both the spelling and the meaning have become slightly altered in general usage. "Extrovert" has become the more common spelling, used to describe a person with a friendly or sociable persona.

Jung used "extravert" to describe an attitude characterized by a flow of psychic energy toward the outer world or toward the object, leading to an interest in events, people, and things and a dependency on them. For the introvert, the flow of psychic energy is inward, the concentration is on subjective factors and inner repsonses.

himself is a disappointment, whatever traits the son shares with his father bring down on him the anger and negativity that others feel toward the father. Then there are expectations that he live out failed dreams that belonged to a parent. Whatever expectations are held for him will interact with what is present archetypally and possible to shape.

If a boy or man tries to conform to what is expected of him, at the cost of sacrificing his connection to his own truest nature, he may succeed in the world and find it meaningless to him personally, or fail there as well, after failing to keep faith with what was true for him. In contrast, if he is accepted for who he is and yet he realizes that it is important to develop the social or competitive skills he'll need, then his adaptation to the world is achieved not at the cost of his authenticity and self-esteem, but helps to round him out.

PEOPLE AND EVENTS ACTIVATE GODS

A reaction that is archetypically or "typical" of a particular god may become activated—or, to use a Jungian term, *constellated*—by another person or an event. For example, a son who comes home with a black eye could without saying a word provoke one father into being a grudge-bearing, vengeful Poseidon who feels an immediate need to get back at whomever did this to *his* son. But the same black eye might evoke contempt towards the son for having gotten in a fistfight at all, if his father reacts as Zeus did toward his son Ares. When Ares was hurt, Zeus was not only unsympathetic but judgmental; he berated his son for being a whiner, and he took the opportunity to say how detestable and quarrelsome Ares was.

Infidelity likewise provokes a range of reactions. What happens in a man when he finds that his wife is unfaithful, or the woman he considers "his," has another lover (even though he may be married and this is an affair)? Does he become like Zeus and try to destroy the other man? Or does he want to destroy the woman, as Apollo did? Or does he want to know the details, as would Hermes? Or does he think up intricate ways of catching the couple and exposing them to public scrutiny, like Hephaestus?

Wider historical circumstances can provide the situation that activates a god in a generation of men. For example, young men with a Dionysian penchant to seek ecstatic experience experimented with psychedelic drugs in the 1960s. Many became psychiatric casualties; many others felt spiritually enlightened. Men who would not ordinarily have had Dionysus in them, did then, and as a result are now more sensual and esthetically aware than they would have been otherwise.

Men who were in the armed services in Vietnam may have volunteered because they identified with Ares, God of War. Or they may have been unhappy draftees. In either case, the situation could activate aspects of Ares. Some men experienced positive bonding, loyalty, and a depth of connection to men that they might otherwise never have felt. Other men became "possessed" by the blind fury of an Ares run amok, perhaps after a buddy was ambushed by a booby trap, or were swept along by an Ares group psychology; as a result, men, who under ordinary circumstances might not even have been in a bar brawl, may have committed atrocities or killed civilians.

"DOING" ACTIVATES GODS: NOT "DOING" INHIBITS THEM

Goal focus and clarity of thought are culturally rewarded qualities that come naturally to men who are like Apollo the archer, whose golden arrows could hit a distant target. Everyone else is schooled to acquire these skills, especially when the emphasis is on the need to do well now in order to get somewhere later.

In contrast, the Dionysian boy has undervalued natural gifts: he can easily become absorbed in the sensory world and be totally caught up in the immediate present. As a youngster, when he delighted in the touch of velvet and silk, or danced to music with his whole body, he was tapping an innate sensuality that probably was not encouraged in him, much less part of required learning for all boys.

There is a saying, "Doing is becoming," that very clearly expresses how gods can be evoked or developed by a chosen course of action. The question so often is "Will you take the time?" For example, a businessman may realize how much pleasure he gets from working with his hands—he can spend hours absorbed in his basement workshop. But if he is to have time for Hephaestus, he can't bring extra work home from his office. Similarly, the man who once joyfully entered the competitive

12

fray on school playing fields will lose touch with the aggressive physical Ares in himself unless he finds time and companions for a volleyball or touch football game or joins a neighborhood team.

GODS AND THE STAGES OF LIFE

An individual man goes through many phases of life. Each stage may have its own most influential god or gods. For example, until his thirties he could be a combination of Hermes, the on-the-go god with winged shoes, and an ecstasy-seeking Dionysus. At that point he comes to a major crossroads: the woman in his life gives him the choice of making a commitment to her or losing her. His decision to make that commitment and stay faithful to it—which (perhaps surprisingly) is another aspect of Dionysus, leads him to clip Hermes' wings, and call on the Apollo in himself to get ahead in the work world. In the next three decades, other archetypes may take their turn. Fatherhood and success could constellate Zeus in him; the death of his wife, or finding that he has been exposed to the AIDS virus, could develop Hades in him.

Sometimes, men who identify strongly with one particular archetype may go through stages, all of which correspond to aspects of that one god. In the chapters about each individual god, these developmental patterns are described.

PATRIARCHAL FAVORITISM

The patriarchy—that invisible, hierarchical system that serves as our cultural Procrustean bed as it enforces values and gives power—plays favorites. There are always winners and losers, archetypes in favor or disfavor. In turn, men who embody particular "gods" are rewarded or rejected.

Patriarchal values that emphasize the acquisition of power, rational thinking, and being in control are unconsciously or consciously enforced by mothers and fathers, peers, schools, and other institutions that reward and punish boys and men for their behavior. As a result, men learn to conform and to stifle their individuality along with their emotions. They learn to put on a correct persona (or acceptable attitude, and manner that is the

13

face they show the world), along with the expected "uniform" of their social class.

Whatever is "unacceptable" to others or to standards of behavior may become a source of guilt or shame to the man, so he may lie on the psychological Procrustean bed. Psychological "dismemberment" follows, as men (and women) cut themselves off from or repress those archetypes or parts of themselves that make them feel inadequate or shameful. Taken metaphorically, the biblical admonition that begins, "If thy right hand offends you, cut it off" is a call to psychological self-mutilation.

What men often cut off are emotional, vulnerable, sensual, or instinctual aspects of themselves. However, in the psyche anything that is cut off or buried is still alive. It may go "underground" and be outside of conscious awareness for a time, but it can reemerge or be "re-membered" when (for the first time ever, or the first time since childhood) this archetype finds acceptance in a relationship or a situation. For men who lead secret lives, unacceptable feelings and actions may retain a shadowy existence and be surreptitiously experienced outside the awareness of others until exposure occurs and scandal follows—as has happened to notable television evangelists, who railed against sins of the flesh, and who then were brought down, when the dishonored Dionysus in themselves was exposed.

KNOWING THE GODS—EMPOWERING OURSELVES

Knowledge of the gods is a source of personal empowerment. In this book, you will meet each of the gods as we move from image and mythology to archetype. You will see how each god influences personality and priorities, and learn how meaning and specific psychological difficulties are associated with each one.

Understanding the gods must come together with knowledge about the patriarchy. Both are powerful, invisible forces that interact to affect individual men. The patriarchy magnifies the influence of some archetypes and diminishes others.

Knowledge about the gods can enhance self-knowledge and self-acceptance, open the way for men to communicate with others about themselves, and empower men and many women to make choices that can lead to self-actualization and joy. In *Cour-*

age to Create, psychologist Rollo May defined joy "as the emotion that goes with heightened consciousness, the mood that accompanies the experience of actualizing one's own potentialities."[2] Archetypes are potentialities. Within us—and within our patriarchal culture—there are gods that need to be liberated and gods that need to be restrained.

NEW PSYCHOLOGICAL THEORY AND PERSPECTIVE

This book presents men and male psychology in a new and different light. By tracing themes in mythology and theology, I found that a patriarchal attitude of hostility toward sons becomes evident. This same attitude is also present in psychoanalytic theory.

I describe the effect of paternal antagonism and rejection on male psychology in chapter two, "Fathers and Sons: Myths Tell Us About the Patriarchy." This chapter incorporates the insights of psychoanalyst Alice Miller, who points out that the Oedipus myth begins with a father's intent to kill his son. In any family or culture in which sons are seen as threats to the father and treated accordingly, the psyche of a son and the climate of the culture will be adversely affected. This is a new psychological perspective that I present.

In addition, *Gods in Everyman* is a psychology of men that considers as important the impact of the culture on the development of archetypes. This is a new emphasis in Jungian psychology.

In chapter twelve, "The Missing God," I speculate about the emergence of a new male archetype, a possibility accounted for by Rupert Sheldrake's theory of morphogenetic fields.

Finally, this book provides a systematic, coherent way to understand men's psychology through male archetypes as personified by Greek gods (which are also present in women). My previous book, *Goddesses in Everywoman,* described Greek goddesses and female archetypes (which are also present in men) as the basis of an archetypal psychology of women. Taken together, the two books present a new systematic psychology of men and women that accounts for the diversity among us and complexity within us. Based on the pantheon of Greek deities, this psychology reflects the richness of our human nature and hints at the divinity we experience when what we do comes out of our depths and we sense the sacred dimension to our lives.

2.

Fathers And Sons: Myths Tell Us About the Patriarchy

At the most private, personal level, the patriarchy shapes the relationship between a father and his son; at the more external level of customs, patriarchal values determine which traits and values are encouraged and rewarded, and thus which archetypes will have an edge over the others, both within a man and among men. To gain self-knowledge, which is empowering, a man must become conscious of the influences on his attitudes and behavior: he must understand what the patriarchy is and how it shapes its sons.

The myths of a culture reveal its values and relationship patterns. A good place to begin an exploration of our own myths is with Luke Skywalker and his father, Darth Vader, from the *Star Wars* films. Archetypal stories and figures—whether from contemporary motion pictures or ancient Greek myths—tell us truths about our human family story and the roles we too may be playing in it. Darth Vader, a powerful father who tries to destroy his son, repeats a theme that is a familiar one from Greek times to the present.

Luke Skywalker, however, symbolizes the hero in Everyman at this time in history. To be a Luke Skywalker, a contemporary man needs to uncover what has happened in the past to him personally and to humankind. He must discover his authentic identity, in a psychological and spiritual sense, ally himself with his sister (as an empowered feminine, an inner and an outer

17

possibility), and join like-hearted men and other creatures in the struggle against destructive power. Only the son (by not becoming like his father and succumbing to fear and power) can free the loving father long buried within Darth Vader, who symbolizes what can happen in a man in a patriarchy.

The large, looming figure of Darth Vader with his black metallic visage is an image of the man whose quest to have and hold power and position has become his life and has cost him his human features. Dark power emanates from him. He resembles an efficient, merciless machine, who carries out orders from his superior and issues orders that he expects to be carried out with the same unquestioning obedience. For Luke, this is what his hostile, destructive father looks like. Darth Vader is an image of the dark side of the patriarchy.

Darth Vader's original face is hidden behind a metal mask that serves as his identity, armor, and life support. He cannot take it off, because he is so damaged that without it he will die—a good metaphor for men who identify with their personas, the masks or faces they wear in the world. Lacking a personal life that matters to them, they are sustained by their personas and positions. Because they lack close emotional bonds and are emotionally empty, they may not survive a major loss of power and status.

Darth Vader is an archetypal father figure in the same tradition as the Greek Sky Father gods. Uranus, Cronus, and to a lesser extent Zeus were hostile toward their children, especially toward sons, whom they feared would challenge their authority. Luke Skywalker, the son, is cast as protagonist on a hero's journey, another archetype.

I was therefore both surprised and not at all surprised to find that Joseph Campbell, the eminent mythologist and author of *The Hero With a Thousand Faces* had a major influence on George Lucas, who brought *Star Wars* to the screen.*

The connections among the mythologist Campbell, the myth-maker Lucas, and Jungian psychology is not surprising.

---

*It was nice to hear an inside story that took place after the enormous success of his films. Lucas with his major celebrity status, yet looking like a graduate student, quietly slipped in a back door to meet Joseph Campbell for the first time, when Campbell was backstage at the Palace of Fine Arts in San Francisco for an event sponsored by the Jungian Institute.

Jung's psychological theory provides the key to understanding why myths have such power to live in our imaginations: whether we are aware of them or not, myths live through and in us. In the Western world, the ancient Greek myths remain the most remembered and powerful.

Mythological stories are like archeological sites that reveal cultural history to us. Some are like small shards that we piece together and infer from; others are well preserved and detailed, like frescoes once buried in the ashes of Pompeii but now uncovered.

I think of Greek mythology as going back to a time that was the equivalent to the childhood of our civilization. These myths can tell us a great deal about attitudes and values with which we were raised. Like personal family stories or myths, they convey to the present generation, something about who we are and what is expected of us—what is in our genetic memory, so to speak, and is part of the psychological legacy that shaped us and invisibly affects our perceptions and behavior.

THE OLYMPIAN FAMILY STORY

Myths about Zeus and the Olympians are "family stories" that cast light on our patriarchal genealogy and on its enormous influence on our personal lives. These stories are about the attitudes and values that have come down to us from the Greeks, descendants of the Indo-Europeans with their warrior gods, who came in invading waves to conquer the earlier goddess-worshiping inhabitants of old Europe and the Greek peninsula. They tell of our founding fathers, and obliterate or only hint at the matriarchal realm that preceded them.

As is often the case in families, after the years of struggle to become established is over people feel the urge or need to record what happened and to construct the family tree. Here we are indebted to Homer (about 750 B.C.) and Hesiod (about 700 B.C.). Homer's *Iliad* and *Odyssey* preserved mythological themes in epics that had some historical basis, while Hesiod first organized numerous mythological traditions in the *Theogony*, which is an account of the origin and descent of the gods.

In the beginning, according to Hesiod, there was the void. Out of the void, Gaia (Earth) materialized. She gave birth to the

19

mountains, and the sea, and to Uranus (Sky), who became her husband. Gaia and Uranus mated, and became the parents of the twelve Titans—ancient, primeval, nature powers who were worshiped in historical Greece. In Hesiod's genealogy of the gods, the Titans were an early ruling dynasty, the parents and grandparents of the Olympians.

Uranus, the first patriarchal or father figure in Greek mythology, grew resentful of Gaia's generativity; the begetting of children was not to his liking. As the later children were born, he hid them in the great body of Gaia, the Earth, and would not let them see the light of day. Gaia suffered great pain and distress over this violence to her newborn children.

So she called on her grown children, the Titans for help. As Hesiod reports it, she was moved by anguish to speak boldly: "My children, you have a savage father; if you will listen to me, we may be able to take vengeance for his evil outrage: he was the one who started using violence."[1]

Thus Hesiod's *Theogony* makes Uranus's violence against his children the initial evil, begetting the violence that followed. It was the original sin of the Sky Father God, which would repeat itself in the next generations.

The Titans were all "gripped by fear" of their father, except the youngest son, Cronus (called Saturn by the Romans). Only Cronus responded to Gaia's cry for help with these words: "Mother, I am willing to undertake and carry through your plan. I have no respect for our infamous father, since he was the one who started using violence."[2]

And armed with the sickle she gave him and the plan she devised, he lay in wait for his father. When Uranus came to mate with Gaia, and lay on her, Cronus took the sickle, cut off his father's genitals, and threw them into the sea. Having castrated his father, Cronus was now the most powerful male god, who with his siblings, the Titans, ruled over the universe and created new deities.

Cronus married his sister Rhea, who like her mother Gaia was an earth goddess. From their union were born the first-generation Olympians—Hestia, Demeter, Hera, Hades, Poseidon, and Zeus.

Once again however, the patriarchal progenitor—this time Cronus—tried to eliminate his children. Forewarned that he was destined to be overcome by his own son and determined that he would not let this happen, he swallowed each child immediately after birth—not even looking to see if the newborn were a son or a daughter. In all, he consumed three daughters and two sons.

Grief-stricken over the loss of her children, and pregnant once more, Rhea appealed to Gaia and Uranus to help her save this last one. Her parents told her to go to Crete when the birth time came, and to trick Cronus by wrapping a stone in swaddling clothes. In his hurry, Cronus swallowed the stone, thinking it was his child.

This last, spared child was Zeus, who did indeed overthrow his father and become supreme ruler. Raised in secret until he was an adult, Zeus got help from Metis, a pre-Olympian Goddess of Wisdom and his first consort, to make Cronus regurgitate his Olympian siblings. With them as allies, he defeated Cronus and the Titans. Violence had begotten violence for three generations.

After their victory, the three brother gods—Zeus, Poseidon, and Hades—drew lots to divide the universe among them. Zeus won the sky, Poseidon the sea, and Hades the underworld. Although the earth and Mt. Olympus were supposedly shared territory, Zeus came to extend his rule over this terrain. (The three sisters had no property rights, consistent with the patriarchal Greek culture.)

Through his sexual liaisons, Zeus fathered the next generation of deities, as well as the demigods, who were the larger-than-life heroes of mythology. And while he actively begot children, he too, like his father before him, felt threatened by the possibility that a son would overthrow him. There was a prophecy that Metis, the first of his seven consorts, would give birth to two children, one of whom would be a son who would come to rule the gods and men. And so, when she became pregnant, he feared she was pregnant with this son, tricked her into becoming small, and swallowed her in order to abort this birth. As it turned out, the child was not a son, but a daughter—Athena—who eventually was born through Zeus's head.

SKY GODS AS FATHERS

The father gods in Greek mythology have characteristics similar to the deities of all patriarchal cultures. As images or ideals, father gods are powerful male divinities, who rule over others. They are larger-than-life versions of the men in power within the culture. As such, they are archetypal figures, whose mythology when viewed metaphorically tell us much about the psychology of such men.

Patriarchal gods are authoritarian males who live in the heavens, on mountaintops, or in the sky; thus they rule from above and from a distance. They expect to be obeyed, and have the right to do what they please as long as they are chief gods. As warrior gods, their supremacy was won through defeating rivals, and they are usually jealous of their prerogatives and demand obedience. And for all their power, they fear that their fate is to be overthrown by a son. As fathers, they are often unpaternal and express hostility toward their young.

In his effort to "bury" his children, Uranus tried to suppress his children's potential by not allowing them to grow and develop as they were created to be. Cronus, in "swallowing" or "consuming" his children, tried to make them part of himself. Metaphorically, this is how a father prevents his children from growing up to be greater than he is, or to challenge his position or beliefs. He keeps them in the dark, unwilling to expose them to the influence of people or education or values that would broaden their experience. He insists that they not differ from him or deviate from his plans for them. If a child cannot think or act independently, he or she will not be a threat. A father who thus consumes his children's autonomy and growth suffers from what I call a "Cronus complex."

Zeus, in turn, tricked his pregnant wife into becoming small and swallowed her. She became diminished and lost her power, and had her attributes swallowed up—just as the matriarchy got swallowed up by patriarchy, and attributes once associated with a goddess became the possession of a god. This diminishment is similar to the way some women change once they marry and become pregnant. They lose the independent thinking and authority they once exercised, as they defer to husbands who are often cast in the authoritarian Zeus mold.

OEDIPUS: NOT GUILTY AS CHARGED

Skipping many generations, we get to the Greek mythological figure Oedipus, who, unaware of what he was doing, killed his father and married his mother. Freud founded psychoanalysis on his analysis of what he called the Oedipus complex, maintaining that this murder and marriage was the unconscious wish of every son. Freud also reacted to men he had mentored (such as Jung and Adler, who developed ideas that differed from his own and whose stature might someday rival his) as oedipal sons to be cast away. When Jung told him a dream that Jung describes as leading to his theories of the collective unconscious, Freud was convinced that it expressed a death wish toward him, Freud.[3]

Freud saw Laius, Oedipus's father, as an innocent victim in the Oedipus myth. But this version was far from the truth, as psychoanalyst Alice Miller notes.*

Laius was king of Thebes. When he went to the Delphic oracle to ask why his wife had borne him no children, the oracle's response was "Laius, you desire a child. You shall have a son. But Fate has decreed that you shall lose your life at his hands. . . . because of the curse of Pelops, whom you once robbed of his son." Laius had committed this wrong as a young man when he had been forced to flee from his own country, and found refuge with King Pelops, who took him in. Laius repaid this kindness by seducing Chrysippus, Pelops's beautiful young son, who then killed himself.

Laius first attempted to thwart fate by living apart from his wife. But in time, in spite of the warning, they had sexual relations and Jocasta bore him a son. Fearing the prophecy, Laius decided to kill this newborn boy by exposing him in the mountains, his ankles pierced and bound by a thong. But the shepherd who had been chosen to carry out the murder, had pity on the innocent baby, gave him to a fellow herdsman, and returned to Laius, pretending he had done what he had been told. Laius could now feel safe, certain that his child must have died of hunger and thirst or been torn to pieces by wild beasts. The herdsman gave the boy, called Oedipus ("Swollen-Foot" because

---

*Alice Miller, a contemporary psychoanalyst, in *Thou Shalt Not Be Unaware: Society's Betrayal of the Child*, focused on the context that led Oedipus to kill his father. From the myth and other evidence, Miller describes the pattern of attributing to innocent children base motivations or an evil nature that must be dealt with, often harshly. Hence abusive treatment of children is rationalized.

of the wounds in his ankles), to a couple. These foster parents raised him and let him believe that he was their own true son.

Grown to manhood, Oedipus was traveling the road to Boeotia when he came to a crossroads, and there was crowded by an old man in a chariot, who brandished his goad at him and hit him on the head. Oedipus, angered by this unprovoked bludgeoning, struck back with his walking staff and toppled his assailant, killing him. After this incident, he continued his journey, not dreaming that he had done anything but take revenge on some commoner who had tried to harm him. Nothing about the old man's dress or appearance showed that he was of noble birth. In reality, however, he was Laius, king of Thebes, and his father.

Alice Miller points out the injustice of blaming Oedipus:

> In Sophocles' tragedy Oedipus punishes himself by putting out his eyes. Even though he had no way of recognizing Laius as his father; even though Laius had tried to kill his infant son and was responsible for this lack of recognition; even though Laius was the one who provoked Oedipus' anger when their paths crossed; even though Oedipus did not desire Jocasta but became her husband thanks to his cleverness in solving the sphinx's riddle, thus rescuing Thebes; and even though Jocasta, his mother, could have recognized her son by his swollen feet—to this very day no one seems to have objected to the fact that Oedipus was assigned all the blame."[4]

Miller further notes that "It has always been taken for granted that children are responsible for what was done to them, and it has been essential that when children grow up, they not be aware of the true nature of their past."[5]

Laius's unsuccessful effort to kill his son Oedipus echoes the myths of the Greek Sky Father gods who attempted to kill their sons. In each case, as in psychoanalytic theory about the oedipal complex the father believes that a just-conceived or newborn baby wants to get rid of him, and so the father treats the newborn as a threating rival. Cronus and Zeus feared they would have sons who would do to them what they had already done to their fathers; Laius feared his son would be an agent of retribution. In mythology, the rationalization for fathers who try to kill sons is always "because of a prophecy." A contemporary psychiatric formulation would be "because of a paranoid idea." In

Jungian psychology, the formulation would be "because of the projection of the shadow" (which occurs when people attribute to others their own repressed or disowned emotions, motivation, or actions).

Projections and the actions that originate from the projections shape the people on whom they fall. A child who is treated as if he were bad, and who is rejected, abandoned, and abused, responds by feeling guilty. He thinks, "I must deserve this treatment I'm getting" (thus doubly suffering, first from the maltreatment, and then from assuming the blame).

Zeus, and mortal kings like Laius, were territorial rulers over others. Each had consolidated their power over an area and its peoples, and ruled as royalty. This form of rule and the values implicit in it is patriarchal; it is a hierarchy of males, each of whom exists in an established order, with Zeus or God at the top, lesser deities below, and then mortal kings who trace their origins to a god, and then loyal vassals and subjects. Large corporations, with the chief executive officer and the board at the top, are contemporary equivalents to Zeus and the Olympians. The armed forces formalize the hierarchy even more, as do the Roman Catholic Church and most fraternal organizations.

POWERLESS MOTHERS IN PATRIARCHAL FAMILIES

All the Olympian gods, including Zeus, had mothers who were powerless and subordinate to a powerful and often abusive father, and most had wives they dominated. Women—whether goddess or mortal, with few exceptions—fared badly in their involvements with the gods. And if women and mothers are devalued, powerless, and unable to protect their sons (and daughters), their sons feel betrayed by them. For the mother who birthed them is the provider, and nurturer; she is the first experience of the world that a newborn has, and she is initially all-powerful. That she later can't protect him, or leaves him, or puts someone else first, is a betrayal and a rejection that he may hold against her, and against any woman on whom he ever becomes emotionally dependent. As a grown man, he may take out on other women the helpless rage that he felt as a child toward his own mother. This chain of events helps to explain one origin of hostility toward women in patriarchal cultures, where women are relatively powerless.

To further complicate matters, when women are oppressed by powerful men, by their fathers, husbands, or brothers, or by a culture that limits them just because they are women, some of them take out their resentment (often unconsciously) on powerless males—their little sons—especially when the little boy begins to emulate his father or express his own inherent assertiveness and boisterous spirit. This may take the form of outright abuse, or rejection, or it may be through sarcasm and humiliation. Sisters who feel the brunt of unfair treatment also may similarly punish their brothers—as long as their brothers are young enough or small enough. This chain reaction is another source of the hostility toward women that originated in their childhood, that many men harbor, and take out on women when they get to be big and powerful.

HOME AS A MAN'S CASTLE

In a patriarchal culture, each man rules over his particular family, with the authority of the king within his own household. The conservative right wing and fundamental Christian sects voice hostility toward legislation or social services that they charge "undermines traditional family values," that undermines this lord-and-master position of the man as king within his own house, which is the patriarchal family model. Patriarchy accounts for "traditional" opposition to women having autonomy over their own bodies or property and reproductive choice in their lives, as well as for the opposition to battered women's shelters, which provide a sanctuary, or a means of escape from abusive men.

A Sky Father who is a dynasty builder takes a major interest in shaping his sons' careers, of preparing them to assume their designated place in the world. In so doing, he may "consume" his sons' lives when such a son lives out his father's ambitions rather than discovering what he wants for himself. The consuming quality is especially strong when the son's own bent differs from the position his father expects him to play.

One larger-than-life example in U.S. politics of a Sky Father, whose ambition for himself might be said to have consumed his sons, was Joseph P. Kennedy. As the son of immigrants, Kennedy felt the sting of social snobbery. His ambition was to rise to the top, if not on his own, then through his sons. Kennedy's consolidation of wealth and power, his quest for recognition, and philandering made him a contemporary version of Zeus. First Joe Kennedy, Jr., for whom the role of extraverted politician may have been natural, was expected to run for president of the United States. When his plane was shot down and he was killed, the next son, John F. Kennedy, was expected to fulfill this role regardless of his personal inclinations and physical difficultes. And after J. F. K.'s assassination, the third son, Robert F. Kennedy, put his life on the line.

SKY FATHERS AND SONS: ESTRANGEMENT AND COMPETITION

That fathers react unpaternally to their children, and view their sons as rivals is not just true in Greek mythology. Listening to many men in my psychiatric practice, I've heard how unfathered they felt, how emotionally distant and judgmental, rejecting, emotionally closed off, competitive or even abusive their fathers were. And how much sadness, pain, and anger this created in their sons (and families) and how the pattern has been passed on through successive generations. I also hear of fathers' intentions to be close and supportive, and of the moments in which they nonetheless unleash a bolt of hostility at a son and then feel guilty and puzzled at how much anger the son touched off in them.

Estrangement between father and son begins with the father's resentment, or with his perception, of his child as rival, which can arise even before the son is born. His wife's pregnancy may activate feelings from his childhood. He may even have a brief affair as a means of warding off depression or feelings of powerlessness. His perception of his pregnant wife may recreate memories of his pregnant mother and the pain that pregnancy and a new sibling brought him as a child.

As a husband now (then, as child), he becomes less central and important to the mothering and nurturing woman in his life. Less availability begins with pregnancy: she turns inward, or she is tired, or she can't do the things she used to do with him. She becomes more absorbed in herself and less in him, she may lose interest in sex, which was a chief affirmation of him and major means of closeness for him.

The rage, hostility, and rivalry he had when he was a child for the new baby that he suppressed, now is revived by his wife's pregnancy. And as a new father-to-be, these same feelings are even more unacceptable and thus need to be hidden as before. Like the Greek father gods, he fears that he will be supplanted by this rival.

The coming of a child, especially the first one, initiates a man into the next stage of his life. It scares many men to take on the responsibility of a family, raising questions about his adequacy as a provider if job stability or potential advancement are questionable. Feelings of inadequacy in this next test of his masculinity may contribute to irrational fears that this baby may not be his.

Moreover, he may feel dread at being trapped. It used to be that "ball-and-chain" feelings were attached to marriage, but now marriage and children are separate decisions and stages in life. Having a child, rather than marriage, is now the point when the dread of being trapped is often greatest. Fatherhood often entails taking on a mortgage, buying life insurance, being the sole provider for a time or from that point on, having to keep an unfulfilling job or moonlight to pay the bills. Thus while others congratulate the couple and fuss over his pregnant wife, the husband may be feeling dread and resentment rather than joy at the coming of a baby.

Then the newborn becomes the center of attention, again perhaps replicating painful childhood experiences for many men. His wife is now more this baby's mother than his wife. As he feared, the baby has indeed supplanted him, at least temporarily. Uncovering feelings men have (through their analysis) reveals that he may be envious of his wife's ability to have a baby and take time off, or envious of the attention and closeness to her body that the baby is getting, especially if the couple is not having sexual relations. The breasts he loved now "belong" to his nursing son. And the coming of the baby has brought an end to their exclusive life as a couple.

In a patriarchal culture, babies and fathers do not have much opportunity to bond. "Never having changed a diaper" used to be a point of pride with men in general. Children—sons in particular—were evidence of their father's masculinity and a means to extend his power, or live out his ambitions; there was little personal enjoyment of them. Uninvolved as he was in caring for the child, a Sky Father's capacity to care for, to care about, the child emotionally may not be tapped.

It's my impression from talking with a generation of men who were present and involved throughout the hours of labor and there at the moment of birth, that a deep, caring bond with their children begins then. However, if bonding does not occur, and a new father does not feel tenderness and protective toward his child and his wife, he is likely to be angry and resentful because he experiences his wife's pregnancy and the birth of a child as a series of deprivations. Rage toward "the interloper," especially if it is a son, and rage toward his wife, who "left" him for a baby, are feelings that may or may not reach consciousness. When uncovered in therapy, these angry feelings are usually found to overlie even deeper fears of abandonment and feelings of insignificance.

A father may then direct corporal punishment, verbal hostility, and ridicule at boys, in the name of discipline, or "helping sons become men." He may strive to beat his son in every game they play. Roughhousing begun in fun may seem to always end with a crying little boy, who then is humiliated for crying. The four- to six-year-old who says, "I wish Daddy wouldn't come home," may be genuinely afraid of his father's competitiveness and anger, and may not just be verifying oedipal theory.

The son who may supplant his father in his mother's affection, and who may reap his father's jealousy, will grow into his power as an adult male as his father's power wanes. Like the mythology of Greek Sky Father gods, unless he is swallowed up in some way a son *will* someday be in a position to challenge his father's power and overthrow his authority.

Doctrines of original sin and the psychoanalytic insistence that all sons want to kill their fathers and marry their mothers, are theories that justify the hostility that resentful Sky Fathers feel toward sons. The "need for" discipline is further supported by sayings such as "Spare the rod, spoil the child."

Sons become first mistrustful, then afraid, and then hostile toward fathers who see them as bad or spoiled from the time they are infants, and treat them accordingly. However, this is not the case if the father nurtures, plays with, and mentors his son, and is a positive role model for him. Then the son may even be closer to his father than to his mother, or may sometimes prefer being with his mother, sometimes with his father.

Often a son has a distant Sky Father who is not abusive, merely emotionally absent and physically not around much. This father experience is common for my men patients, who tell of childhoods in which the son has yearned for attention and approval from his distant father (rather than feeling hostile, as the oedipal theory requires). In their childhoods, these sons missed their fathers, whom they idealized.

As long as a son hopes his father will truly notice him and claim him as his own, the predominant feelings seem to be yearning and sadness. Anger toward the father comes later, after the son gives up his hopes and expectations of being fathered by his father; after he gives up the wish that his father will love him. Anger can also arise from disillusionment, if his distant father turns out not to be worthy of the idealization.

The relationship between emotionally distant Sky Fathers and their adolescent and grown sons often takes on a perfunctory, often ritualized quality. When father and son get together, they have a predictable conversation, a series of questions and answers in which neither gives away anything truly personal, perhaps beginning with "How's it going?" Seen psychologically, such a relationship between a Sky Father and his son takes the form of an apparently comfortable estrangement. Disappointment may lie just below the surface, however.

Frank hostility can also arise when the son feels that all he means to his father is an extension of the father's pride. When the son feels his father doesn't care about him personally, yet basks in his son's accomplishments, estrangement widens. Athletic sons are especially susceptible to feeling used in this way.

Bruce Ogilvie, psychologist and author of *Problem Athletes*, who was the first expert in the field of sports psychology, describes a young man who came to see him who had been a marvelous shortstop and a potential Number One draft choice in the major leagues, whose performance fell apart when he was being examined by major league scouts.

> He was fielding, showing the scouts his skills, when suddenly he bobbled the next ten or so balls. I said, "Stop, I want you to relive that entire experience with me . . . " so he went along, describing every ball he's fielded successfully, until he said to me, "Oh, Christ, there's that son of a bitch! There's my dad, sneaking down into the stands on the right." His dad had never related to him except in terms of his athletic performance. He could see after we finished reliving the situation that if he fulfilled his own am- bitions, he'd also have fulfilled his father's needs. And he couldn't abide that. I can tell a thousand stories like this. I've got a father story from every city in America.[6]

This particular athlete minded that his performance was all that mattered to his father, and he could not stand fulfilling his father's ambitions or need for reflected glory. This is the role that sons, especially first-born ones, are so often expected to play, and thus why they are so valued at birth (over daughters). The proud father, passing out cigars, announces that he now has a "son and heir," who is expected to carry on his name (and his ambitions) and who, just by being born a boy, proves his father's masculinity. The very birth of a son in a patriarchy ful- fills his father's needs to have a son. Next comes the need for that son to live up to his father's expectations—rather than com- ing into the world with particular gifts and talents, emotional needs, handicaps and personality traits, and possibly even a per- sonal purpose of his own to fulfill.

SACRIFICE OF THE CHILD

Besides Greek mythology, which with minor changes be- came Roman mythology, the Old and the New Testaments are the chief sources of the family story in Western civilization. There are many parallels between the two. The Indo-Europeans who invaded the Greek peninsula, and the Israelites who came from Egypt into their promised land, both came as invaders and migrants to an already settled area where the Goddess was wor- shiped. Both invading peoples had Sky Father gods, with war- rior qualities, who ruled from above and communicated from mountains. And, in both, there is an evolution in the character of the Sky God, a shift toward being less hostile toward his children and more parental. In Greek mythology, the change occurs through a series of Sky Father gods, with Zeus the pivotal figure. While the god of the Bible is considered as one entity, he was called by different names—Yahweh and Elohim in the original language of the Old Testament. Over time, the biblical Sky God changed and became less punitive and more supportive of his human "sons."

Looked at as family stories and seen from a psychological perspective, the parallels continue. Greek themes of the Sky Father being threatened by the birth and/or growth of children, his attempt to consume them or keep them contained within his limits, and the hostility toward sons are present in the Bible as well, though hidden in issues of obedience and sacrifice.

To do the will of the biblical Sky God requires the willing sacrifice of the son. Thus Yahweh tested Abraham by ordering him to offer his only son Isaac, whom he loved, as a burnt offering on a mountain. That he was willing to kill his son meant that he passed the test. (Similarly, Agamemnon, leading the Greek warriors against Troy, found his ships becalmed at Aulis. In return for fair winds, he had to sacrifice his daughter Iphigenia, which he was willing to do.)

Although contemporary children are not literally sacrificed on the altar so that their fathers can pass their tests and be successful, children *are* metaphorically offered up as sacrifices. This is true on several psychological levels: successful men are often absent fathers, emotionally and often physically missing from their children's lives. They sacrifice the possibility of closeness to their children to their jobs, their roles. And they also sacrifice their own "inner child," the playful, spontaneous, trusting, emotionally expressive part of themselves.

Patriarchal culture is hostile toward innocence, devalues childlike qualities, and rewards men for their ability to be like Abraham, Agamemnon, and Darth Vader, who put obedience to a higher authority and ambition (or obedience to a demanding god) above love and concern for a child.

Isaac: Sacrifice of the Son

The Old Testament patriarch Abraham was told to go to the land of Moriah and there, on a mountainside, sacrifice his son Isaac to God as a burnt offering. I think of young Isaac, and imagine that he was delighted to accompany his father on this trip, being ignorant of its purpose. Three days after starting out, they reached their destination. There, Isaac eagerly gathered wood and helped Abraham build the altar. Then, puzzled, he asked, "Behold, the fire and the wood; but where is the lamb for the burnt offering?" To which his father said: "God will provide himself the lamb for a burnt offering, my son."[7]

I imagine that Isaac accepted this answer, and wondered how and when the lamb would materialize. When, I wonder, did the young boy realize that his father was going to sacrifice him? Was it when Abraham bound him? Was it when he laid Isaac on the altar, upon the wood? Or was it only when Abraham took his knife to slay him? I can imagine that when it dawned on him that he was to be the sacrifice, he felt disbelief, fear, and betrayal. Maybe Abraham explained that he was obeying a god who demanded the death of his only son; that would have helped Abraham justify what he was about to do, but I doubt it would have given Isaac any comfort. All he knew was that he was not safe with his father; his father was about to kill him.

Then the Lord called to Abraham, and said, "Abraham, Abraham! Do not lay your hand on the lad or do anything to him; for now I know you fear God, seeing you have not withheld your son, your only son, from me."[8] And then Abraham looked up and saw a ram, his horns caught in a thicket nearby, and offered it up in place of Isaac as a burnt offering.

Abraham was then blessed by God, because he was willing to kill his son: "Because you have done this, and have not withheld your son, your only son, I will indeed bless you, and I will multiply your descendants as the stars of heaven and as the sand which is on the seashore."[9]

Iphigenia: Sacrifice of the Daughter

Another success story that hinges on a father's willingness to sacrifice his child is told in the *Iliad*. This time, the father was King Agamemnon, commander-in-chief of the Greek forces in the Trojan War. Gathering together an army, he prepared to sail with a huge fleet to Troy. But there were no fair winds, and with their ships becalmed the men grew restless. The glory, plunder, and power that would be his if his forces conquered Troy, would be lost unless the winds came up. Agamemnon consulted a seer, who told him that if he sacrificed his beautiful, innocent daughter Iphigenia, the winds would blow and the fleet could sail for Troy.

Agamemnon then sent word to his wife to send Iphigenia to him, that she was to marry Achilles, who was the son of King Peleus and the sea goddess Thetis, and who was the most celebrated of all the Greek heroes. You can imagine the excitement at the news of this match, and how the young maiden traveled to her father's encampment, her baggage filled with beautiful dresses and objects, her mind filled with thoughts about her intended bridegroom, as she anticipated her wedding day.

At what point did Iphigenia realize that something was amiss? How long did her father let her believe that she was there to be married? When did she know that he had brought her here to be sacrificed? Was she dressed in her bridal gown? Did she approach the place where she was to be killed, thinking it was where the wedding would take place? At some point, she must have known that her father had deceived her and that death awaited her. When the full realization struck, she must have felt totally betrayed and afraid, forsaken.

Agamemnon did offer her up as a sacrifice, and the winds did come up, and the Greek fleet did sail for Troy to fight a war that would last ten years. In another version of the story, Iphigenia was spared by the goddess Artemis, who substituted a stag in her place at the very last minute.

Agamemnon was thus another father who was rewarded by his willingness to kill his child or have her killed. Looked at psychologically, the father who violates the trust of a daughter and destroys her innocence, destroys a corresponding part of himself. Symbolically, the daughter can represent her father's anima (Jung's descriptive term for the feminine aspect of a man); as can his wife, who represents his other half (colloquially referred to as his "better half"), who in these stories is not consulted, or is deceived, and lacks the power to defend her son or daughter.

I doubt if Abraham told Sarah to say goodbye forever to their son Isaac as they set off for the land of Moriah. I doubt Abraham told her that he planned to heed God, and make Isaac into a burnt offering. Had his mother known what was supposed to happen, we expect that she would have tried to stop it. If she had had the power to prevent it, Isaac would have stayed home. And Iphigenia would have, too, had her mother had known what Agamemnon was up to when he summoned Iphigenia to Aulis under false pretenses.

To be a ruthless soldier or a commander-in-chief, or even a modern executive or entrepreneur, a man (or a woman, who may now take on such a role) usually must be willing to kill or repress his softer feelings, to put his quest for approval or success in the man's world ahead of family ties. There is no place in the military encampment or its contemporary market equivalent for vulnerability, tenderness, and innocence. Nor is there room for empathy and compassion for enemies, in a "Kill or be killed" setting, or for competitors and rivals in which one wins and the other loses. These attributes are seen as weaknesses that must be sacrificed.

The myths that recount the stories of men who were willing to kill their children and how they were rewarded, are very telling commentaries. They speak about what is valued in a patriarchal culture: you must obey authority, and you must do what you need to do to maintain the authority you already have.

This value system has direct, negative consequences on the relationship between fathers and sons. Authoritarian fathers react with anger at what they perceive as insubordination and disobedience, punishing their sons (and daughters) for not doing what they are told to do, or expected to do, for whatever the reason.

The need to maintain a position of authority contributes to "worst-case" abusive father situations. A man may thus become enraged at a baby who won't stop crying or at a two-year-old son in the no stage of development, whom he perceives as being insubordinate or mocking his authority (and not incidentally, also makes him feel his own helplessness to control what is happening). This reaction is considered paranoid. The father does not see his son as a child who is just being himself, is doing what babies and two-year-olds do; the father reacts to what he perceives instead, and abuses the child.

More usually, a son invites the wrath of an authoritarian father later, when he is older. He may not do as he is told, or he may question or disagree with his father, or he may rebel against his authority. Challenging authority is a normal part of learning and finding things out for oneself.

IDENTIFICATION WITH THE AGGRESSOR

From a psychological perspective, the problem isn't that the father has authority and exercises it. Children gain confidence and security when there is an authority who sets firm and appropriate limits. But the child's needs for firmness are not met if, under the guise of paternal authority, the father is expressing jealousy at being supplanted emotionally, or is reacting to his need to show the son who is boss.

The father is then acting the part of a distant and angry Sky Father, who views his son as a threat to his position. Since his rage is irrational, the son initially becomes confused and hurt. This situation grows into mutual resentment and estrangement; paradoxically, it also helps shape the son into behaving like his father when he grows up.

Psychologically, this paradox arises because the son "identifies with the aggressor" instead of with the victim he really was. He came to reject the qualities in himself, that provoked his father's anger, even when they were not bad qualities.

Although a son may dislike his father who criticizes, bullies, and takes his anger out on him, he grows to hate even more feeling weak, incompetent, fearful, helpless, and humiliated. He comes to hate his own vulnerability as the target of his father's punitive judgment and rage. How bad it felt and the idea of "badness" itself get mixed together, which confusion the patriarchal culture enforces by equating awareness of vulnerability with weakness, cowardliness, and "wimpiness." Love of beautiful things, sensuality, and emotional spontaneity are likewise proscribed as unmasculine traits to be hidden from view or to be so deeply buried as to be outside of awareness.

Boys and men learn that showing compassion toward a victim can be dangerous in a patriarchy, that they risk loss of their own acceptable position if they do. This risk is especially high when males in a group are exercising power over others, and are tormenting, beating up, or even gang-raping a weaker person, or hurting an animal. One man in my practice recalled the taunting and ridicule he had to endure as a little boy when he objected to and stopped the torturing of a kitten by other boys his age. Getting picked on was the price he paid for what he did.

Other men have spoken to me of their guilt and shame because they lacked the courage to speak up and intervene. They say, "I didn't lift a finger"; and so gave silent consent to what the group of males they were a part of did to a woman, a homosexual, a Jew, Asian, Mexican, or black. These men came from families where they were not victimized, and so did not identify with the aggressor in the same way that an abused boy might, later on. Yet they went along with what was happening, which is what men in groups usually seem to do.

When a bullied boy grows in size and power and in turn is in the position of being able to intimidate someone smaller and less powerful, he usually does (fortunately, there are exceptions). Fraternity hazings with its paddlings and worse, and the perpetuations of inhumanly difficult medical internships as ordeals to be survived, and how "plebes" are treated at West Point are hostile initiations of the new generation, by the abused previous generation.

The motto to justify these initiation rites is often stated as "What was done to me, I now get to do to you," which is clear identification with the aggressor. Fraternity hazings repeat the experience that many men had as younger brothers at the hands of angry, bigger, older brothers. The younger brother finds himself the recipient of hostility, and is in the same underdog-victim relationship to his older brother, as his older brother was to his father. This underlying repetition of the "what was done to me in the past, I now get to do to you" pattern, is usually not conscious, but operates automatically.

IDENTIFICATION WITH OTHER MEN

That any men come to love and trust each other at all, in a culture that fosters estrangement and competition between men, is remarkable. As reports on the psychological status of men attest, mostly they do not.

There are exceptions, times when men are genuinely close, usually when they are "in the same boat together," and the private subculture in which they temporarily live is egalitarian rather than patriarchal, and all male. From some men, who are now professionals, I hear of a golden age of boyhood buddies that depended on growing up in working-class neighborhoods, of having summers when no one went away, and the group of friends could be together for what seemed like almost every waking moment. This was before girls became important to them, and before they were divided into winners and losers. Later they found themselves going separate ways, yet this experience laid the foundation for seeking friendships with men later. Similarly, upper-class men who went away to boarding schools in adolescence sometimes speak of having been part of a close-knit group of friends, through which they developed a capacity for friendship that continued for the rest of their lives. Enlisted men who come to depend on each other in a battlefield unit also speak of having forged close bonds with each other.

Although all these situations differ, the boys or men felt strongly that "we are in this together." Shared circumstances and similarities made it easy for them to identify with each other. They were in an "equal brother" situation, which temporarily overcame the invisible, divisive, and hierarchal influence of the patriarchy, which usually separates and isolates men from each other.

LUKE SKYWALKER AND "HIS DESTINY"

Just before the climax of *Return of the Jedi*, the third film in the *Star Wars* series, Darth Vader has a telling conversation with his master, the Emperor, who tells him that "Young Skywalker will be one of us." And in the life-and-death struggle between Luke Skywalker and Darth Vader that follows, Luke is tempted to respond in fear and hate and be goaded into giving in to murderous anger—and by thus doing, identify with the aggressor—which the Emperor tells him is "unavoidably, your destiny."[10]

Luke Skywalker has no illusions about the Emperor and the Death Star. He does not want to be part of an empire that seeks to obtain power over all others, represses freedom, and demands blind obedience—which are exaggerated values of the patriarchy—even if he is promised a leadership role.

Because he is not seduced by the promise of power, or overcome by fear that he is naively foolish, and his position hopeless, Luke can resist his "unavoidable destiny." Consequently, he does not give in and become an unfeeling man who gives orders and follows orders, like his father. He does not trade love for power, or loyalty to others for a secure position, or his own belief in a different kind of system in the face of the apparent invincibility of the status quo. And by his commitment to what he believed in and his courage, he is able to resist becoming another Darth Vader, and he wins.

All men and many women in patriarchal cultures face the same temptation: Will they identify with the aggressors and join them? Moments of truth and times of decision continually arise, when the survival of a Luke Skywalker—or of his feminine counterpart, Princess Leia—is at stake in us. As long as we live, life is a never-ending story that presents us with these moments of choice. We can decide not to give up and give in, decide to stay true to what really matters to us, even when we have reasons to be afraid. To stay true, we need to know who we are. Put into a psychological perspective, the active archetypes—in us, connect us to what is most meaningful—to us. Thus knowing which archetypes are the significant ones, tells us something important about our deepest nature, and helps us to hold our ground. We are empowered through this knowledge.

In the following chapters, we meet the gods, those archetypes that live in Everyman and are also familiar to Everywoman. First we meet Zeus, Poseidon, and Hades, the father archetypes, whose separate chapters comprise the first section. Then we go on to meet the generation of the sons—Apollo, Hermes, Hephaestus, Ares, and Dionysus—each of whom represents a distinct personality pattern, that in turn is either favored or rejected by the patriarchy and by their personal fathers.

PART II

The Father Archetype: Zeus, Poseidon, and Hades

Zeus, Poseidon, and Hades were the first generation of male Olympian gods. They represent three aspects of the father archetype. They divided the world among themselves, and each held dominion over his particular realm. As archetypes and metaphors, god and realm need to be considered together: Zeus and sky, Poseidon and sea, Hades and underworld. Earth was dominated by Zeus, but not claimed as his.

Zeus ruled over all. He was chief god, and his personal attributes are those we equate with powerful fathers, kings, chief executive officers of corporations or armies, top-dog alpha males, boss figures. Poseidon and Hades are shadow aspects of Zeus—those parts of the father archetype that men in power suppress or ignore, as well as being two separate patterns.

Biological fatherhood and the father archetypes are not related. You may read about all three of the father gods, for instance, and not recognize your own father in any of them because he isn't there: his pattern may instead follow one of the Olympian sons, each of whom has his own characteristic way of being a father. A Zeus does not head every human family, but his influence is powerfully present in every patriarchal society.

In patriarchies, Zeus is the ruling archetype within the culture—and significant for psychology, in the psyches of men. Like the world in mythology, male psyches became divided—into (1) the conscious mental realm of power, will, and thought (Zeus), the realm of emotion and instinct (Poseidon), which is often-suppressed, less valued, and sometimes split off from conscious awareness; and the dim, feared world of unseen patterns and impersonal archetypes (Hades), which often is glimpsed only through dreams.

Unlike the three gods, who represent fixed archetypal patterns, each defined by his realm, a human being has potential access to all these realms, and can knowingly move through them and integrate their aspects into his (or her) conscious personality.

The conditions under which these three ruling male gods were born still exist as a pattern in many men's lives. Zeus, Poseidon, and Hades had a distant father whose animosity toward them was based on fear that they would eventually overthrow or surpass him and a disempowered mother, who was distressed because she could not protect them or nurture them. Many of us come from such families. Moreover, regardless of our particular family of origin, we all live in a patriarchy that most values acquisition of power and favors men who succeed at this goal. This pattern, as we shall see, plays a significant part in shaping male psychology.

A SPIRAL WAY OF KNOWING

The Zeus, Poseidon, and Hades chapters follow a spiral form: the first time around, we hear about the god and his mythology; the archetypal pattern is the next turn around the spiral; how the god or archetype shapes a man's life is the third time around; the psychological difficulties that are characteristic comes next; and the last time around tells how the man who lives out that particular god pattern might grow.

Like a musical composition or a poem, the spiral form means that a thematic chord or theme runs through each different movement, each turn expands and simultaneously deepens the meaning of the god-archetype for the reader. Each time around, the same god is reintroduced, and with each repetition, the image of the god becomes more fleshed out, seen in more dimensions.

The spiral form invites both halves of our brains to be involved: the understanding that comes through the left half of the brain comes through our linear mind, which absorbs information through words and logic; the right brain is in touch with images, sensations, memories, and feelings that are personal and collective, in time and timeless, and it imposes no order or logic on them. An "Aha!" recognition comes when there is a crossover from right to left or left to right, and suddenly a whole piece of knowledge falls into place—we then know something on multiple levels and are affected or moved by what we now know.

3.

Zeus, God of the Sky— The Realm of Will and Power

He was Lord of the Sky, the Rain-god, and the Cloud-gatherer, who wielded the awful thunderbolt. His power was greater than that of all the other divinities together.

Nevertheless he was not omnipotent or omniscient, either.

Edith Hamilton, *Mythology*

The divine Zeus, who in his glory is the god who appears as light and brings light and consciousness to the humans, becomes in his darkness an enemy of the life-force, locked in his structures and laws, fearing and resisting change and any threat to the status quo.

Arianna Stassinopoulos, *The Gods of Greece*

Zeus was the chief and most powerful of the Olympian gods. As the Olympian Sky God, he ruled from Mt. Olympus, a high and distant mountain, whose craggy heights are often hidden by clouds that gather there. When he and his brothers Poseidon and Hades drew lots and divided up the world, Zeus received the sky, Poseidon was allotted the sea, and Hades got the underworld. The earth and Mt. Olympus were to be held in common, but Zeus from his sky position dominated the landscape and ruled over it all.

The sky is vastly different from the sea or the underworld— as different as are the personalities of the ruling gods of each domain. To venture upward into the sky realm requires leaving the earth, losing touch with the tangible world in order to gain a wide overview of the terrain. From this vantage point, we see the forest, not the individual trees.

Zeus was god of lightning, his symbol the thunderbolt. To this day, when we dare to go against a patriarchal prohibition, we "wait for lightning to strike us dead," and breathe a sigh of relief when it is not forthcoming. As rain-bringer, Zeus also provided what growing things need. Whether he was being punitive or generative, Zeus's power was usually expressed from above and from a distance.

Like all successful rulers, he was adept at strategy, forming alliances through which he defeated the Titans. He established and consolidated his power. And most important—a Zeus characteristic—he could impose his will on others.

We become like Zeus when we want an exalted position and power, either over others or in order to accomplish what we want in the world. It is the realm of powerful men with political and economic power, from the legendary King Arthur and the historical Roman Emperor Augustus Caesar to contemporary political leaders, including Prime Minister Margaret Thatcher of England, who demonstrates by her example that the sky realm is not an exclusively male domain, but is an orientation toward power and a capacity for decisive action.

Most significant psychologically—especially in contrast to Poseidon and Hades' realms—the sky represents a conscious attitude, a perspective that exalts control, reason, and will above all other qualities.

ZEUS THE GOD

Zeus (Jupiter or Jove, as he was known by the Romans) was supreme god among the Greek Olympians. He was the sky god who ruled Olympus and hurled thunderbolts. His symbolic creature was the eagle. Zeus was called Gatherer of the Clouds and Sender of the Fair Winds, as well as Father of Gods and Men (even though within Greek mythology he was not their father: several gods were his brothers and sisters, and he did not create or beget humankind). He gave kings their authority and guarded their rights and power, maintained the laws and punished transgressors.

Zeus was portrayed as a powerful man with a beard, often seated on his throne with scepter or thunderbolt. His most famous statue was one of the seven wonders of the ancient world, made of gold and ivory by Phidias and placed in the Temple of Zeus at Olympia. His majestic visage was one aspect; the other was as a philanderer, whose many amorous conquests were the subjects for artists.

His name is derived from the Indo-European word *dyu*, which means "to shine." Light and power were his chief abstract attributes.

GENEALOGY AND MYTHOLOGY

Zeus's birth story has already been told in the second chapter of this book, on fathers and sons. He was the youngest and lastborn child of Cronus and Rhea. He was preceded by three sisters and two brothers, all of whom were swallowed by Cronus.

Rhea saved Zeus by tricking Cronus into mistaking a stone, wrapped in swaddling clothes, for the baby, which saved him from being devoured. Zeus was then hidden in a Cretan cave and raised by a nymph or a goat (stories differ).

When he grew to manhood, he persuaded wise Metis to give Cronus an emetic, causing him to vomit up his siblings and one stone. And then, with his brothers Poseidon and Hades and other allies, Zeus struggled to overthrow Cronus and the Titans who had ruled from Olympus. He succeeded after a ten-year struggle for supremacy. Here Zeus was a strategist and alliance maker, who eventually succeeded because he had the Cyclopes and the Hundred-handed Ones (who were grateful because he freed them) on his side. The Cyclopes gave Zeus his lightning and thunderbolts, and the Hundred-handed Ones provided him with extraordinary firing power of one hundred throwing arms.

ZEUS AND HIS CONSORTS

After defeating his father Cronus and the Titans, Zeus began a series of liaisons with female deities, nymphs, and mortal women through which he fathered divine qualities, most of the second generation of Olympians, and demigods. Hesiod lists seven official consorts, serial marriages that ended with Hera. They were Metis, Themis, Eurynome, Demeter, Mnemosyne, Leto, and Hera. Most of his consorts were "older" goddesses; that is, worshiped before Zeus came to power, whose people were defeated, and whose divinities became subordinated to Zeus.

The first was Metis, a goddess known for her wisdom and the mother of Athena. The Titaness Themis, a goddess of justice and order, was his second wife; her offspring were the Fates and the Seasons or Hours. Eurynome, his third consort, bore the Graces. By his Olympian sister Demeter, he fathered Persephone; by Mnemosyne (Memory), the nine Muses. His sixth consort was Leto, another Titaness, who gave birth to his twin children Apollo and Artemis.

Zeus And Hera

As an Olympian daughter of Rhea and Cronus, Hera's birth rank was equal to Zeus's. She attracted his roving eye, and determined to seduce her, he turned himself into a shivering cuckoo bird. On seeing the pathetic little creature, Hera took pity, and held it against her breasts to warm it—whereupon Zeus shed his disguise, and tried to seduce her. But she held him off until he promised to marry her. The marriage that resulted had a honeymoon phase that lasted three hundred years. Zeus then reverted to being promiscuous. Greek mythology is filled with his affairs, and with Hera's humiliation and jealous wrath.

Although the "honeymoon's over" version of the Zeus-Hera marriage is best known (thanks to Homer), in her worship Hera was greatly revered as Goddess of Marriage. In her rituals, she was worshiped in the spring as Hera the Maiden. She was celebrated in the summer or autumn—in a sacred marriage to Zeus, as Zeus, Bringer to Completion, or to Perfection—as Hera the Fulfilled One or Hera the Perfected One. In winter she became the mourning Hera the Widow (even though immortal Zeus never died), who annually went into hiding. In the spring, an image of Hera was immersed in a pool, and she returned virginal once more as Hera the Maiden.

ZEUS THE PHILANDERER

Zeus had at least twenty-three affairs with numerous notable progeny as a result, including two Olympians; Hermes the Messenger God, whose mother was Maia; and Dionysus, the ecstatic God of Wine, whose mother Semele was a mortal. And according to Homer, Zeus was also the father of Aphrodite, her mother being the sea nymph Dione.

Zeus's love affairs with mortal women were seductions in which he often took on a nonhuman form. He became a shower of gold to impregnate Danaë, whose son was the hero Perseus; he was a satyr with Antiope, seduced Leda in the form of a swan, and was the white bull who carried Europa off.

The Other Women and their offspring were forever attracting Hera's wrath. Zeus was usually unsuccessful in hiding his affairs, even when he turned Io into a cow, and Callisto into a bear. He invariably saved the offspring of his affairs, but sometimes didn't manage to save the woman, who bore the brunt of Hera's anger.

Zeus and Ganymede

Zeus—like the greek culture he represented—did not confine his sensuality to women. Ganymede was a beautiful Trojan youth, who was carried to Olympus to be Zeus's cupbearer, and according to most accounts to be his lover as well. He was snatched up either by a whirlwind or by Zeus's eagle. Zeus then sent Hermes to console the boy's father for the news and to recompense him for his loss with a pair of fine horses (or a golden grapevine, depending on the version). In Rome, Ganymede was often called Catamitus, which was the origin of our word *catamite*. He was immortalized in the constellation Aquarius as the water-bearer.

ZEUS AND HIS CHILDREN

Zeus fathered many children. His offspring were gods and goddesses, or demigods, the result of his numerous liaisons with both divine and mortal women.

He was the first of the Greek sky gods to be protective, generous, and trusting toward many of his sons and daughters. When Dionysus's mother died while she was pregnant, Zeus sewed the fetus into his own thigh, carrying him there until he could be born. He gave his little daughter Artemis everything she asked for to be Goddess of the Hunt—her bow and arrows, hounds, and choice of companions. He trusted his other daughter Athena with his symbols of power. He settled a dispute between Apollo and Hermes, firmly insisting that Hermes return the cows he had stolen from his elder half-brother, which allowed them to become friends.

The dark aspect of the destructive father was also part of his nature. He was either an incestuous father who seduced his daughter Persephone, or the father who gave permission to Hades to abduct and rape her, and thus did not respond to her cries for help when she called out to him, as Hades was carrying her off. One myth ascribed Hephaestus's deformed foot to Zeus, who threw the young boy down from Olympus when Hephaestus sided with his mother—child abuse. Another son, Ares, was psychologically rejected, the object of his father's hate. And (as noted earlier) fearful that Metis was pregnant with a son who could supplant him, he swallowed her to abort that possibility.

Yet however he treated his children, the generativity of Zeus as the father of many was an essential part of his nature.

ZEUS THE ARCHETYPE

To sit at the summit, with power, authority, and dominion over a chosen realm is the Zeus position. Men who play "king of the mountain" in real life, and succeed at it, are like Zeus. They share characteristic personality traits and susceptibilities; the underlying pattern is the Zeus archetype.

ZEUS AS ARCHETYPE OF THE KING

Zeus had the ambition and the ability to establish a realm over which he was the chief god, and the urge to preside over one's own territory is a major drive of this archetype, which shapes men (and women) to be and behave like Zeus.

When Zeus is the archetype, the need to "establish a kingdom" is a driving force. At the very least, he subscribes to the notion of "a man's home is his castle," and to that end he wants a house and a family. Thus this archetype predisposes a man to want to get married and have children as extensions of himself. He expects his wife to run the household well and do the day-to-day parenting to his satisfaction, while he is minimally involved.

A family is only one part of the larger motivating vision of establishing his own kingdom. A Zeus wants authority and power, and does not mind taking risks to reach his goals. He would rather be his own boss than work for someone else. And if he is a far-seeing Zeus, when he starts his first business he views that as only the beginning.

King Arthur is a legendary version of this archetype. He began as an unrecognized nobody with a destiny to unify a warring feudal land under his banner. Today the battlefields to be won are usually economic realms, and an enterprising ambitious young unknown who becomes an entrepreneurial baron—such as Ross Perot, whose Texas operation grew into a multinational Electronic Data Systems—personifies the archetype of the king.

This archetype is also expressed through "hereditary kingships": in men born to family position and wealth, who inherited a mantle of power, so to speak. When the archetype coincides with an inherited role, the driving force is the man's urge to extend the boundaries of his kingdom, to acquire more and more economic power and prestige.

The big house and the flagship office building are expressions of the same archetype. Once power has been consolidated, Camelot must be built.

ZEUS AS THE ARCHETYPE OF DECISIVE ACTION

The thunderbolt and the eagle are Zeus's two major symbols. They are remarkably apt expressions of the "from afar," quick-to-act decisiveness that characterizes the Zeus archetype.

The eagle soars high above the ground, seeing from horizon to far horizon. Yet he can also detect the movements of his small prey far below, and can descend swiftly to seize that small rodent or rabbit in his claws. Similarly, Zeus characteristically is on the lookout for what he wants or needs to acquire. It may be a particular product, a potential employee, or a company; when he spots what he wants, he goes after it single mindedly. He has both an overview perspective—the big vision—and an awareness of the particular important detail. And when he focuses on the detail, it has his total attention: he has no intention of letting it out of his sight or his grasp. Yet, like an eagle whose prey suddenly darts out of sight or is taken by another predator, for all the energy and effort he put into a particular pursuit, he can change direction easily, cut his losses, and move on.

Zeus's thunderbolt was a symbol of his punitive power. It too, comes from afar to strike decisively—but only after dark storm clouds have gathered and thunder has already rumbled, suggesting a concentration of emotion, a gathering of anger. Jealous Zeus killed Iaison with a thunderbolt when he lay with the goddess Demeter in the thrice-plowed field. Another of his thunderbolts struck Phaëton, when the youth lost control of the horses that drew the chariot of the sun.

The thunderbolt can be a symbol of "firing power," just as the eagle can represent the capacity to acquire or hire decisively. For a chief executive like Lee Iacocca, who brought Chrysler Corporation back from the brink of bankruptcy, the capacity to fire (and hire) is essential to success. It is true that firing may kill a career, may end the work life of a loyal employee, and obviously has an effect on his family. For a Mafia chieftain, "getting rid of the guy" may mean physical death. But these are not Zeus's considerations, and men who personify this archetype do not lose sleep over such matters.

Former president Ronald Reagan, on the other hand, could not seem to fire anyone directly. Although he sat in a Zeus position, he was not noted for acting decisively, which is a hallmark of the archetype.

ZEUS AS ALLIANCE MAKER: THROUGH BUSINESS CONNECTIONS

A successful Zeus figure can work cooperatively with other powerful men. He excels at "summit meetings," in forging alliances and determining boundaries, in arranging *quid pro quo* agreements. His word is enough. He wants to deal with others who have authority and are decisive. He expects others to look out for their own best interests, as he does for his own. For him to consolidate his base of power and expand from there, which are natural goals for the Zeus archetype, alliances are essential.

In contemporary times, the Zeus man's alliances are made with bankers and suppliers, distributors and even competitors, or with referral sources or bureaucrats, or donors, instead of with feudal lords or sovereigns. The titles and realms are different, but the form is the same.

Zeus the god established the Olympians in power with the aid of the Hundred-handed Ones and the Cyclopes, without whose help he could not have defeated the Titans. They helped him because he freed them. In the business world, a Zeus considers when he will "call in his chips": Is now the time to ask for a repayment for favors done? If so, a successful Zeus will do it with subtlety and sensitivity. With each such transaction, a Zeus forges alliances, and consolidates his position, as was so well demonstrated in Mario Puzo's *The Godfather*, who was played on screen by Marlon Brando. Here was the Zeus archetype clothed as Mafia chieftain.

ZEUS AS ALLIANCE MAKER: THROUGH MARRIAGES

For the Zeus archetype, whose primary meaning comes through establishing a realm, marriage is also a means through which alliances are made and power is consolidated. Royal marriages were arranged by prime ministers. Patriarchal marriages in all cultures are alliances between families, in which property and progeny are the main concern. Zeus's seven official marriages reflect this same pattern.

For Zeus, finding a suitable wife is not a matter of heart or soul connection, but a matter of state, an alliance to serve the goal of establishing or consolidating the realm. Other archetypes also need to be present if the relationship is to include passion, friendship, or other aspects that fulfill personal needs.

No wonder the Zeus-Hera marriage turns out to be a model of conflict. When these two powerful archetypes underlie the union, each is motivated by a totally different intention. For Hera marriage is a sacred commitment and has the most important priority, with monogamy and fidelity essential to her well-being. When Hera is the major archetype in a woman, that woman seeks marriage as the means through which she will be personally fulfilled, perfected, brought to completion.

ZEUS THE PHILANDERER

As noted earlier, Zeus was the archetypal philanderer, who seduced nymphs, mortals and goddesses and fathered numerous progeny. He often changed himself into many forms in order to seduce and impregnate whomever he desired. For Leda he became a swan, for Danaë he was a shower of golden rain; for Europa he changed himself into a bull; for Io he was a cloud.

He went after women with the singleness of purpose that is characteristic of his "eagle" nature. Seeing who he wants, he does whatever is necessary to get close to her: changes shape, shows a more vulnerable part of himself, or becomes the ardent lover. Once he has succeeded, his attention most likely again focuses on his work realm. He may unconsciously not protect against pregnancy, for he has a strong drive to be a progenitor. And typically he will "look after his own," financially providing for any progeny, and acknowledging paternity.

ZEUS THE SKY FATHER

A drive to have children is part of the Zeus archetype. His expectation of them is similar to what he expects of his subordinates: to be obedient and carry out his will. His favorite children replicate his ideal of himself as a fair-minded, superior person who does not let emotions ever get "out of control." These qualities are shared by his children Apollo and Athena and are personified by the achievement-oriented, rational son who does well in school and at sports, and the daughter whose mind works like his, who has a special, "father's daughter," mutual admiration bond with him. He is a mentor father, who guides his children's education and careers, as he often does for other, younger people whom he mentors in his business or professional world. He expects loyalty in return, and feels betrayed when a subordinate or child "grows up" and then differs with him.

Zeus is the archetype of a dynastic father, who founds a family. He wants many children and grandchildren to carry on after him, and to this end he tries to impose his will on what his children do in the world, not only in his lifetime but also beyond the grave. Motivated by this dynastic urge, as well as by his nature as a provider father, a multimillionaire Zeus will structure his business and establish trusts to carry out his will through successive generations. A less impressive Zeus with a smaller realm does the equivalent on a smaller scale.

It is a Zeus characteristic for a man to strive to be a father who provides well for his children, and to take pride in how will he does it. The size of his house reflects this trait, as well as expresses his need for a domain. The provider father is usually generous, but his generosity is motivated by his desire to control his children and is tied to his expectations of them. Who gets what in the budgets of Zeus families, as in presidential budgets, reflects the aims of the man at the top.

Zeus is archetypally an authoritarian father who has the final word. He may have open lines of communication with his children, but family and business decisions are made as Lee Iacocca describes: "My policy has always been to be democratic all the way to the point of decision. Then I become the ruthless commander, 'Okay, I've heard everybody,' I say. 'Now here's what we're going to do.'"[1]

ZEUS THE MAN

The life of Zeus the man shows what the archetypal pattern of Zeus looks like when it is lived out. It's a composite picture, intuitively drawn from multiple examples, that can serve as a mirror for the Zeus man to see himself. As we see how the pattern is lived out from infancy to old age, we too can learn to recognize Zeus.

Most men who are like Zeus also have other aspects: there is usually more than one god in every man, which means that a great deal of what follows will fit the Zeus man, but not necessarily everything. Also, the Zeus pattern (as with all others) may become dominant during a phase of a man's life, rather than remain the major inner influence throughout his lifetime. Zeus is obviously present then, but in the background at other times. For example, fatherhood itself may usher in a Zeus phase in a man, if he now shifts gears to establish himself in the world and head a family and if he never espoused these ambitions before. Or a man (or woman) may resemble Zeus in only one area of his life, just in business or just in the realm of personal relationships.

EARLY YEARS

The Zeus baby makes himself known early; he demonstrates a strong will of his own. Diverting his interest is not easy when his mind is set, when he wants to grasp something in his hand, or he has it and won't let go. This is the two-year-old child who has contributed more than his share to the stereotype of "the terrible twos," for he can say "No!" with great authority.

To temper his autocratic nature and develop his innate gifts, a Zeus child benefits from learning about fairness and justice at home and in school, and from being given practical things to think about, and have toys or objects that he can manipulate or deploy. Typically, if he's alone a Zeus child will create a miniature world in which he makes things happen. He builds roads for his fleet of cars, or deploys his regiments of toy soldiers on a battlefield, or builds a city, rather than reads a book or daydreams. He's also not happy with solitary play if he has any choice at all. He's the kid who's always the leader of his troops on the playground, or the kid who wants to be, and when he cannot, feels terribly thwarted.

HIS PARENTS

As a toddler, the Zeus boy intimidates, by the strength of his will, some mothers who have been dominated by authoritarian men. He is a boss by nature, a quality that provokes some fathers—especially authoritarian ones, who may show him who's boss in an abusive way. Parents may "butt heads" with this child; they are challenged by the need not to give in to him, and allow him to become at age two or three a petty tyrant, nor to get into head-on power struggles in which he learns that might makes right.

More so than with other types of children, parents need to remember that he is just a baby or just a toddler—even if he acts as if he were Louis the XIV or Henry VIII. Parents who offer him appropriate choices, rather than getting into power struggles with him, encourage him to think and act, which are innate positive abilities of Zeus. Asking, "Would you like to have this or that? Do this or that? Go here or there?" is better than getting into a contest of will of who can say no and have the last word. It's also better than having the decision rest on who is physically stronger; the rule that might makes right is too easily acceptable to a young Zeus. Set firm limits, and expect them to be tested. He will undoubtedly need to experience a judicious amount of parental power in order to recognize that his parents do have authority and can exercise it.

Once matters are decided to his satisfaction, this child can become very absorbed in whatever he is doing. He usually has an extraverted, positive disposition. After an issue is settled, peace can reign.

The very worst combination for his development is a weak, passive mother and a domineering, abusive father. This child will then identify with the aggressor whenever he is able to—and he can bide his time. Depending on how badly he is treated by a father who shows him "who's boss," and if his mother can't protect him, he can be made to be submissive to those in greater authority. When this is the case, he may lord it over those that are weaker when he has the opportunity. (Remember, too, that the mother can be the abusive parent.)

A Zeus son of a successful, emotionally distant father has a role model who he admires, and who helps him get ahead in the world tangibly as well. If he also has a nurturing mother who loved him, he grows up with a sense of being entitled to have what he wants, with confidence in himself and his place in the world. Nature and nurture reinforce his sense that he is "somebody."

ADOLESCENCE AND EARLY ADULTHOOD

In adolescence, his relationship with authority figures is often the main issue. As a young man, he has a self-assurance that can provoke authoritarian men to show him "who's boss around here." And though he may chafe under them, he can bide his time and cooperate. As a strategist, he sees no point in engaging in power struggles he cannot win.

Usually his male peers recognize him as a natural leader in high school and in college or wherever he is, and he usually dates popular girls and is sexually active. He's a pragmatist, not an idealist; he accepts the world as it is and wants his piece of it. However bright he is, he's not an intellectual. He's not particularly introspective, doesn't waste time dwelling on the past or on his own or anyone else's feelings. As far as he's concerned, he's fine, and life is something to get on with.

WORK

From the time he got his first minimum-wage, after-school job, he has observed and thought about ways he might do things if he were in charge. Many other boys his age see the job as just a source of spending money, do whatever they are expected to do and no more, but the Zeus boy has a lively curiosity about the business as a business, assesses the people he works for, and, usually on his own, learns what works and why. If he grows up in the farmlands or in a ghetto, his attention will be drawn toward whatever the "business" at hand is, from cash crops to drug dealing or other rackets. Characteristically, he sees the bigger picture and keeps adapting his thoughts to what is possible for him. He wonders why older men in charge don't do what he sees as obvious and necessary, or seize opportunities he would grasp if he were in their position. No one has to teach him about initiative and hard work, or tell him to keep an eye out for opportunities; this comes naturally.

Sometimes, he has a specific interest that he is following—whatever it is, the Zeus perspective aids him in getting ahead in whatever his chosen field turns out to be. For example, he has a knack for understanding and using "old boy networks," and is delighted with capitalism because of the opportunity it offers him to get ahead. And he has several innate psychological advantages that give him an edge. Acquiring power and money or property is a game he plays naturally well because he's realistic and confident, and doesn't take what others do personally. If he has to wage a major conflict in his business that may ruin others financially, or require firing people who have worked for him, or make an example of someone, he can give the orders that are equivalent to hurling thunderbolts. In just the same way, a Zeus high up in the Pentagon or in a criminal gang can coolly give orders that will result in deaths. Emotional distance keeps him from losing sleep over such actions.

RELATIONSHIPS WITH WOMEN

As former Secretary of State Henry Kissinger observed, "Power is an aphrodisiac." The "important man" aura of a Zeus does draw some women to him, which is part of his success. He also doesn't go after a woman with his heart in his hand—with women, as in his work, he is a strategist. If he wants a woman for a date, for a job, for a wife—he presents himself in whatever form is most likely to seduce or win her.

He considers his money and power an essential part of his attractiveness; like Aristotle Onassis courting Jacqueline Kennedy, it makes him feel entitled to pursue certain women. He doesn't expect a woman to love him just for himself, and certainly not for his soul, which he doesn't think is even worth speculating about.

He's not interested in an egalitarian relationship with a woman, either for a wife or a friend. He also isn't interested or adept at discussing feelings. And he wants a woman to do what he expects her to do and not bother him otherwise.

RELATIONSHIPS WITH MEN

Men are the players that matter in "the game" to him. Some of the players are his competitors and allies, and he knows that today's competitor may be an ally tomorrow, and vice versa. Other players are like rooks and knights in a chess game whose moves he controls. He will advance one and sacrifice another. It is a mistake for men who are his allies or work for him to think that they matter to him personally—when the chips are down, they are expendable. From his standpoint, he considers everyone expendable, and he expects others to feel the same way and act accordingly toward him. Although he can be ruthless, he often doesn't appear to be because he knows there is no profit in making enemies. And he has no real sympathy when men "take it hard" on finding that they are expendable—they should have known they were, for he considers showing vulnerability or neediness or being emotional signs of stupidity or weakness. (If he were introspective about such matters,—which would be uncharacteristic, he might realize how personally uncomfortable it makes him feel, and wonder why.)

One source of success is his ability to negotiate and come to agreements, which he does all the time. He negotiates well because he has studied men and thinks about what they want and what they will settle for. An especially able Zeus is often very sensitive and up to a point very caretaking of another man's (unspoken) needs, including his need to keep up appearances.

The exclusive clubs where men gather for lunch, play golf, or go duck hunting together are bastions of Zeus power and privilege that serve many purposes. Membership is an important indicator that a man has made it to the top. Here further alliances can also be made to advance family and business interests. And such clubs are refuges where a Zeus man can be among men like himself, men who devoted their energies solely toward acquiring power, and consequently remained immature or undeveloped psychologically. Their idea of fun is exemplified by the Bohemian Grove camp, which is a gathering of the most powerful men in America, from presidents of corporations to past and current U.S. presidents. There they can get drunk and "get laid" (while Bohemian Grove has been off limits to women as members or staff, it is a mecca for prostitutes) cavort, swear, and put on outrageous plays in which men play the parts of women.

SEXUALITY

A successful Zeus man is the equivalent of an "alpha male" in studies of primates in hierarchical species. Alpha males expect success, are aggressive, intimidate lower-ranking males, and (at least among primates) have their pick of the females and are more sexually active than subordinate males. The god Zeus behaved like an alpha male in acquiring and consolidating his power and in impregnating numerous women and fathering numerous offspring. Exercising sexual prowess for a Zeus man can be like having political or economic power in proving to himself and to others that he can have what he wants. Zeus the philanderer may see a desirable woman as a "perk" that he can have as a measure of his status. He may desire her as an acquisition, or want her sexually, or all three.

For all the success with women a Zeus man is reputed to have, one not-well-kept secret is that he is not a good lover. To be a good lover, other archetypes would have to be present in him. Zeus is emotionally distant, does not have an earthy nature, doesn't try to please women, and isn't passionate. He is sexually aggressive and he can be seductive, although his libido can also be totally focused on his work for long periods of time.

Because the Zeus man may focus on achieving power, other aspects of his personality become stunted. Especially likely to suffer is his capacity for emotional intimacy, the lack of which affects his expression of sexuality. His choice of sexual partners reflects this emotional poverty, especially if as he grows older, his partners seem to be getting younger, imitating the classic picture of an aging Zeus with a series of young nymphs.

At the same time that he keeps company with young nymphs, he may also have sexual fantasies of being dominated by a powerful woman, and as prostitutes whose clientele is made up of powerful men report, they are commonly asked to participate in enacting this fantasy. However, if in his erotic life he can only be with someone young enough to be his daughter or granddaughter, or if he feels drawn to being a powerless, dominated boy, then his capacity for sexual relating has stayed immature or confused with power.

If he is a homosexual Zeus, the pattern is the same, only more likely exaggerated: there are greater numbers of partners. And, like Zeus who brought Ganymede back to Olympus, he may share his home with a beautiful youth—or with a series of them.

Marriage

A who's who list of Zeus's consorts reveals that he always married up or married an equal. Historically, these marriages reflected the shift in power, as once powerful goddesses and their attributes came to belong to a male warrior god. Much the same happens in real life when an ambitious man marries a woman from a prominent family and acquires her attributes— status and wealth—through the marriage. Any ambitious man who marries his boss's daughter, and through the marriage gains an advantage he otherwise would not have, has done what Zeus did. The choice of a wife who will enhance his climb upward, may be a calculated one, or may be an unconscious choice "made" by the Zeus archetype. In the latter case, he is powerfully attracted to the woman through whom he can live out his myth of becoming somebody important.

Most Zeus men do marry during the phase of life in which they are establishing themselves. For such a young man, whose life will be shaped by the Zeus archetype (unless life draws on other aspects of himself), this early marriage is crucial. Zeus may not have been the decisive archetype if this man married a woman he fell in love with. From the Zeus standpoint, she could be a very unsuitable choice—yet one who will keep him in touch with an irrational, deeply emotional, earthy, or spiritual part of himself, much as he may consciously resist what she represents. Conversely, her demands on him to be a successful Zeus, when he began life with other, once equally vital aspects of himself, may be decisive for him.

However much potential influence his wife has on his development, his actual power in the relationship makes it much more likely that he will dominate her, and that they will have a traditional patriarchal marriage that revolves around his needs and his need for her to do her job well. Unless she is strong enough to create the conflict that will change him, she will give up her need for intimacy or her dream for herself beyond what they have together.

If he is a philandering Zeus and his marriage had to do with establishing his domain, and if she is archetypally Hera, the combination attacks her deepest values and destroys her potential fulfillment through marriage. Instead, she may end up possessed by the vindictive and jealous shadow aspect of Hera. If he does love her, however, and is distressed by the pain his shallow behavior causes her, then he may grow emotionally as a result.

Most Zeus men—once the courtship and honeymoon is over—don't have time for their marriages or their wives. Such a man may deceptively maintain that all the time he devotes to his work is for her and the children. If it is solely up to him—and in marriages, where he has all the power, it *is* up to him—marriage is not very personal, isn't really intimate, and doesn't get much of his attention. And most women who are married to Zeus men have had to accept his definition of marriage. But this is changing, and women—especially if they do not follow the Hera archetype—are leaving Zeus marriages. But if she has an affair, he will do what he can to destroy his rival in some way, as Zeus struck Demeter's lover Iasion dead with a thunderbolt.

CHILDREN

Zeus men don't just "have children"; many found families and want to found dynasties, which is part of the vision they have for themselves. A successful Zeus may help some of his children get ahead in the world as well as provide for them. He is a distant father emotionally, and may also be an unavailable one. Although he often is not physically present, he is the parent who wields authority.

Zeus fathers can mold the lives of their children and take away the life that child might have been suited for, as well as facilitating the growth of children whose natural abilities are enhanced by access to the education and opportunities he can provide. The force of his personality and his authority make his judgments of his children particularly powerful. His perceptions of them, which may not be accurate, as well as the prejudices or values he has, carry enormous weight—as does the wish to have his approval, which a child may either strive to get (all his or her life) or may despair of ever receiving.

All the second-generation Olympian gods and goddesses looked to Zeus as father. Some were favored, others were abused, nurtured, rejected, or detested by him. We ourselves live in a patriarchal culture where Zeus values are pervasive, regardless of the archetype of our personal fathers. How a particular child fares with a Zeus-type father depends on his or her archetypal pattern and the strength of the ego through which the child expresses that archetype.

MIDDLE YEARS

Sometime in midlife, the Zeus man takes stock and can see how successful he has been in his ascent, whether there will be a place at the top for him, and if he wants to climb this particular mountain. He may find himself temporarily in the doldrums, without his usual drive, as this questioning goes on, often outside his consciousness. He may declare that this is the time he needs to take that long-promised vacation or sabbatical, or he may flirt with making a major change. It is uncharacteristic of him to introspect about himself and his own motives, yet he may feel some nagging doubt about whether this whole personal expedition to the top, to which he has singlemindedly devoted himself and subordinated others (and their needs) is worth the effort. He may know, deep within himself, that it is not.

Midlife is a time when other successful Zeus men know that they have arrived at their particular summit. He may have set his sights on owning his own small company or ranch, or heading his own division, or chairing a particular department, and made it—goals that another Zeus man might not even consider much of a way station to his particular top. To be a successful

Zeus does not require being Donald Trump (the spectacularly successful billionaire developer); it only requires reaching a personally set, meaningful goal and finding that it gives a sense of satisfaction. Then midlife may be a time to "pause to enjoy the view."

For a Zeus man, midlife can also be a time of major emotional difficulties, when neglected parts of himself or neglected relationships dramatically assert themselves. His adolescent children may get into major difficulties, his wife may leave him, he may have a heart attack, he may act out a shameful fantasy. His arrogance may make him blind to his limitations, and after all his hard-earned success, he may overreach himself and fail spectacularly. He may consequently find himself rejected and embittered, without any close relationships, or humbled and able to learn from painful lessons and reconstruct portions of his life differently.

Midlife may also mark important shifts of emphasis in men who, while they were predominantly Zeus-like in the first half of their lives, grew through their relationships as well. He now can and wants to spend more time with people he cares about, and even in work he finds himself taking an interest in mentoring others, or in deepening friendships. When such is the case, chances are that a crisis of someone close to him—his spouse or a child, or a parent—made him aware of how precious people are to him.

LATER YEARS

If he ever becomes introspective, the Zeus man will note that his need to impose his will and be in control has come up at every turn in his life. In his later years, he faces this need once more, especially if he had been a successful Zeus. Can he let go of control? Whether it's the family grocery store or Columbia Broadcasting System—as it was for Bill Paley—giving up control or having it wrested from him is usually a troublesome issue, unless he has grown beyond this one archetype and become wise.

Like the series of Greek father gods who feared sons would supplant them, a controlling Zeus struggles to avoid the inevitable. He may have prevented a real son from ever challenging him, by viewing his boy as a competitor from the very beginning.

He may have so undermined his sons, that he has no competent heir. Still, other men will move in to take over when he weakens his grasp on whatever scepter he holds. And he probably will attempt to control his assets beyond the grave through his testamentary will. This losing struggle to maintain control is the fate of the man who subordinates his entire life to the Zeus archetype.

PSYCHOLOGICAL DIFFICULTIES

Every god or archetype has the potential for creating certain specific kinds of psychological difficulties. For the man who would be Zeus on Mt. Olympus, certain problems and limitations "go with the territory" of the sky realm. Emotional costs are involved for himself and others in his ascent, and once he reaches the summit, his lack of consciousness, coupled with power, can prove a destructive combination.

A TALKING HEAD IS AN INCOMPLETE MAN

Zeus's realm was the sky, and the Zeus archetype predisposes a man to live in his head and express himself through his words and power to make things happen. He has a natural advantage in an industrial patriarchal culture, where a superior man is supposed to be "a talking head," who works with ideas and abstractions (like money and investments, or law, or power), not with his hands or body—a man cut off from his heart, who will not be moved by sympathy, for that would make him "a bleeding heart" or "a weak sister." Such a man has a superior position that gives him the power to use words and have them believed and obeyed. That power is as commonplace as being able to pick up the phone and make a call that puts his will in motion—to have his word be law in his home, in business, or on the battlefield, or to realize a concept of his, to say, "Let there be light, and there is light."

A man dominated by the Zeus archetype in himself (which is also the ruling archetype in our culture) often gets cut off from experiencing his body as a receptive or as a giving sensual part of himself. He may pride himself on how many miles he can run, what good shape he is in, or his stamina. Such pride concerns mastery over his body, not enjoyment of it. He is also likely to be cut off from his heart as a giving and receiving emotional organ. The Zeus man is often out of touch with his own sensuality and emotional responses, which makes him unable to communicate or connect at these levels with others or know these aspects of himself. This emotional immaturity easily leads to distorted sensual and sexual expression, shame and guilt, and condemnation or devaluation of others who are not cut off as he is. He is an incomplete person, undeveloped in ways he usually cannot even appreciate.

"HE CAN'T SEE THE TREES FOR THE FOREST"

The Zeus man prides himself on seeing the bigger picture, of his grasp of the issues, which gives him an overview perspective. He may lead a war on poverty and never have anything to do with a poor person (and smile wryly, if he knows himself at all, at the *Peanuts* cartoon character who says, "I love humanity, it's people I can't stand"). Or he may be a leading expert on child rearing without ever having taken full responsibility for a single child or having whole-heartedly loved one. He considers his perspective superior, and as he is listened to as an authority, he has no reason to doubt his position. When he is challenged by someone who has firsthand experience and who also takes an emotional stance, he dismisses that person with the comment "She (or he) can't see the forest for the trees." He might instead consider that he himself "can't see the trees for the forest"— much less love one.

In Vietnam, for example, Zeus's expertise failed miserably. Men who had risen so swiftly to the top that they had once been referred to as "whiz kids" ran the war from Washington, D.C., and assumed that the superior U.S. firing power would be decisive. They did not take into account how individuals in Vietnam would behave and why, making this war unwinnable. The suffering they caused was unfathomable. Whoever thought up the idea that the nuclear war button should be behind a human heart, and require that the president take a dull knife and kill that person personally before he could push the button, realized that a Zeus man does not "see the trees for the forest," and thus needs to become conscious about the suffering and killing he can order from afar.

"MIGHT MAKES RIGHT" MENTALITY

Zeus is an archetype that predisposes men (and women) to seek and use power. Danger arises when power is acquired. Lord Acton, a nineteenth century historian who was deeply opposed to the doctrine of papal infallibility, wrote: "Power tends to corrupt, and absolute power corrupts absolutely." His statement has become an aphorism, a concise statement that expresses a principle that we recognize as true, and one that Zeus men in small and large ways often validate.

Historically, men in power have believed that they rule by divine right, which is not surprising, given that Zeus is their underlying archetype. Law has developed as a counterbalance to the excesses of men in power, but even now Zeus men often feel and act "above the law."

The man who exercises abusive power over others is corrupted further by this same "might makes right" mentality. Self-deluded justification—the right to do it—at its worst, often accompanies acts of wife beating, child abuse, and incest in the family.

"UNEASY LIES THE HEAD THAT WEARS THE CROWN": FEAR OF THE USURPER

Power and paranoia often go together. Men at the top fear being overthrown, become suspicious of motives and loyalties, thwart the growth of others lest they become too strong, and help create the very enemies they feared. This is the story of Uranus, Cronus, and Zeus, and is a shadow part of the father archetype.

INFLATION AND GRANDIOSITY: THE EMPEROR'S NEW CLOTHES

A man with authority and power, who sits on top of his particular mountain, is susceptible to thinking that being an authority in one situation makes him an expert on everything. For example, doctors are apt to become psychologically inflated, possibly because they routinely make life-and-death decisions, and because others also attribute expertise to them in areas where they have none. Falling victim to their own inflation, for example, doctors may think of themselves as knowledgable, expert investors even though they have devoted very little attention to investments—a mistake that usually leads to losses.

The Zeus man's inflated view of himself makes him susceptible to being manipulated by others who play up to him, and to repressing others who refuse to. This was of course, what happened in the fable of "The Emperor's New Clothes." If the man feels entitled to flattery and believes it, he will reject honest people and the truth, and suffer the consequences. Like Gresham's law, which says that bad money drives out good, flattery drives out truth. Inevitably, men who have power over others and "don't want to hear the truth," will be cut off from it.

PSYCHOLOGICAL PROBLEMS FOR OTHERS

The combination of emotional distance from others, lack of emotional maturity and the power that a Zeus man holds, creates a variety of problems for others. A wife who wants intimacy and communication from such a man is disappointed, because he neglects relationships once he has secured them (to sustain and deepen relationships, he needs to have developed other archetypes). If she is like Hera, and he is a philandering Zeus, then she will suffer deeply from his betrayal. Her character may suffer, too, if she is taken over by jealousy and vindictiveness.

Children are also negatively affected by this father's absence and his judgmentalism. They feel emotionally abandoned or rejected, and often have troubles with self-esteem if they cannot live up to his expectations.

Victims of an abusive Zeus obviously suffer, and have emotional scars that predispose them to either become abusers themselves (which is more likely for a son) or to be in other abusive situations.

WAYS TO GROW

A Zeus man often remains unaware that he has problems and needs to grow until a major crisis makes it impossible for him to ignore feelings, either those of others or his own. Growth for the Zeus man often begins only after he experiences humility and vulnerability.

WHERE IS THE REST OF ME?

The message that something is wrong needs to get through to the Zeus man. As in former President Reagan's most notable scene as an actor, he has to wake up and realize that parts of him are missing and be distressed: Where is the rest of me? (Reagan was cast as football star, George Gipp in *Knute Rockne: All-American,* who awoke in a hospital to discover that his leg had been amputated, and said, "Where is the rest of me?")

Given his lack of introspection (for introspection involves going down to Hades' realm), and his emotional distance, he is not likely to get the picture that he is dreadfully cut off from himself or others until something drastic happens, and he becomes painfully aware that something is wrong. When he finally wakes up, the message usually comes from someone close to him: the wife he betrayed by his affairs or neglected for work, leaves him; the child he has not bothered to know confronts him or will have nothing to do with him. Only after they cut themselves off from him, does he feel the pain of what is now missing.

Awareness of how cut off he is from his feelings and from others may dawn more gradually in psychotherapy. But because he needs control and assumes that everything is a matter of will, Zeus men don't usually seek help. His more usual reaction to psychological distress is rising above the situation by throwing himself into work. Usually a Zeus man comes to see a psychiatrist only because his spouse insists, and often then he comes "for her." Or he may come because his child's therapist requires both parents to be in therapy.

GETTING THE MESSAGE: A HEART ATTACK

Although a Zeus man might have any kind of serious medical problem, a heart attack often is what fells him. It is a most apt symbolic ailment and one that requires him to make major change in his life. Metaphors abound here: "ignoring his heart," which is traditionally the organ of emotion, has almost killed him. To save his life he needs to come down from the summit, because the oxygen that his heart needs is too thin there. This man may finally get the message that it isn't just a physical problem, but a physical expression of an emotional problem.

FALLING IN LOVE

His heart may abruptly disrupt his life in yet another way. He may fall in love. As if struck by a love arrow of Eros, he may be irresistibly and passionately drawn by his unconscious to a woman he cannot do without. Reason deserts him, and he deserts his responsibilities. In what Jung calls an *enantiodromia,* a too one-sided position flips over into the opposite: the realm of instincts and emotions that he has discounted and kept down, now rise and overturn reason. A crisis ensues that destroys the status quo of his psyche and shakes his marriage; it also brings vitality and life into his constricted heart. A need to be in the emotional realm, which was not acknowledged, now consciously presents itself as fate.

LOSING HIS HEAD

A major loss may also change the Zeus man, by breaking through his emotional barriers and taking him out of his head. He temporarily goes "out of his mind with grief" and plunges into depth. As painful as his sorrow is, as bad as whatever the precipitating situation was, he no longer is isolated from suffering humanity, he comes down off the mountain and becomes "more human."

The experience may change him by opening him to Poseidon's realm of emotions, which puts him in touch with his own feelings and his need for others. (Or, like a temporarily toppled head of state, the Zeus aspect of himself may reassert itself, judge what happened as humiliating, and now anxious that it could happen again, clamp down even harder on his emotions.)

HEALING WHAT AILS HIM

In the Grail legend, there is a king—a Zeus figure—with a wound that will not heal. As long as his wound remains unhealed, his kingdom will stay a wasteland. In his castle is the Grail, which can heal him—but that will happen only if a young man, an innocent fool, comes to his court, sees the Grail and the wounded king, and asks a question. In one version, that question is "What ails thee?" The recognition that something is wrong must be achieved before any healing process can begin. The question "What is the matter?" has to be asked and answered.

In the legend, the symbolic wound that will not heal is either in the king's thigh close to his genitals, or in the genitals themselves. Such a wound affects expression of instinct and passion, and impairs sexuality, generativity, and creativity. No wonder his kingdom is a wasteland, for no new life is possible with this wound.

The wounded king can represent the Zeus archetype, or power as the ruling principle in a patriarchy. The wounded king can also represent the patriarchal father in a dysfunctional family, or the ruling archetype in a man's psyche. Whenever a wounded Zeus rules, there is an oppressive need to maintain control that stifles growth and expressiveness. Emotional aridness, lack of creativity, and depression results. The kingdom—which may be the culture, a family, or a man's psyche—then becomes like a desert wasteland where nothing grows or thrives.

For healing to take place, an innocent fool must enter his psyche or the situation. Seen from the Zeus perspective, acting naïve or being an innocent is to be the fool. Invested in his position as an authority, it takes courage for a Zeus man to risk looking foolish or to turn to others in his vulnerability, or to encounter new experience with the openness of a child and the ineptness of an amateur. Yet this is what he must do if he is to grow and be healed.

4.

Poseidon, God of the Sea—The Realm of Emotion and Instinct

Riding his chariot of horses across the sea, Poseidon, god of the oceans and god of horses, embodies the two age-old symbols of the unconscious: horse and water. Water has always evoked in man the infinite mystery, infinite possibilities and infinite dangers of our fluid unconscious. With no predetermined shape of its own, it is constantly in movement, never changing yet never the same for two successive moments. And the horse personifies in its primitive potency the instinctive drives of our own raw nature. . . . Poseidon was the most primitive of the gods, the earthshaker, the god of storms and earthquakes, of the sudden devastation of tidal waves—the dangers unleashed when the forces slumbering under the surface of consciousness erupt."

Arianna Stassinopoulos, *The Gods of Greece*

The mover of earth and the empty sea
the great water god . . . earth-shaker
whom the gods gave double honors
you are controller of horses
saviour of ships
hello Poseidon
earth-carrier dark-haired and happy god
your heart is good

Homer, "The Homeric Hymn to Poseidon"
(translated by Charles Boer)

Poseidon lived under the sea, the kingdom that became his when he and his brothers Zeus and Hades drew lots to divide up the world. To grasp the emotionality that he personifies and the psychological domain he rules, we need only think of the powerful moods of the sea. It can be turbulent, with roaring waves that indiscriminately batter everything in its path with tremendous destructive force. Like intense emotional affect that floods the personality and drowns rationality, Poseidon would arise from his undersea residence and rage, and then retreat once more to his underwater home. He was also called Flood-bringer and Earth-shaker, to express the enormous disturbing and destructive power of nature and human nature.

The sea in dreams and metaphor represents the unconscious. In its shallows, just below the surface, lie the emotions and memories that are readily retrievable and personal; in its dark depths are primitive creatures and myriad forms beyond what can be personally known, the collective unconscious. Water and emotions are linked symbolically, which makes the sea an apt realm for Poseidon, who reacted emotionally and intensely when he was provoked. His symbolic animal was the horse, which often represents the power and beauty of physical instincts, a land animal attesting to Poseidon's pre-Olympian origins as an Earth-Father god.

As will become clear when we meet Hades, the underworld also represents the personal and collective unconscious; the undersea is the realm of repressed personal feelings and instincts, and the emotional realm we humans share collectively. Families of Poseidon men often know this aspect of the father archetype in its most frightening form, when his raw feelings erupt and raging emotions periodically flood the household. The patriarchal culture allows fathers as lord and master of their households to unleash fury there—and often nowhere else.

Although we may have been the recipients of a father's Poseidon emotionality (especially an alcoholic father), it may also exist in ourselves. Anyone who has found him- or herself unexpectedly overwhelmed by waves of intense feelings that well up from the depths, or has had his or her body tremble and shake with grief or rage or revenge, has had a firsthand experience of Poseidon.

We are trained, in this world ruled by Zeus, to devalue and submerge our feelings and instincts, to keep a lid on them if we can. And if we are like rational Apollo or cool-thinking Athena (Zeus's favored children), we repress feelings very well—up to a point. We often dream of tidal waves or floods and obsessive fears of earthquakes when Poseidon's world threatens to break through the defenses erected (by our Zeus, Athena, and Apollo tendencies) against feeling our feelings and expressing them.

But even in a world dominated by Zeus, some people know Poseidon's realm well. They are like sailors who go down to the sea in ships, or people who would not dream of living anywhere else but next to the sea. These men (and women) live and work with the tides of emotion and instinct. For example, I think of Dylan Thomas's powerful, emotionally evocative poetry and his turbulent life, of the line "Do not go gentle into that good night ... / Rage, rage against the dying of the light," and feel his familiarity with Poseidon's realm. This quality also can be heard in Beethoven's music, and experienced through Eugene O'Neill and Tennessee Williams plays—men who found a way to express and give form to the terror, beauty, and power of Poseidon's dark emotions.

POSEIDON THE GOD

Poseidon (whom the Romans called Neptune) was the Greek god of the sea. He was portrayed as a powerful male with a beard, a lookalike of Zeus, holding a trident.

For all that he is identified with the realm of the sea, the name Poseidon meant husband of Da (*posis Das*), a name for the earth. He was linked with earthquakes and called Earth-shaker. His major symbolic animals were bulls and horses.

Poseidon's temperament is his most characteristic feature. He is bad-tempered, violent, vindictive, destructive, and dangerous—a god accompanied by tempest and turbulence, like the raging sea. But he also could calm the sea: storms instantly ceased when Poseidon drove his golden chariot drawn by his white horses with golden manes over the waves, and sea monsters frolicked around it.

GENEALOGY AND MYTHOLOGY

Like all of his siblings except Zeus, Poseidon (the son of Cronus and Rhea) was swallowed by his father, who feared he would be overthrown by his son. In some versions of his birth, Poseidon escaped this fate, as Zeus did. In one, a foal was substituted for him and swallowed by Cronus. In another, instead of swallowing him, Cronus flung him into the sea, to an intended watery death, as soon as he emerged from the womb. In the usual account, however, he was consumed by his father, and freed only after Zeus challenged Cronus and managed with Metis's help to make him regurgitate his three sisters and two brothers. Then the Olympian brothers and their allies fought Cronus and the Titans, and won. They drew lots to divide the universe, and Poseidon's portion was the sea.

Poseidon was not content with his lot. He competed with Athena for possession of the cities of Athens and Troezen, and with Hera for Argos. In a contest for Athens, the competition was to give the citizens a gift. Athena presented them with the olive tree, and then Poseidon stuck his trident into a rock on the Acropolis and produced a brackish spring. When Athena's gift was judged the more useful and he lost, he flooded the surrounding plain. He also flooded Troezen. He fared no better in his struggle with Hera over Argos, and when he lost, in revenge dried up all the rivers. He tried unsuccessfully to claim Aegina from Zeus and Naxos from Dionysus. In his dispute over Corinth with Helius, he fared a little better: he got the isthmus, and Helius got the acropolis. Poseidon also rebelled against Zeus and plotted against him unsuccessfully.

POSEIDON AND WOMEN

Poseidon first set his sights on marrying Thetis, a Nereid or sea goddess, vying with Zeus, who also desired her. However, when Prometheus revealed that Thetis would bear a son who would be greater than his father, both gods deserted her and arranged her marriage to a mortal. (The Greek hero Achilles was the son of this union.)

Next he approached Amphitrite, another Nereid, who viewed his advances with repugnance. He overcame her by force and raped her, and she fled to the Atlas Mountains to escape him. Finally Delphinus (or Dolphin), pleaded his case charmingly, and she consented to marry Poseidon. In gratitude, Poseidon placed Dolphin's image among the stars as a constellation.

The marriage of Poseidon and Amphitrite followed the same pattern as that of Zeus and Hera, for Poseidon was also a philanderer. Amphitrite's jealous vindictiveness, like Hera's, was directed against the other woman. One dreadful example occurred when Poseidon was enamoured of Scylla: Amphitrite threw magical herbs into Scylla's bathing pool, which changed her from a beautiful woman into a barking monster with six heads, each with triple rows of teeth and twelve feet. Scylla inhabited the Straits of Messina, devouring sailors snatched off the decks of passing ships.

Medusa suffered a similarly awful fate because of Poseidon. Because Poseidon had made love to Medusa in a temple dedicated to Athena, the goddess turned Medusa into a repulsive monster with snakes for hair; merely gazing on her face turned those who gazed at it to stone.

When Demeter was searching over the whole earth for her abducted daughter, Poseidon spied and desired her. To escape, Demeter turned herself into a mare and hid herself in a herd of horses. Poseidon persisted in his pursuit, however, changed himself into a stallion, and raped her.

POSEIDON AND HIS CHILDREN

Amphitrite bore Poseidon three children, a son and two daughters, and he had numerous other offspring, many of whom were monsters in mythology. Poseidon fathered both destructive giants and ferocious sons of normal size. His sons inherited his violence, and could count on their father's fierce loyalty to them.

When Odysseus blinded his one-eyed son Polyphemus the Cyclops, Poseidon pursued Odysseus with implacable hatred and punished those who aided him. For example, Poseidon blocked (with a huge mountain) the harbor of a seafaring people who helped Odysseus, and he turned the rescue ship into a rock. The Odyssey was as long and difficult as it was because of Poseidon's grudge.

POSEIDON'S HOSTILITY TOWARD THE TROJANS

As a grudge holder, Poseidon had no equal. His rage at the Trojans was so great that he intervened on behalf of the Greeks, against the express command of Zeus. His hatred sprang from an earlier time. Poseidon and Apollo had an agreement with King Laomedon (who was Priam's father and Paris and Hector's grandfather, and long dead at the beginning of the Trojan War) to build the walls of his city of Troy in return for a certain sum. But when they had finished, he refused to pay the fee. Thus Poseidon avenged himself "unto the second and third generation" (which the Old Testament also held as a standard of revenge).

POSEIDON AND CRETE: THE BULL FROM THE SEA

King Minos of Crete asked Poseidon to send him a bull to sacrifice. The bull that came from the sea was so fine that Minos decided he would keep it instead of sacrificing it as he had promised. Enraged at King Minos for not keeping his word, Poseidon caused Minos's queen, Pasiphaë, to have a passionate affair with the bull. The progeny of this union was the Minotaur, a half-bull, half-human monster, who was kept at the center of the labyrinth beneath his palace.

POSEIDON'S PEACEFUL ASPECT

Although Poseidon was noted for his anger, destructiveness, and otherwise stormy disposition, he also had a less-noted peaceful and merciful aspect to his personality. In his quieter moods, for example, he visited his faithful Ethiopians, who gave him rich sacrifices, and for a time forgot his pursuit of Odysseus. In an act of mercy (and an earthquake), he turned Thessaly, which had been an enormous lake, into dry land. He also changed Ino and her son into sea gods when they threw themselves into the sea, and appointed Castor and Pollux as protectors of sailors who could lull storms.

POSEIDON THE ARCHETYPE

Imagine looking out on a placid sea and knowing that an emotional, angry, and resentful god lives under the surface, who may erupt in fury and pound against whatever is in his way, and you will immediately grasp some main characteristics of the Poseidon archetype. This archetype is a part of the father archetype "that lost out" to Zeus, and is repressed in men who are like Zeus and who work at keeping everything under control.

When the realm of emotionality is repressed, this archetype goes underground, and remains unintegrated into the man's personality. Emotions are bottled up instead of allowed expression in the moment. Eventually, however, Poseidon can no longer be contained, and in rage and grief, the primitive urge to wreak havoc on whoever caused the pain, no matter what the circumstances, takes over.

Poseidon is also the archetype through which a psychological realm of great depth and beauty can be known. Poseidon's undersea world cannot be seen from Mt. Olympus, and it was not described in Greek mythology. Access to emotional depths is an unappreciated aspect of men's psyches, and it is devalued and repressed in patriarchal cultures. Ordinary American middle-class men, for example, are expected to keep their emotions under control, just as upper-class Englishmen are expected to keep a stiff upper lip.

A less well-known aspect of Poseidon is symbolized by underground water. It is the emotional depth hidden under the earth, unexpressed and unseen but nonetheless there as deep introverted feelings that need to be tapped or expressed to be known of at all.

ARCHETYPE OF THE DEEP-SEA DIVER

Poseidon was the only Olympian god who had access to the watery depths. He could plunge deeply and stay under the sea as long as he wanted, or rise swiftly to the surface merely by commanding his golden-maned steeds who pulled his chariot, and could have the creatures of the deep frolic around him—a scuba diver's dream. Poseidon is also a metaphor for the man or woman who can go deeply into the realm of feeling and emotions, and gain access to what is down there: soul and sorrow, great beauty and monsters of the deep, places so deep and so dark that clear vision is no longer possible and one can only dimly sense what is there. Here there is a sense of vastness, profoundness, depth, far greater than one can ever plumb or fully know.

The man who is cut off from his Poseidon nature, until he drinks and weeps when he is "in his cups" or is plunged into this realm through his grief and anger, enters Poseidon's realm and is temporarily overcome by it, flailing around like a drowning man.

The deep-sea diver aspect of the Poseidon archetype, in contrast, is expressed by the poet, playwright, novelist, composer, musician, or psychotherapist who is drawn time and time again to descend deeper into the realm of emotions, where he (or she) taps into collective human depth. People from cultures that have experienced suffering historically, where art and literature are valued, and whose national natures are more emotional (for example, Russia and Ireland) seem to respect this realm more and allow their men to be more emotional, irrational, and expressive.

ARCHETYPE OF THE KING

Like Zeus and to a lesser extent Hades, Poseidon also seeks power over a domain and the respect and control that come with being a king. The Poseidon man feels a drive to "be somebody important." However, a man who is archetypally Poseidon lacks the impersonality, strategic thinking, and force of will that is needed in a sky god patriarchy to be a success and establish "a kingdom." His efforts in business may then resemble those of the god Poseidon, who repeatedly lost contested land to other deities, was publicly humiliated, and reacted in anger.

Given the intensity of feelings associated with this god, a man who lives out this archetype is usually not a good loser. From the Zeus standpoint, each contest was decided "fair and square" by appropriately appointed judges. Like men who do not understand the rules that take property and honor from them, and who do not lose gracefully, Poseidon reacted with rage. Most characteristically, he brought floods, just as his archetype can flood the man's psyche with feelings, drowning out rational thought.

If such a man fails to establish himself in the world, home becomes the sole domain where he is king.

TRIDENT BEARER

Poseidon's symbol was the trident, a phallic symbol that along with the meaning of his name, husband of earth, places him historically as a pre-Olympian god, a consort of the Great

Goddess, who had three aspects: maiden, mother, and crone. Poseidon's trident was the symbolic triple phallus, signifying his function as mate of the triple goddess. Like his two animal symbols, the horse and the bull, the trident is a statement about his sexuality and fertility, although more abstract.

The carrier of the trident is sexually potent, able to impregnate. This impregnation is specifically not limited to the childbearing aspect of the feminine (to the Goddess as mother) but is extended to the virginal, intact, innocent feminine (Goddess as maiden) and to the wise woman (Goddess as crone). Lived out in its most literal archetypal form, this indiscriminate, promiscuous, sexually expressed, psychopathic masculinity is embodied in men who make no distinctions between young and old women. Lived out in a committed human relationship, the carrier of the trident is a man who is husband of the maiden, mother, and wise woman, who coexist within his wife. As her mate over the duration of a lifetime, he is husband to the maiden he married, then to the mother of his children, and in old age to the old woman she becomes.

In its most abstract meaning, Poseidon is the husband of earth, as life-giving moisture that is needed for earth to be fertile. He represents underground water, and just as the god Poseidon struck the earth to bring forth water, the trident is symbolizes the power to tap this source.

POSEIDON THE IMPLACABLE ENEMY

The story of Poseidon's relentless ten-year pursuit of Odysseus is the story of a father's wrath at the blinding of his one-eyed monster son. Never mind that Polyphemus had intended to eat Odysseus and his men, and that only Odysseus's wiles and courage had prevented this feast. This is an eye-for-an-eye justice, that takes nothing else into consideration. Such "justice" is really vengeance, to pay back harm done to oneself or to one's own. Poseidon waits to settle old accounts, harboring grudges that do not fade with time. It may take three generations, as with the Trojans; but someday he will get even.

Many stories and many men follow this archetype. Movie stars, such as Charles Bronson in the *Death Wish* series and George C. Scott in *Hardcore*, have played Poseidon fathers on personal vendettas, who take retribution into their own hands, filling the screen with violent retaliation. Similarly, William "Bull" Halsey, Admiral of the Pacific Fleet in World War II, pursued Japanese warships over vast stretches of ocean with the implacable hatred of a Poseidon hunting down a treacherous Odysseus. For him, "The only good Jap was a dead Jap." And Yahweh, the god of the Old Testament, who declared "Vengeance is mine," was likewise claiming and voicing this aspect of the Poseidon archetype.

POSEIDON AS ARCHETYPE OF THE WILD MAN

Robert Bly, a major American poet and leader of the men's movement, speaks of the masculinity that men—especially men who matured in the 1960s—must reclaim, as "the wild man at the bottom of the pool." This imagery is taken from the story of Iron Hans in *Grimm's Fairy Tales*: There was once a forest that all men avoided, because huntsmen who entered it never came back. One day a strange huntsman who knew no fear went into the wood with his dog. The dog chased some wild game near a deep pool; a naked arm appeared out of the water, seized him and drew him down. When the huntsman saw this, he fetched three men with pails to empty the pool. When they got to the bottom, they found a wild man, whose body was as brown as rusty iron, and his hair hanging down over his face to his knees.

Bly makes the point that the wild man is a symbol of masculinity that is instinctive, untamed by women, in touch with nature and part of nature—that will be dishonored and disregarded, even feared, until men seek to know and bring this source of strength and masculinity into consciousness, and into the culture.

I think of the wild man at the bottom of the pool as an image of a rejected and devalued Poseidon, a repressed archetype in the unconscious, known here by another name. In the fairytale, the wild man is freed from captivity by a young boy. And in return, the wild man promises to help the boy: whenever he is in great need, the boy is to return to the forest and call on him. The wild man is a source of strength and power, an archetype that the boy does call on when he is tested. In the process, the boy becomes a courageous and loving man, and the wild man emerges as a proud king.

POSEIDON THE MAN

Poseidon's sphere is the realm of emotions, and the man for whom Poseidon is the archetype is directly in touch with his instincts and feelings, which he expresses spontaneously and immediately if he's extraverted, and may harbor within if he's introverted. In either case, he feels deeply and, intensely. And he grows up in a culture that prefers boys and men to be unemotional.

EARLY YEARS

The Poseidon child feels strongly about everything that matters to him. Especially if he is an extraverted child he responds immediately, intensely, and spontaneously to whatever affects him with feelings and action. He wants what he is attracted to, and throws himself into expressing his need to have it now! He has a hunger for what he wants, and howls with frustration and anger when he can't have it now! His whole body and voice also expresses his great pleasure on getting what he wants, if he gets it then—getting it later, it's no longer the same. The desire in the moment passes, and it no longer is imbued with the desirability, his emotions had given it. When he is caught by in his emotions, as intense as they are over a particular need, his focus can be diverted, and channeled toward something else, much as a flash flood will follow a flood control course. Unlike his Zeus brother, Poseidon can lose sight of what was so important to him, and find himself now caught up in something else.

A child who has had to stifle his emotions because he is afraid of a punitive parent may learn to mask his feelings. But they are still intense, only held in. He then shares the still-waters-run-deep qualities of an introverted Poseidon, who may maintain a surface calm and yet harbor intense, tumultuous feelings.

If the Poseidon boy has not been criticized for his spontaneity and emotionality in his home, he is sure to encounter disapproval when he goes to school. Teased if he cries, told to sit still when he exuberantly jumps out of the seat to volunteer, always being told to clean up the clutter that he seems to generate, he finds himself continually being criticized for not living within other people's much narrower expectations of how he should be. He and his emotions and his stuff seem to spill over and upset others.

HIS PARENTS

A fortunate Poseidon was born into a family that was temperamentally suited to welcome him—a family that also welcomes emotions, drama, tears and laughter, and is physically demonstrative. This household also tolerates the clutter that collects when many individuals do many different things in various states of completion and doesn't "run on time" (you can't set your watch by when dinner is put on the table, or when people come to and go from the house). If this describes his folks and his household, then Poseidon grows up in a family atmosphere that is accepting and validating of who he is. But it may not have helped him to adapt to the demands of the outer world, as he finds out immediately on entering most schools.

Some Poseidon children come into families that are not emotionally expressive, spontaneous, or demonstrative, and instead value manners, intellect, obedience, neatness, the completion of tasks and putting everything away afterward. Such a child is temperamentally a round peg in a square hole (or a right-brained person in a left-brain world). In such a household, he may be continually reprimanded for what he does (or doesn't do): the messy state of his room, doing his appointed chores when he is supposed to, clutter in other parts of the house are all chronic issues. (He maintains he knows where everything is in the clutter and can't find things after he has had to clean up his room.) His emotionality also is likely to meet with disapproval: if so, he will get the message that the "Big boys don't cry" (when he cries), and "Don't act silly" (when he's happy). If he needs too well what he is told, he will repress his natural self and shape himself into what his parents want.

In an ideal situation, "who he is" is seen, accepted, and valued, and with parental patience and effort he also learns to be more orderly and manage time and sequence—the need to plan ahead does not come naturally to him. The poster message "It wasn't raining when Noah built his Ark" belongs on the wall of a Poseidon boy's room. (As we will see, none of the gods who draw us into the inner world or the emotional world heed linear time, thus many people would do well to heed this message).

In worst-case situations, the Poseidon son polarizes an overly punitive parent, who demands obedience, and becomes enraged when he persists in being himself and isn't ready on time, isn't neat, and does not complete tasks. The parent considers his behavior insubordination, to be beaten out of him. In this situation, he is likely to be punished or treated with contempt for his natural emotionality as well. Adding to his behavior and further getting him into trouble, is his sense of having authority or being entitled, which provokes "I'll show you who's boss" situations, that he cannot win. (The Zeus boy is better at hiding such feelings.) In this setting, the Poseidon boy may learn all too well to hold in and hold back—only to have his own anger later erupt against someone weaker.

ADOLESCENCE AND EARLY ADULTHOOD

A Poseidon teenager is usually an emotional, intense young man, very much affected by his changing hormones and in hot pursuit of sexually attractive young women. Sowing wild oats is what he has in mind, not a steady girl. During this time of life, for a middle-class Poseidon expected to go to college, school is supposed to be the chief focus, but this doesn't interest him.

Besides, Poseidon temperament and talents are not appreciated in most schools: he reacts emotionally and bases decisions on how he feels, so he's a fish out of water in the intellectual academic world. The beauty of logic escapes him, he dislikes analytic or repetitive work, hates test taking, and finds most of the required courses boring. To do well in school, he requires other archetypes.

An athletic Poseidon may actually be found in water, playing water polo or swimming. Or he may find his niche in drama production, where he can tap into his emotions, channel them into a role, and become appreciated.

He doesn't set his own sights on getting good grades, although he may end up buckling down, doing the work, and doing it well, when others impress on him that this is a necessity and that he has the intelligence. Yet however well he does, academic achievement doesn't hold much meaning for him. And he usually doesn't know what he wants to be when he grows up.

If he does poorly in high school, as college application time or the work world beckons he feels increasing resentment at being left out. This pattern may repeat itself at other stages of his life, when his goal-oriented peers start reaping material possessions, and he becomes increasingly unhappy with his lot.

WORK

Finding work that matters to him and that also provides income, self-respect, and respect from others is often difficult in industrial and corporate nations like ours. A Poseidon man is out of his element in offices and factories. To do well in these spheres requires him to suppress his emotional nature, to develop and act the part of another god. If he can adapt and succeed at this, doing what would give another type of man personal satisfaction, he feels that he is just working for a paycheck even at the highest levels of power and prestige. If he never did develop the left-brain skills the workplace requires, and has an emotional temperament he hasn't learned to contain, as well as difficulty with authority, he will have marginal employment, and neither get pleasure from work nor get his share of the materialistic "good life"—which enrages him.

Work that means something to him allows him to fulfill his own nature by letting him develop his capacity to assess and act out of deep feeling. Poseidon's aptitudes often lie in the direction of working with nature (including human nature) where time is measured in cycles, tides, and seasons. Here he learns to trust his instincts and experience with plants, living creatures, currents, weather, or people.

RELATIONSHIPS WITH WOMEN

Two aspects of the Poseidon man make it likely that he will dominate women: his patriarchal attitude and the power of his own emotional intensity. Thus he may consciously or unconsciously override her feelings and violate her boundaries. Beginning in adolescence, he may not take no for an answer once he s sexually aroused and has ventured on some physical intimacy. This attitude may result in various degrees of date rape, from not heeding her need to go slower, to forcing intercourse if she makes out with him" and lets him kiss or fondle her.

He usually does not fare well with contemporary women who are themselves on a career track. He does not do well as a young urban professional, yet he often acts as if he is entitled as a male to be in a dominant position over career women. This combination leads to competitive situations in which the woman has an edge and is likely to win. Like Athena in her competition for Athens with the god Poseidon, she can figure out what the situation calls for, while he does not take this into consideration, and thus loses to her.

RELATIONSHIPS WITH MEN

Poseidon is at a disadvantage in the Zeus world of Western industrial culture. He reacts emotionally rather than rationally in a culture that sees such behavior as negative. Although he is usually not "picked on," because he carries himself with some authority, he may find himself left out of the competition for achievement and status. He "speaks a different language," and unless he adapts very well, suppresses his emotions, and develops a linear, goal-oriented mental focus, he does not do well out in the world, where detachment and strategy win.

Sometimes long-lasting ties develop between a Poseidon man and a man who is his psychological opposite. Each is drawn to the possibility of developing what is unconscious in himself. Poseidon men have a capacity for loyalty and emotional depth, neither of which are qualities that are encouraged in a Zeus world, where the man on the way up moves often, is competitive, and leaves behind people who cannot keep up the pace.

SEXUALITY

Poseidon's sexuality starts out as a force of nature. Emotional intensity combined with his powerful instinctual nature make this so. The bull and the stallion are symbols of Poseidon the god and images that express his innate, indiscriminate sexuality: he can personify the Stud, ready and able to perform.

The Poseidon man can be as insensitive as Poseidon the god, who pursued and forced sex onto a distraught Demeter, who was searching for her abducted daughter when he spied her. Many women married to Poseidon men find that his sexual appetite comes first, regardless of what is on her mind or weighing on her heart. Like Demeter, she may try to hide herself, to avoid him, by downplaying her sexuality—and, like the goddess, not succeed.

As long as he is in the grip of the archetype and behaving sexually as a force of nature, he is "inhuman," unrelated psychologically to his partner. He is swamped and taken over by forces inside of him as he in turn seizes others.

If Poseidon is a homosexual man, especially prior to AIDS, he much more than his heterosexual counterpart could live out the role of the sexual stallion among readily available partners. An older homosexual Poseidon might also reenact the myth of Poseidon and Pelops. The god Poseidon had a sexual love for a young man named Pelops who was so beautiful that Poseidon took him to Olympus. The parallel occurs when an older, powerful, well-established homosexual becomes patron and lover of a young man whom he elevates into his world.

Both Zeus and Poseidon were portrayed as powerful men who had lusted after many women, married, and fathered many children. Yet both acted on their attraction to beautiful young men, as men often did in ancient Greece. Contemporary heterosexual Zeuses and Poseidons, powerful men who feel themselves aging, sometimes are disturbed and very threatened by dreams about and attractions to young men.

MARRIAGE

The story of Poseidon's courtship and marriage to Amphitrite provides us with metaphorical details necessary before a Poseidon man can make a commitment to one woman. Poseidon saw Amphitrite dancing and fell in love with her. (He fell in love, which is much more than sexual desire; she attracted his inner image of his beloved—which Jung called the "anima.") When he courted her—raped her—she took fright and fled to where she was safe from his power. He behaved toward her as he was used to, imposing his desire and overpowering her with his intensity, violating her. Then he felt the loss of this particular, special woman that he in his usual form could not win back. The human Poseidon who realizes too late that his beloved has fled from him is in this same position.

To win her back, Poseidon needed the help of a dolphin who found where she was hiding and persuaded her to marry

87

the sea god. Poseidon the man often finds that he needs to develop the "dolphin" in himself that can attune himself to another person (can "find her" although she was hiding) and be sensitive, caring, and communicative at a deep level. He must do so if he is to persuade the woman he loves to voluntarily return to him; she will not stay and be dominated.

If this happens to the Poseidon man and he evolves and marries a woman who can have this effect on him, then they will "live in a beautiful undersea palace"—be together in emotional depth.

However, many Poseidon marriages are far from deep or beautiful if the man hasn't evolved and if he takes out his resentment and anger (from work or lack of it) on her. Lack of emotional control, issues of power or the lack of it, feeling that marital sex is an entitlement all contribute to making bad Poseidon marriages among the worst there are, especially when combined with alcohol or other substance abuse.

Like Zeus and Hades men, the Poseidon man is marriage-minded. These three archetypes seem to foster the establishment of patriarchal households that the man definitely heads.

CHILDREN

Given his readily accessible feelings, the children of a Poseidon man may either fare very well or terribly. A Poseidon who himself was accepted as a child, had other aspects of himself fostered, and has a comfortable place in the world, can be a wonderful father. He can be emotionally responsive and physically demonstrative; a model of a strong man who laughs and cries, and a father who is present—not a distant or absent father, which is the more usual model in our culture.

However, he can be terrible; as father and husband, usually both, when this is the case. His emotional and sometimes physical assaults on his wife carries over to his children. His sons are traumatized by the onslaught of his rage, cower before him, and then most likely act just like him when they have the upper hand. Most of Poseidon's sons were offspring of his own worst nature. One was noted as a rapist, and was referred to as the "satyr of the sea"; others were destructive monsters or giant and savage.

Poseidon's daughters usually become unnoteworthy persons. Their childhood makes them prime candidates for further bullying. And because they tune into the pain that underlies their father's behavior, they may cast themselves in the role of rescuers.

MIDDLE YEARS

By the middle of life, most heterosexual Poseidon men have married and fathered children, and it is clear whether the family life that has resulted is a best-case or worst-case example. Whether very good or terrible, his family is usually the center of the Poseidon man's emotional life. Thus he usually will be precipitated into a major midlife crisis if his wife leaves him at this time. If this should happen, his tidal waves of feelings inundate others and himself, often stirring up emotional complexes that had lain quietly in the unconscious until this point.

Midlife may also bring about depressions or dramatic shifts in men who repressed their Poseidon nature and who adapted well to expectations that they repress their feelings, to fit in and focus on becoming successful in the world. The trouble is, they may achieve positions with status and power that are the envy of others, only to find that the power is personally meaningless. They lived as if they were someone else, not themselves. And that bad bargain catches up with them at midlife.

Such a man may say, "So what if I'm a vice president, and get to spend half my time jetting around the country? My kids are growing up without me around." What now? Quit the job, with the standard of living that goes with it? Some Poseidon men do—and precipitate a marital crisis, if they are married to women who cannot accept the financial change.

An unconscious effort to reconnect with the emotional depth that a Poseidon man is innately capable of reaching may be what makes a woman irresistibly attractive to him. He may also find himself attracted to a young man who represents either the neglected boy in himself or a repressed sexual orientation. This homosexuality may produce an internal crisis for him even if he didn't act on his feelings. In any case, the intensity with which repressed feelings eventually emerge is disruptive, and the adaptations he so ably achieved and constructed may come crashing down. Dramatic shifts happen when a strong Poseidon nature has been repressed for the first half of life, to emerge—almost as if with a vengeance—in the second half, now demanding its due.

LATER YEARS

As the Poseidon man rounds the last turn of his life to go into the home stretch, the image of his symbolic stallion once more comes to mind. Did he stay connected to his instincts and feelings while at the same time developing the ability to see the track ahead and consider strategy? Was he at one with the horse—his instinctual nature—and yet could he think, observe, make decisions? If he did, he has lived life authentically and fully.

Or did he abuse and kill the "horse," because others did not value it, and devalued him for being emotional? Or was the horse condemned to die via repression, because (like the adolescent protagonist in Peter Shafer's play *Equus*) he acted from this deep level in himself and it got him into trouble? In his last years, is he cut off from his source of depth and meaning, an alienated, shallow man?

Or did his "horse" nature tyrannize him, so that he never developed judgment and restraint? Reacting instinctively and from his appetites as life becomes more complex invites failure, retaliation, and pain. As such a person grows older, he becomes less and less attractive, less and less human, unlike the Poseidon man who in his life both keeps faith with his authentic nature and evolves that potential to a higher level.

The highest human potential for living out this archetype is represented by the image of Poseidon himself in his chariot drawn by his white-maned horses, calming the sea, with creatures from the deep frolicking around him. This Poseidon man (or woman) can descend into the deep sea, where he is at home, and can experience its beauty and serenity, unafraid of what others consider monsters that lurk in its dark places.

Fear makes "monsters" out of the dimly perceived elements in the depths of the human collective psyche; bringing them up to the surface where they can be seen and related to transforms them.

We all sense the presence of inarticulate, inchoate, enormously powerful forces in our own depths, and may fear them until a Poseidon poet, writer, composer, psychologist, dancer, or artist brings them to the surface. Such a man (or woman), astride his own instinctual nature, and at home in his emotional element, translates our fears into conscious human qualities.

PSYCHOLOGICAL DIFFICULTIES

Psychological problems arise when Poseidon's emotionality and instinctual urges flood the man's personality and are uncontained and unmediated. Difficulties also arise when Poseidon characteristics are devalued, and "who one is" is consequently not acceptable.

Poseidon is Zeus's shadow—the emotional aspect of the father archetype that is repressed or buried and thus is undeveloped and inaccessible in a man whose conscious identification is with Zeus.

TOO MUCH FLUIDITY: EMOTIONAL INSTABILITY

The instant emotional responses that are natural for a baby present a psychological problem for an adult. A baby cries when he is hurt, hungry, uncomfortable, afraid, in distress for any reason. He coos with contentment when all is well and may shift from one emotional state to another in a moment. He has no observing self, no capacity to wait, no understanding: distress is distress, need is need, comfort just is or is not available, and nobody else matters. The baby emerges from the watery realm of amniotic fluid into the world as an emotionally reactive being who is center of his universe. He perceives no reality other than his own subjective experience of comfort, need or distress. And it is perfectly all right for a baby to be this way.

The adult equivalent is quite another matter. A man (or woman) taken over by his fluctuating subjective feelings, who takes no one else and no situation into consideration is self-centered, emotionally inappropriate, and lacks a sense of proportion. Others consider him emotionally immature or unstable. Bear in mind, however, that social standards for appropriate male behavior require the suppression of emotions—so much so that shedding some tears cost a front-running presidential candidate, Senator Edmund Muskie, the lead in the primaries.

When it comes to showing emotions, what is "too much" is a social and political judgment as well as a psychological one, and the cultural stereotype is strong. Poseidon men can vary from emotional expressiveness up to a point when an emotion or emotions "take over." When a man is "possessed" by a feeling or feelings to such an irrational degree, he is rightly considered "out of his mind."

TIDAL WAVES AND EARTHQUAKES: DESTRUCTIVE EMOTIONS AND UPHEAVALS

Poseidon was the mythological sender of tidal waves, and he was also called Earth-shaker. In the psyche, the equivalent is an emotional complex of so great a magnitude that it hits with such force that it overwhelms and destroys the usual personality. Rationality topples, reality is swallowed up or flooded over, and—like King Lear out in the storm—he goes mad. Only after the waters recede, or the earth becomes stable once more, can new construction or reconstruction begin. Then there is some calm for the observing ego, who may be able to understand the experience and reconstruct himself and the relationships he undoubtably destroyed at least temporarily.

The "tidal wave" may have been an amplified version of his usual emotional nature. For example, a man (or woman) may react to a current loss or betrayal by opening the floodgates to more grief and rage than he ever has felt before; yet the feelings are not new, only greater.

"Earthquake" describes the emotionality of the man who has kept his feelings underground. Introverted feelings can exist like water in underground caverns; they run deep, and blind creatures who have never been exposed to light may live in the depths, the equivalent of repressed and thus undeveloped primitive emotional complexes. The underground water follows fault lines, and as the pressure builds up underground, some mild tremors are felt; but before the first big quake they are are usually disregarded. Only after a major quake do we remember the precursor "rumblings" that hinted at the instability and emotionality below the surface. If his life takes a turn for the worse around a particularly vulnerable point, or a fault line, an earthquake results and the emotionality that has been repressed that goes back to childhood and even infancy floods his psyche. The primitive rage with which he may irrationally attack others may devastate not only them but also (and even more) the man himself.

Just as there are people who live close to a raging sea, some live in earthquake country. Both must learn to read the weather or seismological reports, and from experience learn what to expect, and how to prepare, and what to build that is likely to survive a potentially destructive wave or quake. Men (or women) whose Poseidon emotionality can overwhelm their egos must become conscious of their own susceptibility, and must learn as much as is possible about its conditions and warnings. They must develop ways to live with this powerful part of them. Similarly, people who are affected by the destructiveness of Poseidon, as lived out in someone else, must learn to detect the warning signs. They can also decide to move away, just as people leave California if they don't want to be around for the next big quake.

An Eye for an Eye

Poseidon's mythology emphasizes his resentments and retributions. Homer's Odyssey frames the story of Poseidon's implacable hatred toward Odysseus for blinding his one-eyed Cyclops son. Poseidon was responsible for the length and difficulties of Odysseus's journey home. This dark aspect of the father archetype seeks revenge—an "eye for an eye." Often he makes no allowance for neutrality in his feeling judgment: "He who is not with me is against me." Retribution is not based on justice or rightness, and it doesn't spare innocents—children and children's children suffer alike for the sins of the fathers.

As a negative emotional complex, Poseidon vengeance can become all-consuming, destructive to the personality of the man it takes over as well as toward whom the hostility is directed. A man so possessed plants bombs, attempts to ruin someone financially, or directs his efforts toward destroying another man's reputation—or may only obsessively fantasize doing so. But the inner situation is the same—he has been taken over by a powerful negative aspect of Poseidon.

POOR SELF-ESTEEM

Whenever a man's innate qualities do not fit the stereotype of "masculinity" that is modeled after Zeus, his self-esteem suffers. Poseidon men are criticized for being "too emotional" or "not rational enough," and such a man may internalize the criticism so that long after people cease saying this to him, he continues to do it to himself. And when he doesn't get the approval or get ahead with the ease that is the birthright of men who "fit" the ideal, his criticism is compounded and his self-esteem suffers further. He may not be guided into work that suits him, and instead try to be other than he is. If he succeeds, this repression makes him feel that he is a fake or gives him a sense of doing something meaningless—all of which affects his sense of self-worth. Furthermore, should he harbor feelings of resentment or dwell on revenge, he cannot feel good about himself, for when we are full of negative feelings, it adversely affects our own sense of well-being and worthiness.

PSYCHOLOGICAL DIFFICULTIES FOR OTHERS

A Poseidon man is a "marrying kind" (as Zeus, Poseidon, and Hades men all are). Like Zeus, he may have affairs, which can turn a susceptible wife into a jealous Amphitrite, whose vindictiveness resembled Hera's.

He can be a terror to live with, if he's a resentful, angry Poseidon, who reacts out of proportion to whatever sets him off. His difficulty in holding back his emotions and instincts, coupled with frustration and rage, may turn him into an abusive spouse or parent, especially when alcohol further loosens his controls.

WAYS TO GROW

With Poseidon the major influence, psychological growth occurs when a Poseidon man's innate connection with the emotional realm finds a means of expression through work, relationships, or creativity. Because he is susceptible to being taken over by strong emotions, the Poseidon man needs to develop abilities to observe, reflect, and think objectively.

DEVELOPING AN OBSERVING "I"

Most of us have a sense of the contrast between "being ourselves," and either "being beside ourselves, with. . ." or "not in our right mind." We recognize that there are times, when we are in some significant way "not ourselves." In Jungian psychological terms, these expressions describe what it is like when an emotional complex takes over the personality, temporarily submerging the ego that is usually in charge. Ego is the consistent, observing, remembering, and deciding element in the psyche—what you mean when you say, "I." A complex is an archetypal pattern that has become charged with emotion. When it temporarily has more power or energy than the ego, it can for a time "take over" or "possess" the personality.

For example, a father may become "like a man possessed" and bent on vengeance when a child of his is brutalized. He becomes like Poseidon in relentless pursuit of Odysseus: his rage and revenge is all that matters; he is not even available to support or comfort and help heal the child in whose name he acts. This same complex may be activated by the same situation in another man but may have less power because the man's ego is stronger, relative to the complex. Such a man may have vivid fantasies of retribution, of taking to the streets with a "Saturday night special" handgun, but he realizes that he must struggle with the hatred that threatens him, knowing that what must truly concern him is what his child is feeling and needs from him. This same complex might "take over" another man with minimal provocation, perhaps even an imagined one.

When an emotional complex takes over, the "I" is put out of commission. The person may be unconscious or blind to what is happening, while people around him react in different ways. He may be humored, avoided, or feared, or his complex may provoke an equivalent unconscious complex in others. Or the person may struggle with the complex, as he feels himself overreacting or behaving in ways that are not like him. In psychotherapy as well as in life, the complex may become evoked and known. The very act of observing a complex shifts energy from it to the ego, and gradually as the "I" sees what is happening, and resists being taken over by the complex, the complex loses energy and influence and recedes. When compassion for himself, and for others who are affected by the complex, accompany this process, the individual and his relationships grow in depth.

A man (or woman) who lives in the watery realm of Poseidon and gets taken over by emotions needs to develop the ability to see circumstances dispassionately and objectively (a Zeus perspective). He may also need to recognize that his emotions are often connected to archetypal images (patterns that exist in the collective unconscious, which, as we shall see in the next chapter, is part of Hades realm).

LEARNING FROM THE DOLPHIN: GIVING UP THE NEED TO DOMINATE

When Poseidon fell in love with Amphitrite, he thought he could overpower her and dominate her. She fled from him, and would not have married him if it had not been for the intercession of Dolphin, who was persuasive. In gratitude, Poseidon made him a starry constellation.

If a Poseidon man learns from Dolphin—a creature at home in his own realm—he does not try to dominate and overpower or vie for territory that belongs to others. Instead, he may focus on his affiliation with others. When feelings and emotions are the natural medium through which one swims, so to speak, it is easy to develop skills that enhance rapport and empathic understanding. Furthermore, such a man has an innate potential for emotional expressiveness, which also needs encouragement and development. In the same way that artistic or mental skills require encouragement and opportunity for development, so must a talent for feelings.

CREATIVE EXPRESSION

For Poseidon's depth and intensity to be expressed through drama, poetry, and literature, the archetype of Hermes needs to be developed. Hermes is the Messenger God, who communicated words (and guided souls) from one level to another. Being a Poseidon with innate musical or artistic talent can result in emotionally expressive music or art. Whatever the medium, it characteristically evokes strong and tumultuous feelings, as the Poseidon man's otherwise potentially disruptive emotions find a creative outlet. What goes on deep in the psyche is given form and made conscious as art.

Hephaestus, God of the Forge, is another archetype that can help transform Poseidon's emotions into creative work. Even more than Poseidon, Hephaestus was a rejected god; but instead of erupting, he made beautiful and useful objects. His anger was transmuted instead of becoming destructive.

DILUTING POSEIDON'S EFFECT

When other archetypes are active, Poseidon usually loses his power to flood and take over the personality with emotions. Thus a major way to grow is by developing other gods (and goddesses). Especially helpful are Apollo, God of the Sun, Athena, Goddess of Wisdom, and Zeus. The three deities who represent the ability to think of consequences, to become objective, and achieve some distance. These are qualities that a Poseidon man needs to develop.

5.

Hades, God of the Underworld—The Realm of Souls and the Unconscious

Although a ruler of the dead, Hades is not to be confused with the Devil or Satan. As a death-god, Hades is grim, inexorable, sternly just, irrevocable in his decrees; he is not evil in himself, not an enemy of mankind, nor a tempter of evil.

Philip Mayerson, *Classical Mythology in Literature, Art, and Music*

Hades' other name was Pluto, which in Greek means wealth, riches, and the god's invisible fullness was symbolized by the image of the cornucopia that he held in his hands, overflowing with fruits and vegetables or with jewels, gems, gold and silver.

Hades is the god presiding over our descents, investing the darkness in our lives, our depressions, our anxieties, our emotional upheavals and our grief with the power to bring illumination and renewal.

Arianna Stassinopoulos, *The Gods of Greece*

The God of the Underworld and the domain over which he ruled were both called Hades. Least personified and least known of the gods, he was the "invisible one."

We must make a descent to become familiar with his realm. Only then is it possible to discover that there are riches to be found in the dimness, coldness, and darkness of what mystics refer to as the dark night of the soul, and what more psychologically minded people know as a profound depression in which one is cut off from ordinary reality, unable to feel or to bear being in the "sunlight" of everyday life.

The specter of death brings one to Hades. Death of a relationship, death of a way of being, death of purpose, of hope, or meaning can bring one there. The prospect of physical death itself, faced as a probability or certainty, is an experience that takes one to the underworld.

Most enter Hades or meet Hades involuntarily. Like Achilles at Troy, the hero—the man (or woman) whose ego and worth is identified with success—may die through a major defeat on a competitive battlefield. The event is a death knell for his heroic attitude and his sense of immortality. Or the involuntary descent may come through being a victim. A woman (or a man) may be raped or beaten, be violated, feel helpless, experience terror, and enter a numb, cold, cut-off underworld. Through victimization, an "abduction" occurs, as was Persephone's fate.

Some enter the realm of Hades or meet Hades voluntarily. For Psyche, it was the last of her *heroinic* tasks, done because it was the only way through which she might be reunited with Eros. Love was the motivation for Orpheus, as well, who went to Hades seeking his wife Eurydice; Dionysus made a descent to find his mother Semele. And in Sumerian mythology, Inanna-Ishtar voluntarily journeyed to the underworld to Ereshkigal, her dark sister. Besides love, wisdom was a motivation: Odysseus had to venture into the underworld to seek information from the blind seer Tiresias, which he needed in order to find his way home. Voluntary descents are done at great risk, for there is never a guarantee of a safe return.

Hades' realm is the unconscious, both personal and collective. Therein reside memories, thoughts, and feelings that we repressed, everything too painful or too shameful or too unacceptable to others to allow to be visible in the upper world, yearnings we never embodied, possibilities that remained dim outlines. In the underworld of the collective unconscious exists everything possible to imagine becoming, everything that has ever been. It is the realm that the Roman poet Terence must have known in order to say, "Nothing human is foreign to me."

Hermes, the Messenger God, guided souls to the underworld, and fetched Persephone back. Iris, the less-known Messenger Goddess, also entered and left the underworld at will. Once Persephone had eaten the pomegranate seeds and returned to the upper world, she returned periodically to the underworld, and as queen of this realm was there to receive and guide those who voluntarily ventured into the underworld. And though Hades could and did leave the underworld—though in his mythology, he did only on two occasions—this was his allotted realm, where he resided.

In life as in mythology, some figures can descend and return, some can accompany and guide other souls, and some know the realm itself because they reside there, or live there periodically. Psychologists, for example, are familiar with Hades. Both psychology in its original meaning (from the Greek word *psyche* meaning "soul") and thanatology (from Thanatos, the Greek god of death) are fields related to Hades' domain.

Psychotherapists need to be archetypally connected to Hermes, Persephone, Dionysus, or Hades to do depth soul work. These archetypes make it possible to be at home with the unconscious and all that is there, including madness. These same archetypes make working with death and dying meaningful. C. G. Jung in analytical psychology and Elisabeth Kübler-Ross in thanatology became guides for others in their respective fields, but only after they had made descents themselves. Depressions and near-death experiences are the usual initiations into the realm of Hades. After that, as was said of the initiates of the Eleusian Mysteries, one no longer fears death.

However, on Mt. Olympus where Zeus reigns, Hades was much feared. The patriarchy and patriarchal religions see Hades as a place of evil where Satan rules, a place to be avoided in death as well as a dimension devalued in life. As long as the culture and the individual identify only with Zeus and sky gods, the underworld will remain a fearful place, rather than a source of riches. Whatever we need to become whole exists in the underworld; equated with the collective unconscious, the shades that live there are like archetypes, forms that require vital energy, unfleshed-out potentials awaiting birth.

The underworld in its most negative, Christian designation is called *hell* and associated with fire and damnation. Hel was the Norse queen of the underworld, and her name became the English word "hell." The Celtic lord of death had the title of Helman. As with Hades, the name of the deity and place became one and the same. Barbara G. Walker's research indicates that the pre-Christian "hell" was a uterine shrine or sacred cave of rebirth, denoted by the Norse *hellir*. The earlier notion of *Hel* was as a cauldron-womb filled with purgative fire. The underworld, originally a mother realm, later became a father realm. And as the sky god values became more and more dominant, the realm itself grew more and more negative and feared.

Hades is also a repressed aspect of the father archetype. In the patriarchy, as on Olympus, Zeus dominates. His version of the father archetype prevails. In individuals and in the culture, Hades exists as a force in the unconscious, met and valued only through a descent.

HADES THE GOD

Hades was the ruler of the underworld, the subterranean kingdom in which the shades of dead humans resided and where certain mythological immortals were confined as a consequence of losing the struggle for supremacy to Zeus and the Olympians.

To say his name was considered unlucky, so he was called by a number of alternative titles. He was "the Unseen One" (Aidoneus) or "the Rich One." The latter name in Greek was "Plouton" (from which the Latin Pluto was derived) and Dis (from *dives*, "rich") in Latin. Other, less-favored names were Good Counselor, the Renowned One, the Hospitable One, the Gate-Fastener, and the Hateful One. He was also known as Zeus of the Underground or Zeus of the Underworld.

Although the Greeks thought of Hades as grim, cold, and ruthless, they never thought of him as evil or Satanic. Like Zeus and Poseidon, Hades was portrayed as a mature man with a beard. He had a cap of invisibility, given him by the Cyclopes, and when seen as the god of riches, he was pictured with a cornucopia or horn of plenty.

GENEALOGY AND MYTHOLOGY

Hades was a son of Cronus and Rhea who was swallowed at birth by his father. When Zeus and Metis made Cronus regurgitate the children he had swallowed, the brothers—Hades and Poseidon—joined Zeus to fight against Cronus and the Titans, and won. After their victory, the brothers drew lots to divide the world, and Hades' portion was the underworld.

Hades fathered no children and little mythology. He spent most of his time unseen in the underworld, leaving it only twice.

Once, according to Homer, Heracles wounded him with an arrow, and he went up to Olympus for aid, an incident little elaborated on. His one significant departure was to abduct Persephone.

THE RAPE OF PERSEPHONE

The rape of Persephone is Hades' only significant myth. Hades desired Persephone for his bride, and with her father Zeus's consent, he abducted the young maiden. She was gathering flowers in a meadow with her companions, and left their company, drawn toward a beautiful hundred-flowered narcissus, which had been created specifically to lure her. As she reached down to pick it, the earth opened up before her, and out of the dark vent in the earth Hades came in his chariot pulled by black powerful horses. Hades seized the terrified maiden, who screamed for her father Zeus, who, knowing all along what was to happen, ignored her cries.

Hades' horses then plunged downward, carrying Hades and Persephone deep into the underworld. Then the earth closed over, as if nothing had happened.

Persephone languished in the underworld, while her mother Demeter, grieved and raged at her loss. Eventually Demeter withdrew to sit in her temple. As a result, no crops grew, no births occurred, no new life of any kind sprang up. Famine threatened the earth and its inhabitants. Only then did Zeus heed Demeter and send Hermes to bring Persephone back.

Hermes descended to the underworld, where he found a disconsolate Persephone, unreconciled to her fate, sitting on a low couch with Hades. When she realized that Hermes was there to fetch her, she was overjoyed. But before she stepped into the chariot that would bear her back to the upper world, Hades gave Persephone some pomegranate seeds to eat.

Persephone was then restored to her mother, and spring returned bringing new life and greenness to the earth. Had Persephone eaten nothing in the underworld, she would have been returned to her mother as if nothing had happened. But because she had eaten the pomegranate seeds that Hades had given her, Persephone would now spend part of the year—the winter months when the earth lies fallow—in the underworld with Hades. Thus she came to be queen of the underworld.

HADES AND DIONYSUS

An almost invisible thread connecting Hades with Dionysus the Ecstatic God, was traced by noted mythologist Walter F. Otto in *Dionysus: Myth and Cult*. He quotes a line from Heraclitus, "Hades and Dionysus are one and the same," and notes that when Dionysus went to the underworld seeking his mother Semele, he turned the myrtle over to Hades. Thus myrtle came to be associated both with Dionysus and with the dead. Karl Kerenyi, in *Eleusis: Archetypal Image of Mother and Daughter*, notes that Dionysus and versions of Hades appear as doubles, again suggesting some interchangeability or connection between the two deities.

Dionysus's origins were as a god of vegetation and fertility. As such, his worship would have taken the seasons into account, and like Persephone he would have had an underworld life part of each year. Then he and Hades would have been connected. Dionysus knew suffering, dismemberment, and rebirth as well as periods of madness. Thus he descended into the underworld, into Hades' realm.

THE UNDERWORLD

The dead inhabitants of the underworld, who dwelt there forever, were regarded as mere shadows of their living selves. It was a dreary place, and most lived on the Plain of Asphodel (named after a flower). A very select few inhabited Elysium, "the Islands of the Blessed." At the very bottom of the underworld was Tartarus, a place of eternal blackness where the wicked were tortured, and the Titans were imprisoned.

Besides being located underground, Hades was associated with the distant West. Odysseus sailed west to Persephone's grove, a wild sunless coast at the edge of the world to find the entrance to Hades.

The dead were escorted by Hermes to the underworld. They needed a small coin to pay Charon the ferryman to take them across the river Styx, and then entered through gates guarded by Cerberus, a huge, three-headed dog, who readily let them enter but prevented them from leaving. On entering Hades, they were met by three judges, Minos, Rhadamanthys, and Aeacus.

A few living mortals entered the underworld and returned: Heracles fetched Cerberus for one of his labors; Psyche came seeking to have a box filled with a beauty ointment from Persephone; Odysseus came to talk with the shade of the seer Tiresias; Aeneas sought the shade of his father. Some mortals, however, did not return: Theseus and Pirithous came to kidnap Persephone and were imprisoned by Hades in chains of forgetfulness.

HADES THE ARCHETYPE

As noted before, Hades was both the name of the god of the underworld and the name for the underworld itself. There are also two archetypes of Hades: an archetypal personality pattern and an archetypal realm.

Significant in defining the two archetypal Hades are these characteristics: the god wore a cap of invisibility, and thus was an unseen presence. He rarely ventured out of the underworld and did not know what was happening above him in the world of mortals or on Mt. Olympus. He lived in his own realm with the shades who were shadowy, unsubstantial images, like visual echoes of themselves when they were alive, imaginable as colorless holograms. Hades however, was also called the "rich one," and his realm a source of underground wealth.

HADES AS ARCHETYPE OF THE RECLUSE

The human recluse who withdraws into seclusion, neither caring nor noting what is going on in the world, is leading a Hades existence. He may have lost whatever once had meaning for him in the world, and now he may live like the shades in the underworld, going through motions, and lacking vitality especially if he is also depressed. He may become an isolated and paranoid Hades, as billionaire Howard Hughes did in his last years. Hughes's wealth made it possible for him to occupy a floor of his own hotel in Las Vegas, where no one he did not authorize could enter, and bodyguards kept him safe—or virtually a prisoner in his own realm.

Hughes in his younger years had not appeared to be socially inept and unable to garb himself in a suitable persona, as was the case later on. He headed a major studio, ran an airline, built aircraft, and appeared with beautiful movie stars on his arm. Hughes had no trouble then responding to that basic question asked of men, "What do you do?" A Hades man who cannot respond with an acceptable answer and who does not have position and wealth, is a man without a persona, which makes him an invisible man in the world of men. If he does not have a family, he may live alone in a transient hotel room in the part of every big city that is the netherworld, where pornographic stores, streetwalkers, and drug dealers do business and where the homeless and the down and out sleep in doorways. This place is like Hades the underworld, much as he himself is like an invisible Hades.

If a man has no choice but to live like Hades, because of his personality pattern and circumstances, his lot seems sad. However, if he is physically safe and has the basic necessities of physical life, he may be relatively content with his lot. He may by nature prefer to be alone and to not be noticed or bothered.

HADES AS PLOUTON, ARCHETYPE OF THE RICH ONE

A different type of reclusive Hades may have sampled the outer world, and know that he prefers the subjectivity and richness of his interior world—the Plouton or "riches" aspect of Hades. In our extraverted culture, which emphasizes productivity, people are not encouraged to spend time alone "doing nothing." Thus the introverted recluse is judged negatively or considered peculiar for spending so much time alone. This rejection is compounded by his subjective responses to people, things, or events in the outer world, which can be peculiar because they are so subjective.

Hades the reclusive Plouton is, however, a "missing" part in many people, who do not value opportunities to be introverted in the way that this archetype can be. Introverts can live an interior life in touch with their own subjective reactions to outer experience. A type of introversion (introverted sensation, in Jung's psychological typology) may be experienced as inner dialogues, visions, or bodily sensations.

To have Hades as part of one's psychological nature can be very enriching. Hades the recluse is a source of creativity that can be expressed through the arts, often in visual arts. Fellini's films, especially *Juliet of the Spirits* and *8 1/2* exemplify the richness and subjectivity of this inner realm.

Hades can also be that part of a person's psyche that informs him of his subjective reaction to a person, a thing, or a situation. A dream can function in the same way. For example, when one Hades man unexpectedly encountered a woman who had betrayed and hurt him two years before, a technicolor picture flashed in his mind: he saw her with knives sticking in her body, an image followed immediately with the physical sensation of having a gaping hole in his heart. Instead of feeling hostility, anger, and emotional pain, he had these sensory experiences, which were vivid waking equivalents of dreams.

From the outer-world perspective of that same person, thing, or situation, this introverted idiosyncratic way of perceiving is judged to be a distortion of reality. Very early, as children, people who naturally and normally perceive in this fashion learn to mistrust their perceptions because they receive no validation from others. If they can, they often cut this aspect of themselves off as unacceptable, or crazy; and thus what could be a source of riches and depth is no longer accessible. Hades people need to tap into their inner lives.

However, without access to Zeus's view of objective reality, and Poseidon's emotional responsiveness, which are needed to balance and make sense out of Hades' subjective perceptions, the person runs a danger of emotional isolation and withdrawal into a world of one's own.

HADES AS THE GOOD COUNSELOR

Good Counselor was another one of Hades' names that describes a potential aspect of this archetype. As a source of subjective knowledge, Hades can indeed be a good counselor. We do need to look inward when we make crucial decisions because no one but ourselves can say what the subjective value of an experience is. An objective, sensible choice may be empty of meaning, nothing but a superficial choice that looks good to others. How we learn which choice truly matters to us personally differs from person to person. Hades helps us through our bodily sensations, our visceral reactions, inner voices, and visual flashes to know what our subjective reaction is to something or someone. When it comes to the truly important personal decisions in our lives, the subjective factor is of crucial importance, which Hades can give us.

HADES THE INVISIBLE MAN: INADEQUATE PERSONA

With his cap of invisibility, Hades was the unseen god even when he ventured above ground, which befits a god without much persona. (A persona is the surface covering of our personality, a composite of what we look like, how we dress, what we do, how we act—the stuff first impressions are made of.) Besides, as lord of his particular realm, he would cast a pall on any party.

Hades is an archetype that governs a deep interior life and is unexpressive, either in emotion or words. When this archetype is the major one, social invisibility results. Others don't see the riches underground and are often uncomfortable in his presence.

HADES AS "ZEUS OF THE UNDERWORLD": ARCHETYPE OF THE RULER-KING

Hades, Zeus, and Poseidon ruled over their own realms, and each is an example of the archetype of the king. Personalities and domains differed, but these gods shared fundamental similarities. Each established his authority over his particular territory, each sought a wife who became his official consort, each was a patriarchal figure (although Hades had no children).

HADES THE ARCHETYPE OF THE ABDUCTOR: INCESTUOUS SHADOW OF ZEUS

When Hades decided he wanted Persephone, he did not court her—he abducted and raped her, with Zeus's permission. And when Persephone cried to her father Zeus for help, Zeus looked the other way. In many incestuous fathers, Zeus and Hades are versions of Dr. Jekyll and Mr. Hyde. As Zeus, such a man is the prominant pillar of the community and an authoritarian (and often puritanical) father who provides for his family; he is the father who "looks the other way and disregards her cries," who consents when (as Hades) he himself rapes or seduces his daughter.

In this psychological situation, Hades is the archetypal shadow of the father, that which is evil in him and acted out in secret on the daughter who cannot escape. He himself is the rapist father, who abducts his daughter into the underworld. Once raped, her innocence is betrayed; she is no longer the virgin maiden in a sunny, safe world; she becomes captive in his secret, dark world and often exists thereafter in her own netherworld as well.

HADES THE ABDUCTOR AS THE IMAGINARY LOVER

Hades the abductor can be totally invisible as a ghostly lover, an archetype that has become autonomous with a "life" of its own in the psyche of a woman. An easily understood parallel in childhood is the imaginary playmate. Now in the life of an adult woman, he is an imaginary lover. He keeps her company and has conversations with her, he may write poetry, give her advice, make promises. He becomes her only confidante and may contribute to her withdrawal from the world by his comments, which increasingly inhibit her from interacting with others.

It's not uncommon for ordinary people who are introverted sensation types (in Jungian psychology terms) to hear voices or sounds. Many musicians, for example, ordinarily "hallucinate" music, and lots of people have inner voices or have had visions. To develop an imaginary lover, a capacity for this kind of vivid inner experience must be present, along with a personal life that lacks significant relationships. She may be a person with an inhibited social life, due to a lack of physical attractiveness and/or social skills or fearfulness.

The "abduction by Hades" is into this private world where she has an inner relationship with this ghostly lover. This has the same effect on her life as a real but secret relationship; it cuts her off from others, although she may continue to work at a humdrum job and be little noticed.

A man who lives as Hades the Recluse may also have an imaginary Persephone. She may be a real person that he was attracted to at a distance who gradually becomes an autonomous "presence" in his inner world. If this happens, and the line between the imagined woman and real woman becomes blurred in his mind, he may intrude in some inappropriate or crazy way on the real woman.

HADES (THE PLACE) AS THE ARCHETYPE OF THE UNDERWORLD

Hades was the underworld realm, the netherworld, the underground world where souls go after death, a place that some gods and mortals could visit and return. Thus Hades is an archetype of place, as well as a personality pattern.

HADES (THE PLACE) AS AN ARCHETYPAL IMAGE OF DEPRESSION

When Persephone was abducted into the underworld and was captive there, she could have been clinically assessed as depressed: she did nothing but sit, ate and drank nothing, and thought that she would never see the light of day, pick a flower, or see her mother again. Meanwhile, in her absence, the whole earth was turning into a wasteland, as nothing would grow.

Depressed people act and feel like Persephone did when she was abducted. They feel cut off from everything that used to give them meaning; everything is emotionally gray. Sometimes even the perception of vividness and color is gone, and the world looks literally gray. This type of depression can be associated with a descent into an inner world of images and voices, well described by Joanna Greenberg, (who as Hannah Green) wrote her autobiographically based novel *I Never Promised You a Rose Garden,* which is about an adolescent's withdrawal from reality.

Minor descents into the underworld are the stuff of everyday life. Those are the times we might say, "I'm in a bad place today," meaning that we are depressed.

THE SHADOW WORLD

In Jungian psychology, the contents of "the shadow" are twofold. The shadow contains those parts of ourselves that are unacceptable either to us or to our idea of "what other people will think" if they knew about it, and so we keep these thoughts, actions, attitudes, feelings hidden, sometimes from ourselves as well as others. This part of the shadow corresponds to Freud's concept of the id, and to dark Tartarus, that part of Hades where defeated Titans and others who had offended the gods of Olympus were kept imprisoned.

However, the Jungian idea of the shadow also includes "positive" shadow material, positive potential on the verge of becoming conscious, which is thus still in the shadow, not yet in the light. This material corresponds to the underground riches that are associated with Hades.

THE AFTERWORLD: REALM OF THE DEAD

For the Greeks, Hades was the realm of the dead. Here souls went after death to exist as ghostly shades forever, or they might drink of the river of forgetfulness (Lethe) and be born again, with no memory of their previous existence. As an archetypal place, Hades is the afterworld, a concept that assumes the existence of a soul that survives after death.

Mediums who believe they are in touch with the dead, hospice workers who work with the dying, and spiritual practices based on the assumption that the soul may need help to make the transition, all function like Hermes the Messenger God, who could move between levels and who guided souls to Hades.

THE PERSONAL AND COLLECTIVE UNCONSCIOUS

The underworld also corresponds symbolically to the personal and collective unconscious. Everything that we have forgotten is there in the personal unconscious: Some memories need only a little conscious effort to be nudged back into conscious awareness; other, more painful memories may have been actively buried or repressed. They have an "existence" in this realm, even though we cannot recall them.

The collective unconscious is the realm of archetypes, or universal human patterns, that can be constellated, precipitated, or evoked by circumstances that energize them. These patterns have existed through time, lived out by people who have long since died. In a sense they exist as "shades"—or archetypes that indeed are repeatedly born again.

HADES THE MAN

The theme for Hades the man is how to adapt: Can he stay true to himself and also fit into the outer world? His innate subjective predisposition is not encouraged; on the contrary, he is measured against a personality standard that is the very opposite of who he is. He usually grows up in a culture that is foreign to him, that requires him to grow beyond the confines of this one archetype if he is to find a place in it.

EARLY YEARS

An introverted child such as Hades does not usually make a strong impression. The invisibility for which Hades was noted sets in early, because he does not have either a strong will or a get-into-an-uproar personality like his brothers. Occasionally he may stand out because he reacts "peculiarly." As far as others are concerned, he often seems to react unexpectedly, especially to new people and situations. How something or someone appears to others isn't what he is reacting to; how it subjectively affects *him* is responsible for how he reacts.

For example, suppose a new babysitter comes to the house or he's meeting his grandmother for the first time. Instead of smiling back at the gray-haired woman, he may withdraw in alarm and cry because she evokes an unpleasant sensation, or he may see something frightening in her face instead of her ordinary features.

Even if he does nothing out of the ordinary, he prefers to hold back and take in experience rather than reach out for it. So he will appear shy as a little child, and serious and withdrawn as he gets older. This reticence is judged negatively, especially in a boy. From the beginning, the Hades child usually is not bathed in approval, as some extraverted, social children are. His development of self-esteem is difficult, hampered at best; he often develops a negative sense of himself.

HIS PARENTS

There are some very difficult matches between Hades sons and their parents. Hades just doesn't fit the mold of what boys are supposed to be like, and both he and his parents feel rejected and misunderstood.

There is something autistic about the Hades personality that shows early. When he is distressed, the sensations he perceives or the impressions he experiences may be purely subjective, so that others don't fathom what is going on. This peculiarity makes many mothers feel first inadequate and then angry.

Father-son combinations often fare worse. One sad mismatch (especially if he is a man for whom *introvert* means "sissy") is between an extraverted, hail-fellow-well-met father, who passes out cigars and buys a miniature baseball and bat for his newborn son and the often serious, inward boy he got for a son. He anticipated having a son be a chip off the old block, a boy to be proud of, his buddy, a little guy that he would coach and take to games. And this is not who his Hades son is. If, further, he needed a son for his own self-esteem, then anger may lie just below the surface of his affable persona and may be directed against the son who did not live up to his expectations.

So the Hades boy may thus feel unwelcome in the world as he is and find that his interior world is, in contrast, a refuge. The Hades boy enjoys his own company, anyway, and wants to spend time by himself—or perhaps with an imaginary friend. From nursery school onward, he is intruded on by others' needs for him to be more social, and he probably continues to thwart the nurturing needs that his mother may have for him to be dependent on and responsive to her. Usually he gets the message that something is wrong with him for being the way he is.

He does well when his parents can respect his individuality, and can appreciate that a capacity for solitude is a strength, not weirdness. Even so, he usually receives no help with the subjective ways he has of perceiving and has to manage how to interpret his own experience or repress his subjective reactions.

For example, a child who sees auras around people feels very strange when he realizes that other people do not, and he may never associate the colors he sees with information about the person. Similarly, if he has the sensation of pressure in his solar plexus in certain settings, he may think he's vaguely unwell and not know that this feeling is his response to something specific that literally makes him uncomfortable.

Although parents may not be equipped to help with these subjective experiences, they can help him adapt to the world in which he lives. They can provide patience and encouragement, and specific guidance—an approach similar to that one might use to raise a child from a foreign culture or one with a perceptual handicap. With loving support, he can emerge from childhood feeling competent and safe in the world. But this won't happen if he is ridiculed for his subjective responses and lack of knowledge—then he'll just clam up. Education is also very useful for his psychological development, because objective perceptions and reason can be developed as a balance to his interior subjectivity. And he develops trust in relationships if he is loved as he is and given space. He is not a standard-model child and needs some special consideration.

ADOLESCENCE AND EARLY ADULTHOOD

A Hades adolescent follows a very different drummer and runs into trouble when he tries to conform to the beat of adolescent conformity. He doesn't know how others just seem to know what the fads are, doesn't get caught up in having the "right" clothes, and would just as soon miss most of the "right" parties even if he were invited. If he has developed an extraverted side to himself that is "good enough" to let him get by, and has the inner security to be himself, he knows by now that he is a distinct individual and has tested the conversational waters enough to conclude that he prefers his own company to most people. By now, he may have one or two friends, which is as many as he wants.

For him to get to college or into a career requires development of other archetypes. Education promotes Apollo's rational thinking and objective perceptions and teaches writing and speaking, which are Hermes qualities. Both gods help him to be more extraverted. He runs a danger if he does this too well and tries to be what others expect of him—a risk of entering a work world in which he can be competent, but that has no depth of meaning for him.

WORK

The key that can connect inner and outer worlds for him is to have an interest that grows out of his inner experience develop into an occupation. This interest provides him an in-the-world identity and a means of making a living through doing something that has meaning for him.

This archetype is unempowering, in that ambition, communication, and persona are all lacking. Unless he develops other archetypes, he could "drop by the wayside" in his high school years—and at anytime thereafter. He may not be hired for anything other than unskilled work at marginal pay. Whatever he does do, he often does quite seriously. He often stays at a repetitious job that offers no challenge, because his "real" life is the interior one.

If a Hades man also has a well-developed Hermes (the archetypal communicator—who can move between worlds and carry information between them—and the conductor of souls to the underworld), then he may bring the depth level to which he has access up into the world. These two archetypes function together in film making, depth psychology, literature, hospice work with the dying, theology, and other fields. Here he may find that he has special gifts to do deeply meaningful work that he loves to do for its own sake.

RELATIONSHIPS WITH WOMEN

Hades strikes out in meeting women at social gatherings. He might as well be an invisible man for all the warmth and chemistry he will generate under these circumstances. Dating rituals and flirting are totally out of character for him, and he does them badly if at all. Lack of experience with women or rejection by them is the common experience of Hades men.

Yet like Dante, who saw Beatrice once and was then inspired by his inner relationship with her to write the *The Divine Comedy*, Hades men can be deeply affected by their subjective inner experience of a real woman whom they hardly know. A Hades man is also capable of having a deep soulmate connection with a woman, who can share the riches of the inner world. Fate seems to draw these two souls together, because the chances are very slim that either set out to find one another.

Failing at sociability, he may lead a reclusive life without much contact with women at all.

RELATIONSHIPS WITH MEN

The reclusive, even secretive Hades does not know how to enjoy camaraderie with other men. He feels apart and makes his way in the world pretty much as a loner. Other men let him be. Something about him keeps him from being picked on—or included. Being one of the boys doesn't matter to him, which gives them no shunning power, and something about his inner orientation conveys strength. He is "different" but not in a way that invites being a victim. The few friends he might have in his life will have to enter his realm, perhaps drawn into discussions about his perceptions.

SEXUALITY

There is a very complex range to Hades' sexuality. He can lead the celibate life of a monk more easily than any other type, and may do so if he becomes a recluse. However, if a soul connection with a woman grows into a sexual one, it becomes a powerful initiatory experience that is an inner multisensory experience as well as physical intercourse. As a result, he may connect with an ecstatic Dionysian potential.

However, potential parallels also arise with the sexual history of Hades the god, who abducted and raped Persephone. He also cast a lustful eye on Minthe, but she was transformed into a mint plant before he could do anything amorous. The same story was repeated with Leuce, who became the white poplar tree. Thus his only sexual relationship was with Persephone, whom he did abduct and also married. Both Zeus and Poseidon forced women sexually repeatedly, yet it was Hades who got the bad reputation; the others got away with it. Life may follow myth, because marital and date rape, incest, and sexual harassment by powerful men is not uncommon. They get away with it when the woman is dependent or has less credibility and power than them. But when a Hades man does the same, he is more likely to be exposed and labeled, because he does not live within a context of power. Instead, his actions may have come out of a rich fantasy life that involved a real woman, whom he then approaches, mistakenly thinking she wants a sexual relationship with him. Whatever he does under this misapprehension will be inappropriate, and she or others may make it public.

MARRIAGE

If he finds a woman to love who loves him, he will get married. Like Zeus and Poseidon, Hades men also want to establish households, and have stability and order. Marriage is crucial in determining the course of his life. Without marriage, he will stay a loner and an outsider, maybe a recluse. With a wife and children, he becomes part of a family and community through them. His wife mediates between her introverted husband, who is often inaccessible to others, and other people. Often, she interprets him to his children as well.

If he is part of a large, extended traditional patriarchal family within a closed ethnic or religious community, others may help "arrange" a marriage to a much younger, sexually inexperienced woman. She is thus "abducted" into marriage, through a courtship that she may not feel free to resist.

CHILDREN

Although the god Hades did not have children (he was the only major deity who did not), a Hades man may become a biological father. If he runs true to type, he will be a rather grim, humorless patriarchal father, who expects orderliness and duty, isn't emotionally expressive, and can't mentor his children into being successful in the world.

A Hades man who himself was loved as a child is an undemonstrative loving father, whose children must (and seem to) pick it up through his emanations. He might also share the riches of his inner life with them and encourage their imaginativeness, through his selection of picture books and stories when they are young and later by talking about how he perceives things. Most often, he shares his presence, one to one. His child spends time being in the same physical space, in comfortable silence if they are also introverted. A more extraverted child does the talking and showing to a receptive Hades father.

MIDDLE YEARS

There is a wide range of how Hades the man's life shapes up at midlife. Much more so than with almost any other archetype, his life depends on outer circumstances and, even more important, on developing other archetypal patterns.

A pure Hades is a loner who lives in his own inner world. At midlife, and without a family or ability to do well in the outer world, he may inhabit his own underworld full-time. He may be a recluse who lives in a cheap hotel room, or a chronic mental patient withdrawn into his own world, or a monk or brother in a religious order like the Trappists who maintain silence.

If he has the support of family and community, and works, then most likely he is the stable, patriarchal head of a family. If he developed his intellectual life, he may be an academician, absorbed in an interest that allows for a rich interior life. If he has developed an expressive ability in the arts or literature, his work is highly subjective.

If he has developed and lived out several other archetypes through his significant, enduring relationships and work, he may have entered both the emotional realm and the realm of the mind and will as well as the interior realm. Without Hades as a primary or major archetype, a man may not naturally develop a familiarity with this realm. Many men do not, especially those who find the outer-world tasks of the first half of life easy. Thus, the Hades man who has had to adapt to outer life is at midlife often more fully integrated in these three spheres than most men.

LATER YEARS

The pattern a Hades man has established by midlife will most likely continue into the later years. His familiarity with the inner world of dreams and images and the connection with the collective unconscious often makes the prospect of death an unfeared transition. Jungian analyst Jane H. Wheelwright wrote of the analysis of a dying woman in *Death of a Woman,* noting that the dreaming psyche does not fear death and showing the value of intensive psychological work based on dreams as one faces death.

When people die over a period of time, they invariably disengage from the outer world; loosen emotional ties to events, people, and things; and go inward. They become then like a man (or woman) or that part of a person that is Hades, who is naturally detached and more at home in the underworld than the outer world. Perhaps this same process is going on in people with advanced Alzheimer's disease or who are in coma. Are they in the inner world, watching images, hearing, sensing, in Hades' realm? Perhaps they are even, as many dying people report, meeting "the shades" of people who preceded them in death.

PSYCHOLOGICAL DIFFICULTIES

The psychological problems that plague a man (or woman) with a Hades disposition are those that result from having an introverted, subjective perspective.

PERSONA PROBLEMS: THE INVISIBLE MAN

Often, like the god who hardly ever left his realm, and had a cap of invisibility when he did, a Hades man is unseen because he avoids people or, if he's present, he doesn't show himself. Besides, he's not interested in whatever is going on in the world anyway, so that he's not up on sports, current fads, political news, the chit-chat of cocktail party and backyard barbeque. And his reactions are subjective, anyway, which strikes others as peculiar, so he's learned to be quiet and invisible rather than inappropriate.

THE LONER PERSONALITY: A SCHIZOID PERSON

The Hades man has a predisposition to be a loner. If circumstance and people confirm his tendency to mistrust others and feel inadequate in a competitive world, he will withdraw into himself. He keeps to himself what he perceives and how he reacts. There is an emotional barrenness to his life, a lack of relationships and emotional spontaneity. Others let him be reclusive, since his nonverbal and often verbal message is "Leave me alone." As a loner, he can live in a closed-off inner world, leading a schizoid existence based on a stable but constricted psychological disorder.

INFERIORITY COMPLEX

The Hades man in a Zeus world has the same difficulties as does a black man in a white world. In a white world, the black man does not see positive images of himself; he is treated as an inferior, is always the outsider, and is the recipient of negative or shadow projections. The psychological world follows similar dynamics. If we use Jung's descriptions of psychological types and accept his observations that the "inferior" function is usually devalued and the opposite of the most conscious, utilized "superior" function, Hades represents the inferior function in the

Western patriarchal industrial world. What is valued are hard facts or objective reality, and logical thinking; what is rewarded is the ability to get to the top, to successfully compete for status, power, affluence. So Hades is likely to suffer from feelings of inferiority, low self-esteem, and lack of confidence, because he is not up to "the standard" of what a man should be like.

Inferior performance in this culture is also a source of low self-esteem. It is hard to compete in a foreign culture, and this situation is equivalent. The dominant extraverted, competitive culture is foreign to the Hades man. Yet it is possible to compensate, to develop a second language, adapt well to a different culture, and even excel. Still, he often has an underlying feeling of inferiority, a continual monitoring of himself, and a feeling of somehow being a fake when success comes.

DEPRESSION: EMOTIONAL ARIDNESS

Hades is cut off from the realm of emotions. Although we all have to venture into the realm of objective reality and thinking just to get through the bare requirements for a basic education, and we have to learn the language of this outer world, it's quite possible to remain the equivalent of an emotional illiterate. It is not required that we learn how others feel and why, nor are we tested or given special education if we have problems in accessing our own feelings or perceiving those of others. These skills either come naturally, or develop through strong emotional attachments, which are not innate predispositions for Hades. Thus the problem of emotional aridness, which contributes to a chronic, low-level depression (for many men in general, but for Hades men in particular). The inner nonverbal, subjectivity of Hades can also be considered to stem from the right brain, the cerebral hemisphere, which is more pessimistic in mood.

DISTORTIONS OF REALITY

Introverted perception is colored by subjective influences; this is it's nature. The best situation for anyone is to have both objective and subjective perceptions, to perceive accurately what is out there and then to have an inner subjective response that enhances the experience. (Accuracy and objectivity concern what is consensually or collectively perceived and decided on as "reality."

However, with reclusiveness and mistrust, subjective perceptions can become pathologically distorted and out of touch with reality. It is not the degree of distortion in his perceptions that brings "the men in white coats" to cart him off for a psychiatric examination, but what he does with those perceptions (what he says and how he acts, and who is affected) and whether there are other people with either enough concern or enough power to intervene in his life.

SLEEP DISORDERS AND THE REALM OF THE SHADES

Narcolepsy is an unusual condition in which rapid eye movement sleep intrudes on conscious awareness. Sometimes it's possible to be awake and in the middle of a dream state, which is alarming. More usually, the person is overtaken by sleep in all sorts of situations, including highly emotion-laden moments. It's as if sleep (or Hades) sneaks up and abducts the subject into its realm.

The adolescent or adult who suffers from narcolepsy can also find that dreams intrude into waking life. For example, a person can be in the middle of a conversation and phase in and out of a vivid dream state, which includes smells and tactile sensations as well as seeing and hearing. This is what we experience when we are asleep and dream, but it is very disturbing as a hallucination if we are awake and nobody else is having the same experience.

Fantasies and active imagination are voluntary descents to be entered and left at will. Taking psychedelic drugs provides another voluntarily chosen access. And every night when we go to sleep we enter the world of the shades, though we may not recall the dream on awakening. People who have lucid dreams not only remember dreams, but are aware that they are dreaming and can make decisions that change the course of the dream, including waking up. When we muse, reflect, and free-associate about something in the outer world, we also enter this realm. And if it is our nature to take all experience in, as do introverted types of people, then Hades' realm may be very familiar. It's a matter of when and where, how deep we descend, whether we stay conscious, and if we have the choice of being there or not, that determines whether we experience problems with Hades' realm.

DIFFICULTIES FOR OTHERS

The difficulty Hades creates for others by being himself is that he lives in his interior realm, and the rest of the world usually lives elsewhere. The direction of his psychic energy or libido is inward. And his significant others want some of that energy to flow outward into their relationship or into the world. At the very least, they want Hades to communicate about what is going on down there. Loving someone with a reclusive nature is especially hard for extraverts, who may take their exclusion personally and think that they have done something wrong when an introverted partner or child withdraws. That very tension and the tendency for opposites to attract can draw Hades out—or can make the other person more introverted or lonely.

WAYS TO GROW

A Hades man will be an isolated person unless he develops other aspects of himself. He needs to develop a persona to be approachable and visible, and to find the means to express his inner experience.

DEVELOP A PERSONA

A persona is the face we wear into the world. The Latin word *persona* meant "mask," and referred to the masks that were worn on stage, which made the role the actor was to play immediately recognizable. A persona is how we present ourselves, the initial impression we make. A Hades man who lives more in his inner world than in the outer world must consciously craft himself an appropriate persona, putting some thought into how he presents himself. Since the small talk that allows strangers to be at ease with each other does not come naturally to him, he'll need to put some thought into what he says and how he wants to come across. A well-functioning persona—like the clothes we wear—needs to be appropriate to the situation, as well as reflect the person. Hades needs to make an effort to be both visible and approachable, in other words.

FINDING PERSEPHONE

A Hades man will do well to find a receptive woman who can mediate for him with the world. A Hades man will gradually open up and share his perceptions and the richness of his inner life, but he must first be accessible. "Persephone" does this for him, either as a real woman, or as his anima—which Jung described as the unconscious feminine aspect of a man through which he expresses gentleness, emotionality, and sentiment. This expressiveness softens his more forbidding aspects and makes him more approachable.

ACTIVATING HERMES

Hermes was the only god that freely both entered and left Hades' realm. As Messenger God and psychopomp (which means guide of souls), Hermes delivered messages, guided souls to Hades, and came for Persephone. He was noted for the suddenness of his appearance—which is how an intuitive insight arrives on the scene—as well as for the quickness of his mind and his facility with words. When Hades and Hermes are present together, Hermes is the means through which the images or shades in the underworld of Hades are understood and then communicated to others. This is what C. G. Jung did when he described the archetypes of the collective unconscious. If through reading Jung and other analytical (Jungian) psychologists, or poets such as T. S. Eliot, a Hades man finds the vocabulary to convey the riches of his inner experience, then his own Hermes has been activated.

DRAWING ON THE OTHER GODS, GOING OUT INTO THE WORLD

The man who is predominantly and innately an introverted Hades usually has ample opportunity to develop other archetypes, which is the way he grows. All the years of compulsory education draw on Apollo qualities. Living in linear time, meeting schedules, thinking scientifically, rationally explaining cause and effect help develop this archetype. Putting ideas into words is also part of school that develops Hermes. And if he is loved or loves anyone, then the realm of emotions also becomes a place in which he grows.

A Hades man who recognizes himself in these pages and realizes that his family was so dysfunctional that he withdrew too much into himself, can grow psychologically beyond Hades as an adult. It begins with a decision and a commitment to do so. Then it takes courage, to venture out of the world of his own in which he found safety and isolation. He might go to meetings of Adult Children of Alcoholics (the commonest cause of dysfunctional families), knowing that he can just listen for a long time until he begins to relate to the experiences others speak of, and then make contact with a few people. He might decide to return overtures others have made to him at work. He might seek a therapist. If he realizes that he is spending too much time in his inner world, he might structure his time to focus more on the outer world: he could take courses that will teach him what he feels he does not know, or take up a skill and concentrate on it.

PART III

The Generation of the Sons: Apollo, Hermes, Ares, Hephaestus, Dionysus

The Olympian sons were Apollo, God of the Sun; Hermes (whom the Romans called Mercury), the Messenger God; Ares (Mars), God of War; Hephaestus (Vulcan), God of the Forge; and Dionysus (Bacchus), God of Ecstasy and Wine. These second-generation Olympian gods were the generation of the sons. Although they did not rule over realms, they were associated with particular locations, situations, or kinds of places. Travelers felt Hermes' presence on roads and at boundaries, Ares on the battlefield, Dionysus in the midst of a mountain revel. Hephaestus was hard at work at his smithy under the volcano, and Apollo was in residence at Delphi during most of the year. The sons were defined by what they did, which in turn had to do with their attributes and temperament.

Zeus was father of this generation. Apollo, Hermes, Ares, and Dionysus were his sons, and he was a father in name only of Hephaestus, whose mother Hera was his sole parent and the wife of Zeus. Zeus favored Apollo and Hermes, rejected Ares and Hephaestus, and was the surrogate mother as well as the father of Dionysus.

FAVORED SONS: APOLLO AND HERMES

Those sons Zeus favored are the same two that as archetypes help men to get ahead in the patriarchal world. Apollo and Hermes were mythologically comfortable in Zeus's sky realm. As God of the Sun, Apollo drove his chariot across the sky. As Zeus's messenger, Hermes could freely and easily travel to the top of Olympus. These two gods, like Zeus, are associated with emotional distance and mental activity. As archetypes, they are the two most at home in the realm of the mind. Both were associated with words, negotiations, and commerce, and appealed to Zeus to settle disputes. Both avoided physical conflict. Neither had a wife or consort.

REJECTED SONS: ARES AND HEPHAESTUS

The sons he rejected, Ares and Hephaestus—in contrast to Apollo and Hermes—did not use their mind or words. They both expressed themselves through physical action. Both were, in a sense, manual rather than mental. And both were motivated by their emotions. Ares would be stirred to fight by rage or loyalty, using weapons for a destructive purpose. When Hephaestus was rejected and betrayed, he put his feelings into the objects he made, using tools for a creative purpose. Zeus rejected Hephaestus and detested Ares. Both gods were also ridiculed or called names by others, and men who are like them are likely to suffer a lack of self-esteem. Both were sons of Hera, a devalued, angry, and impotent mother.

As archetypes, their characteristics are not valued by the patriarchy, and hence men who resemble these gods have difficulty being successful.

AN AMBIVALENTLY VIEWED SON: DIONYSUS

Dionysus is in a category of his own, as the only Olympian with a mortal mother, and the only one that was both nurtured or mothered by Zeus as well as fathered by him. When Dionysus was a fetus too small to survive on his own, Zeus sewed him inside his thigh, which served as an incubator or second womb, until he had grown enough and could be born.

Dionysus was the only god who preferred to be with women, and women were major people in his mythology. Dionysus brought his mother out of the underworld to Olympus, where she could have a place of honor. He came to Ariadne after she had been deserted, married her, and was a faithful Olympian husband.

The last god to join the Olympian pantheon, Dionysus was the son who changed Zeus from a distant father into a nurturing father. Dionysus is ambivalently viewed: men in power react to Dionysus as a foreign influence that should not be allowed into the culture or to their psyches, while women and the feminine aspect of men are likely to welcome his influence. Men who are like this god find that others react to them with strong ambivalent (hardly ever indifferent) feelings.

THE GODS AS FAVORED, REJECTED, OR AMBIVALENTLY ACCEPTED PARTS OF OURSELVES

The American patriarchal culture differs in one major respect from that of the Greeks: the classical Greeks were not puritans and hence have no puritanical mythical father, as in our culture and our psyches. For Zeus, sexuality was an expression of power, an instinct he could gratify because he had the power to do so; the Greeks did not consider sex prurient and dirty. By nurturing Dionysus, on a metaphor level Zeus nurtured the possiblity of relating to the Dionysus in himself, through which his sexuality could take on an ecstatic dimension, or through whom his relationship to the feminine and to women could change. Thus while Zeus had positive feelings for Dionysus, and the Greeks viewed him with ambivalence, the American version of the patriarchy judges Dionysus negatively.

We live in a patriarchy that plays favorites, and that bias is incorporated within our psyches as well. Thus our accepting or rejecting attitudes toward parts of ourselves are shaped by culture and by family. "Who" we individually resemble most closely, or which of these archetypes are most "us," begins as inherent predispositions that are welcome or not.

When we learn the names for these patterns, and they come alive in the chapters that follow, we're able to recognize the presence or absence of each particular god in our psyches, as I imagine has already happened with the three preceding father gods. Like the "Aha!" culmination of the detective story, which hinges on the discovery of the real identity of a significant person in the story, the most important "Aha!" in this book may come when you discover something about your true identity or an important piece of yourself that now can be "re-membered."

6.

Apollo, God of the Sun—Archer, Lawgiver, Favorite Son

Beauty of every sort, whether of art, music, poetry or youth, sanity and moderation—all are summed up in Apollo.

Under his most important and influential aspect may be included everything that connects him with law and order. Primarily he represented the Greek preference for "the intelligible, determinate, measurable, as opposed to the fantastic, vague and shapeless.

W. K. C. Guthrie, *The Greeks and Their Gods*

Apollo rejects whatever is too near—entanglement in things, the melting gaze, and equally, soulful merging, mystical inebriation and its ecstatic vision.

Walter F. Otto, *The Homeric Gods*

Apollo is the embodiment of a masculine attitude that observes and acts from a distance. As god, archetype, and man, he "shines"; he was the most important son of Zeus, and his attributes lead to success within a patriarchy. He is very much at home in the sky realm of intellect, will, and mind. Yet although he is noted for clarity and form, there is nonetheless, both a hidden and a dark aspect to Apollo.

APOLLO THE GOD

Apollo was second only to Zeus as the most important Greek god. He was the God of the sun, of the arts (especially of music), of prophecy, and of archery. He was the lawgiver and punisher of wrongs; the patron of medicine, who could also bring plagues; and the protector of herdsmen. He was known by the

130

Romans as well as the Greeks as Apollo, or Phoebus ("bright," "shining," "pure") Apollo.

He was portrayed standing or striding, as a handsome, beardless youth with virile strength and flowing, golden hair. Inscribed on his temple at Delphi were his two famous precepts: "Know thyself" and "Nothing in excess." The bow and the lyre were dear to him, the laurel his sacred plant.

For all his solar brightness, he had a lesser known darker aspect, with both light and dark reflected in his symbols. Apollo was known as the pure, holy, and cleansing god, whose attributes were analogous to the sun, which was his most important symbol. Singing swans, Apollo's sacred birds, circled around Delos seven times as his birth became imminent, and Zeus gave him a chariot with swans when he was born. Even so, the raven and crow—the dark birds—were also associated with Apollo, as were the snake and the wolf. His punishments could be cruel, and he could act vindictively.

GENEALOGY AND MYTHOLOGY

Apollo was the son of Leto and Zeus, and twin brother of Artemis, Goddess of the Hunt and Moon. When Leto (a Titan, of the ruling generation that preceded the Olympians) was pregnant with Apollo and Artemis, she wandered over the earth trying to find a place where she might give birth. No place would welcome her because people rightly feared the wrath of Hera, Zeus's jealous wife. Finally, in labor, she came to the barren island that was later called Delos. For nine days and nights, Leto suffered terrible labor with Apollo (Hera had prevented the goddess of childbirth from going to her aid). Apollo was finally born under a palm tree, on the seventh day of the month. The number seven was sacred to him, and that palm tree was one of the famous tourist sights of antiquity.

APOLLO AND ARTEMIS: THE TWINS

Apollo and his twin sister Artemis were both archers. Apollo's bow and arrow shafts were golden, and he was god of the golden sun. Artemis's weapons were silver as was her silver moon. Artemis was the older twin, and it was she, according to Homer, who taught Apollo archery. Both shot from afar their invisible and unerring shafts, which brought sudden and pain-less death. The two were honored for their purity, and known for their remoteness, unapproachability, and for disappearing (she into the forest, he to the mysterious realm of the Hyper-boreans).

Both Artemis and Apollo watched over growing youth on the threshold of maturity, and meted out swift and merciless punishment. For example, when the foolish woman Niobe hu-miliated their mother Leto by bragging that she had six beauti-ful daughters and six handsome sons, while Leto had only Artemis and Apollo. Leto called on her divine children for help, whereon Apollo killed all six of her sons and Artemis all six of her daughters. Niobe was changed into a weeping pillar of salt.

Artemis once loved a hunter named Orion. Jealous Apollo challenged her to try to hit a far-off speck in the distant sea, doubting that she could do it. Competitive Artemis rose to the challenge and with unerring aim hit the target, finding out too late that she had killed Orion, who had waded out into the sea until only his head was above the water.

In the *Iliad's* famous battle of the gods during the Trojan war, Poseidon challenged Apollo to a duel. Apollo declined, deigning not to fight for insignificant mortals, and would not be provoked by Artemis who angrily reproached him as a coward.

APOLLO AND HIS UNSUCCESSFUL LOVES

Daphne was Apollo's first love, and Eros (also known as Amor or Cupid) the cause of his difficulties. After Apollo jeered at Eros's power with bow and arrow, Eros shot a golden love arrow into Apollo's heart, and a leaden love-repelling arrow into Daphne's. Apollo, now burning with passion, pursued Daphne, and as he was about to overtake her, she prayed to her father, the river god, for help. He turned her into a laurel tree. Apollo loved her still. The laurel became his sacred tree, her leaves made into wreaths adorned his hair.

Cassandra is the best known woman who rejected Apollo and paid a price. She was the daughter of Priam and Hecuba, king and queen of Troy. Apollo taught Cassandra the art of prophecy on the condition that he would become her lover. Cas-sandra promised, but didn't keep her word. Although he could not take back the gift of prophecy, Apollo's revenge was that he decreed that no one would believe her. With the onset of the Trojan War, Cassandra continually saw the calamities that would occur and, unbelieved, was shut away as a madwoman.

Apollo was a little more successful with Coronis, a beautiful young woman who became pregnant with his child. The god assigned a white raven the task of keeping an eye on her for him. The raven reported back that she was cheating on him. Apollo's response to this was to change the raven's feathers from white to black, and to kill Coronis. This murder be committed in haste, and later regretted. But there was nothing he could do to bring her back to life. When she was on the funeral pyre, Apollo snatched his unborn son from her body, and gave him to Chiron the centaur to raise. This son was Asclepius, who became the god of healing and medicine.

In his love for a man, Apollo also suffered. Once he was taken with a young man, Hyacinth, son of the king of Sparta— so much so that he abandoned Delphi to spend all his time with him. One day, when the two competed in discus-throwing contest, Apollo's discus ricocheted off a stone, struck Hyacinth, and killed him. In anguish at the death of the man he loved, Apollo vowed that Hyacinth would be remembered. From Hyacinth's blood sprang the flower that bears his name.

APOLLO AND PROPHECY

Apollo was the god of prophecy, though he himself did not prophesize as part of his mythology. This was an attribute that he expropriated. He took over the oracle of Delphi, a site with a long history of prophetic divination. Prior to Apollo, Delphi was a pre-Hellenic sanctuary of a Goddess, possibly a snake goddess. In his mythology, Apollo killed a great she-dragon or serpent named Python to gain possession of Delphi. Thereafter he was called Pythian Apollo and his priestess was Pythia.

Apollo's mediums were all women under his control, and their psychic divinations were attributed to their communion with him. In practice, control was exercised by an exegete, a priest-interpreter who attended the priestess. When the Pythia went into a trance, the priest put questions to her and took down her words. The response was then turned over to another priest, who usually put it into metrical form. The meaning of the words was often obscure and ambiguous, and the oracle was often used for political purposes.

DELPHI

At the foot of Mt. Parnassus, in the innermost chamber filled with the fumes of smoldering barley, hemp, and laurel leaves, the elderly Pythia would sit on a tripod and enter a trance state.

In this inner chamber was also the Omphalos, or navel stone (the word *delphys* means "womb"). Delphi was considered the navel or womb of the earth and center of the world, even before Zeus—in the spirit of scientific inquiry—decided to mark the center of the world. He turned two eagles loose, one flying from the easternmost edge of the world, the other from the westernmost boundary. Released at the same time and flying at the same speed, they met over Delphi.

Also in the inner sanctuary of Apollo's temple was the grave of Dionysus. For the three winter months, Apollo handed over his temple to Dionysus, while he went away far north, to the fabled land of the Hyperboreans.

People came to Apollo's temple for two major reasons (other than to honor the god): to consult with his oracle and to obtain purification after committing a crime. Lawmakers sought advice from Apollo as both the giver and interpreter of the law. And Greek states attributed their constitutions to him. He was the divine authority for law and order.

Besides his two most famous precepts, others were also inscribed on his temple, which convey Apollo's values of moderation and authority:

> Curb thy spirit.
> Observe the limit.
> Hate hubris (pride).
> Keep a reverent tongue.
> Fear authority.
> Bow before the divine.
> Glory not in strength.
> Keep women under rule.[1]

Apollo was a pan-Hellenic god, whose influence was second only to Zeus throughout Greece. Not only did cities send emissaries to Delphi for advice, but ministers of Apollo were also sent to the cities of Greece from Delphi as the interpreters of civil and religious law.

APOLLO THE ARCHETYPE

Apollo could see clearly from afar and observe the details of life with an overview perspective; he could aim for a target and hit it with his bow and arrows, or create harmony with his music. As an archetype, Apollo personifies the aspect of the personality that wants clear definitions, is drawn to master a skill, values order and harmony, and prefers to look at the surface rather than at what underlies appearances.

The Apollo archetype favors thinking over feeling, distance over closeness, objective assessment over subjective intuition. The man who most closely conforms to the Apollo archetype has attributes that will hold him in good stead in the world. He can succeed in a career and can master a classical art form easier than most people can.

THE ARCHER

To be an archer takes will, skill, and practice. An accomplished archer can aim for a distant target and be confident of hitting it. Metaphorically, this is what a man who is archetypally Apollo is naturally drawn to doing.

The Apollo mind is logical and easily relates to objective reality. For him, the laws of cause and effect are not lessons to be learned by dint of experience and parental admonishments, but principles that an Apollo mind seems to have programmed in from the start. That preprogramming is the archetype: the little boy who knows what he wants and has the will to accomplish that goal is being true to his Apollo nature.

To aim at a target requires having a sense of future time, which an Apollo man has. Other types of men may have difficulty setting goals, but not Apollo. He knows where he wants to go, what he wants to accomplish, that he wants to win. He is not a dreamer. His targets are realistic ones that will require effort. They are also usually goals that are visible to others. A boy may aim at becoming an Eagle Scout, or winning first place in a competition. Later he may decide to go to Harvard, MIT, or Oxford and then take a prestigious position in his chosen field. Apollo qualities favor achieving recognition.

Possibly the high school and college years are where the Apollo archetype exists in its most untarnished form, in young men who are clearly marked for success, and have not yet either been emotionally wounded nor had much opportunity to learn humility. You probably can recall an all-round accomplished Apollo: A nice-looking, graceful, clean-cut young man, with excellent grades, who played a musical instrument, did well at a gentleman's sport, and probably was a class officer—just who the Ivy League college director of admissions wanted.

Fittingly, most of the best-known *Apollo* space program astronauts resemble Apollo. I think of John Glenn, Edgar Mitchell, or Neil Armstrong, and see the god Apollo. They and the space program were like the god Apollo was to his father Zeus, carrying out the will of the father. They were extensions of the will of the president, and were the brightest reflections on a series of administrations.

FAVORITE SON

Apollo was Zeus's favorite son, and next to Zeus, the most important Greek god. Described as having golden hair, Apollo was indeed a fair-haired son whose purpose was to carry out his father's will.

In the United States, the Republican Party is the political party that espouses traditional patriarchal values. George Bush and Dan Quayle, the Republican presidential and vice-presidential candidates in 1988 were cast in Apollo molds. Bush, the son of a powerful senatorial father, and Quayle, whose family newspapers dominate his home state of Indiana, were privileged, good-looking men, used to having advantages. Bush needed to overcome an image problem as a perennial second-in-command Apollo if he were to attain the position of Zeus; and it was almost unimaginable to voters that an archetypal fair-haired boy such as Quayle could take over as president. Favorite sons usually rise only so far, because they are perceived as lightweights, cast in the archetypal role of a son or brother, lacking the driving ambition and capacity to consolidate power and rule as a father figure with the ruthlessness of a Zeus.

The favorite son archetype appears untarnished by pain and struggle. His propensity to mentally distance himself from the suffering of others and be out of touch with his own feelings makes this likely. However, when a man is perceived by others as an Apollo, the attributes of the archetype are projected upon him and it is difficult to see him otherwise.

THE MUSICIAN

Apollo was associated with two stringed intruments, the bow and the lyre. His touch on one let loose the arrow; his plucking the other brought forth music. W. F. Otto, author of *The Homeric Gods,* noted that the Greeks saw a kinship between the two: "in both they saw a dart speeding to its goal, in one case the unerring arrow, in the other unerring song."[2] The song from the most alert of all gods does not arise dreamlike out of an intoxicated soul but flies directly towards a clearly seen truth.

In his music, Apollo was again associated with clarity and purity. In contrast to Dionysian music, which expresses chaos, ecstasy, turbulence, emotional conflicts, and passion, Apollonian music values that clear note, the purity of music that is like higher mathematics, which brings harmony through time and measure and lifts the spirit. Bach's classical music echoes Apollo. Those who have heard twentieth-century master cellists Pablo Casals and Yo-yo Ma play, similarly often describe the experience as a spiritual epiphany, as if the god came through the music and unerringly hit the mark.

Moderation and beauty were the essence and the effect of Apollo's music. It restrained all that was wild, charming even predatory beasts. When the tormented biblical King Saul commanded the young shepherd David to play a stringed instrument for him, so that he might be soothed, David must have played the kind of music Apollo played to have this effect.

UPHOLDER OF LAW AND ORDER

Apollo gave cities their legal institutions, interpreted law, advocated order and moderation, provided the structure for a community to work together, and means to settle disputes. The lawgiver and the musician both express this archetype's instinct for order and form. Apollo is uncomfortable with chaos or turbulence, the discordant note, or passionate intensity, in behavior as well as in music. Through rules and laws, as through measure and time, Apollo's intent is to provide form and bring order.

The law-and-order aspect of Apollo is certain about what ought to be. Through his ordinances, Apollo decreed what was allowable and what was not. Accordingly, the Apollo lawyer prefers arguing constitutional law or cases where he (or she) can apply principles and precedents, rather than plead motivation or special circumstances. Not surprisingly, when men and women are nominated to the U.S. Supreme Court, their Apollo qualities are stressed by their advocates.

Both the idealist who envisions a time when all people might live peacefully under the rule of law that would guarantee justice and fairness and the contemporary upholders of "law and order" who have a strong conviction that they know what is right and good for everyone, are deriving this sense of authority from the Apollo archetype.

Meaning as well as authority comes from doing work that has an archetypal basis. The jurist or law enforcement officer—every bit as much as the musician or astronaut—may sense this inwardly, and find that Apollo gives his work a sacred dimension.

THE FAR-DISTANT ONE

In many different ways, the Apollo archetype predisposes a man to be emotionally distant. He can live in the future as the goal-oriented archer or prophetic one, he can rise above the situation to see everything objectively rather than remain in touch with what he personally feels, or he can bypass his emotional and relationship difficulties by seeing all experience as spiritual lessons (which they can be, of course).

The ability to see things rationally or spiritually, at a distance from one's own immediate emotional response, is therefore part of the Apollo archetype. This gift predisposes Apollo-like people to respond to their own emotional pain by distancing themselves from these feelings and "going skyward," through intellectual understanding, a mindful spiritual practice, or repeating their precepts to themselves.

There was a remote otherworldness about the god Apollo that has to do with his connection to the mysterious Hyperboreans. The mythologist W. F. Otto noted that when Apollo was

born, Zeus gave him a chariot with swans on which he rode not
to Delphi, but to the Hyperboreans with whom he remained for
a whole year. Thereafter he periodically went to "this blessed
land of light"[3] for a portion of each year. In contemporary times,
with New Age emphasis on worlds of light, we recall the image
of Apollo and the Hyperboreans again. Today, that "northerly
realm beyond the mountains" envisioned by the Greeks as the
land of the Hyperboreans is placed in the Pleiades constellation
or in another dimension. The Hyperborean aspect of Apollo has
a similarity to the netherworldness of Hades. On a psychological
level, whether that distant place of retreat is a star world or an
underworld, or a world of higher mathematics, the effect is the
same: it leads to feelings of isolation from others and to periodically disappearing from this world into another.

THE BROTHERS

Apollo's role as a brother is his most significant within-the-
family designation, with sibling rivalry and sibling friendship
emphasized in his relationship with his younger brother
Hermes, the Messenger God, and with his sister, Artemis, Goddess of the Hunt and Moon.

Many mythological incidents link Apollo and Artemis.
Artemis, born first, helped their mother Leto during her
prolonged labor with Apollo. Later, Leto would call on the two to
avenge Niobe's insult. Apollo's jealousy of Artemis's affection for
the hunter Orion, as mentioned, led him to challenge her, so that
she unknowingly killed him. Competition also arose between
Apollo and his younger brother, Hermes, whose first act was to
steal Apollo's cattle, and from whom Apollo received the lyre.

As an archetype of the sibling and favored older brother,
Apollo predisposes men to be part of a team effort. He fits easily
into the role of a corporate man, who can be second in command, without feeling the resentment or chafing at the bit that
a man who is archetypally a father or king, in need of having
his own kingdom, might feel. He also finds it natural to work
with competent women or compete against them. As a competitor, Apollo participates in the give and take of politics as well as
of sports and usually does not hold grudges. Because of his
emotional distance, he can play politics like a game and do well
against others who become emotionally caught up in it. He may

not win the top position, however, because he appears cautious and doesn't inspire others to see him as a chief. Apollo was the most important god *after* Zeus.

THE NONHERO

Apollo, whose physical appearance of virility and nobility gave him the look of a hero, was opposed to acting the part. Specifically, he would not be drawn into a duel unlike heroes in this culture from the Trojan War to the quick-draw shootout in the Western cowboy movie. To angry Poseidon, Apollo calmly replied, "You would have me be without measure and without prudence, if I am to fight for insignificant mortals, who now flourish like leaves of the trees and then fade away and are dead." And when his sister Artemis called him a coward, he still would not be drawn into combat.

Moreover, Apollo was antagonistic to heroes. Apollo refused the hero Heracles help through the Pythian Oracle. And he opposed Achilles, the most famous and favored of Greek heroes. Achilles died when he was struck in the heel by an arrow, in that one vulnerable place that had not been bathed in the river Styx. In several versions, it was Apollo who killed him, either in the guise of Paris or as himself. But it was not done as a heroic act—not in direct combat, but by shooting an arrow from a distance.

Apollo values prudence, avoids physical danger, is unriled by emotions, and prefers being an observer. This is the profile of a side-liner, not a hero. When generals had to lead troops into battle, there were probably no Apollos among the generals. But probably many Apollo generals now rank high among the successful organization men who have risen in the Pentagon. When war games are thought out, as they are today, and various options and plans are considered, and the ultimate weapon is unleashed from a distance, perhaps by pushing several buttons on a computer, the armchair general is very likely an Apollo, who considers statistical probabilities instead of the passions and allegiances that motivate people. This was the case in the Vietnam War, with the Pentagon directed by Secretary of Defense Robert McNamara, and his staff of young, bright men who came with him who were earlier referred to as "whiz kids."

CULTIVATING APOLLO

In this culture, Apollo traits are cultivated vigorously from the time a boy is a young child. From prekindergarten through graduate school, people are expected to think and express themselves verbally and logically. The lessons of cause and effect are repeated in life as well as in science. Good grades and good impressions are made today in order to get a rung higher tomorrow. In all but alternative schools, every classroom and grade usually promotes Apollo's values and characteristics.

In spite of the heavy emphasis on developing Apollo qualities, if another archetype dominates the person, the need to consciously develop Apollo, may arise only in adulthood. To develop Apollo characteristics, an individual may seek help to learn how to organize time, how to budget money, or how to organize work. The help needed may also be more specific, such as how to write a résumé. Whatever the task, in Apollo's realm education and practice is likely to lead to success. An expert always seems to be available to teach how to systematically learn anything.

APOLLO THE MAN

A man who resembles Apollo ordinarily finds it easy to be in the world. He has qualities that make gaining approval from others and achieving success quite likely. However, difficulties and deficits may arise in his relationships and inner life.

EARLY YEARS

The Apollo child is usually (as is appropriate to the myth) sunny in disposition. Typically, he is extraverted in attitude, and, being curious and inquisitive, he enjoys looking around at the world. He likes the elevation of being a baby in a backpack.

Apollo gathers information about his surroundings. He's interested in what something is or what somebody does. He wants to know the names of things. Never much of a dreamer, he doesn't indulge in fantasy, imaginary playmates, or imagined monsters.

In nursery school and kindergarten, he's one of the boys or one of the gang, a brotherly, give-and-take child, who gets along and who may even be a leader. Others often want him to be their best friend, but he often doesn't have a favorite, special friend.

As the various Little League sports come along, he may do well or even excel. If he has some talent, he will enhance it by practicing. If his talents lie elsewhere, so will he.

He seems to have a built-in clock and knows he needs to do today what will be due tomorrow. So homework and practicing his music lessons, a newspaper route, being a Cub Scout or an altar boy, each get his attention.

Although he actually may be as good a boy as he appears to be on the surface—he's often considered a "straight arrow"—it's not unusual for him to have friends who get into trouble even though he doesn't. Other boys may get carried away by boisterous, excessive make-a-mess, do-something-bad behavior, and may not consider that they could be asking for trouble when they go beyond the limits. But not the Apollo boy: he thinks of such things and looks out for himself.

His Parents

The god Apollo was the second-born twin, and Leto labored for nine days and nine nights to give birth to him. After great effort, he was born, "and Leto was happy, because the son she made was strong, and an archer."[4] Her words from the Homeric Hymn to Delian Apollo echo those of women who have "succeeded in producing" a son and heir and who later are validated by the achievements of their Apollo sons.

Following such an ordeal, perhaps even a goddess would have been exhausted and unavailable to nurse him. What we know is that Apollo "was not given his mother's breast. Instead Themis, with her divine hands poured [him] nectar and lovely ambrosia."[5] Apollo's earliest nourishment thus was the food of the gods, given him by Themis, pre-Olympian Goddess of Prophecy, whose mantle Apollo's oracles would later wear. The parallel for an Apollo man was to have a physically undemonstrative mother, who didn't provide the holding and merging that a nursing baby experiences from an "earth mother."

From the beginning Apollo described his life mission thus: "I will reveal to mankind the exact will of Zeus."[6] Here is a father's son, who will grow up basking in parental approval: "And a brightness casts about him, the flashings of his feet and his carefully woven gown. And they are delighted in their great hearts, Leto, with her gold hair, and wise Zeus, as they look upon their dear son playing with the immortal gods."[7]

The Apollo boy is likely to be rewarded with approval, especially by a traditional father, for being exactly as he is. An Apollo son is a success in the making, a positive reflection on his parents, an achiever in a culture that values accomplishments. He is used to being in the limelight of parental pleasure, which is the "brightness cast about him." This is the traditional position of an Apollo boy especially the first-born son in a patriarchal culture, expected and able to carry on the traditions of the family; that is, "to live out his father's will."

It is not unusual for an Apollo boy to be a winner, and be used to receiving love and approval for what he does. At each level of life (or of competition), however, he encounters others who also do very well. He thus feels great pressure to excel, and he may no longer be at the head of his class, or the star quarterback of the team.

Now the psychological questions emerge: How much do his parents need him to do well for them? Is he loved for himself, or is the love he gets actually tied to achievement? Does his own sense of worth depend on the latest achievement? Does losing devastate him? If so, he takes doubt or challenge too personally, though he will usually hide his sense of being threatened, and the hostility this generates in him, behind a sunny, smiling mask.

Sometimes an Apollo boy has narcissistic parents who indeed need him to be an extension of themselves, who feel better about themselves when he "wins" and demand that he reflect well on them. Such a boy carries a very heavy burden. His own will to win makes him a competitor; needing to win in order to retain his parents or a parent's conditional love may add a counterproductive anxiety to the situation, which makes him less able to do well. On practice days, he's fine, but when it counts, he doesn't perform up to his ability.

When exceptional ability and the Apollo personality are both present in a youngster, whether he will become all that he could be—as chess player, musician, math genius, doctor, lawyer, archer, scientist, and human being—will depend to a great extent on his parents and his teachers. As a child with exceptional talent, and the will to excel for himself, the Apollo child thrives when learning is a game to be mastered and when the greatest satisfaction is personal mastery and love of what he is doing.

ADOLESCENCE AND EARLY ADULTHOOD

How good "an archer" he is sets the theme for these early years of manhood. If he is able, and not handicapped by anxiety, he will excel at repeatedly reaching goals he aims for. Good grades, class offices, honors and awards, scholarships are all prizes that go to young Apollos. If he comes from an underprivileged household, he'll look like a Horatio Alger. He works hard and uses his time well, managing to get good grades, excel at extracurricular activities, and hold a part-time job.

He has an affinity to seek out a father Zeus, if life did not provide him with a real father who could be this. He has an archetypal affinity, a wish to be a favored son, an attitude of wanting to excel and to please that draws the approval of Zeus men, who help him to get ahead in the world.

The tasks of the first half of life, which for men is to succeed in the world of work, so coincides with Apollo's own drive to achieve, that this phase of life is unusually smooth for an Apollo. Adolescence is not a time of turmoil, of antiauthoritarian rebellion, or mystical, sexual, or inward preoccupation for most Apollos—at least as far as other people can see.

The major difficulty of this period occurs when an Apollo man is unable to succeed because of psychological, social, or intellectual problems or handicaps. A dyslexic Apollo with learning disabilities is greatly frustrated in his wish to accomplish. He may be successful at overcoming the handicap because he will work at it systematically. The discrepancy between what he wants to do and his inability to do so may create so much internal rage and frustration, however, that he can't keep his focus on one goal at a time, and so cannot overcome the handicap.

WORK

The Apollo man is at a distinct advantage when it comes to work. Doing well at work comes easily for him, because he has an inherent ability to focus on a task, to want to practice until he masters something, and to see the end product of what he is doing. Given his objectivity about himself and the outer world, his goals are likely to be realistic, as step by step he advances according to plan.

Apollo men often go into professions that take years of education and the ability to set long-term goals. Medicine and law attract many Apollo-minded men. Law is especially fitting. In the trial of Orestes, who had killed his mother (Orestes killed her at Apollo's instigation because she had killed Orestes' father Agamemnon), Apollo was the articulate defense lawyer.

The Apollo man adapts easily to working in institutions and corporations. He has a propensity to develop competitive brother relationships with peers and to assume a leadership role within his peer group. He seeks the approval of men in positions of authority and carries out their directives easily. An additional plus today, in a time of women's equality, is that he works well with competent women, toward whom he relates easily, forming alliances with women who are like Artemis or Athena in themselves being goal-oriented and competitive. He is the ideal organization man.

An Apollo man often does not make it to the top, or succeed as an entrepreneur because he lacks the drive to amass either power or money, the vision, decisiveness, or ruthlessness of a Zeus. He is the archetypal son in a patriarchy, and although he aspires to make it to the top and his success on the way up seems to lead there, he usually either doesn't make it, or he fails to consolidate power and extend his authority once he gets there, and so is toppled.

When the Apollo man gets as far as he (and the archetype) can take him, and it is not what he aimed at, work no longer serves as the source of gratification it always was before, and instead becomes a problem. When the Apollo man gets above his level of competence, and is no longer the bright star, trouble occurs. He is unprepared to fail or falter. He has put his energy into his work, sacrificed development of other interests, and has expected his family to also defer their needs to his career. There may be no ready-made alternatives for him to fall back on to give him meaning.

RELATIONSHIPS WITH WOMEN

An Apollo man is often attracted to an independent, competent, attractive woman, who is a highly complementary match—they then look like an archetypal two-career, young urban professional couple when they go out on a date. He likes working with the same kind of woman, as well.

Often the relationship has a competitive flavor, and their fun together may be in playing games or doing things that involve skill. Or they may share interests in the arts or music. A work-related relationship can function very well as they challenge and support one another to excel.

Living in his head, rather than either in his body or emotions, the Apollo man is not a lover. There's characteristically a lack of passion in his relationships with women. Also, a relationship with him often doesn't have much emotional depth, for he prefers to maintain his usual emotional distance. Consequently the woman in his life may decide that theirs is a brother-sister relationship and may reject him as a lover, either directly or by becoming attracted to someone else. That was the fate of the god Apollo.

The sister competitor needs to be wary of one possible facet of the Apollo man. A devious and hostile potential can be a hidden part of his personality. While maintaining a friendly competitor attitude, he can do something very underhanded, just as Apollo tricked Artemis into hitting the far-off target that turned out to be the head of her lover Orion.

The attraction of opposites seems to exert a magnetic pull, when—like the god who loved Sybil and Cassandra—an Apollo man is drawn towards a psychic woman, who is emotional, irrational, impractical, and often unimpressed with him. He finds her fascinating, frustrating, and unpredictable. Many Apollo men are drawn to such women whom they try to control.

RELATIONSHIPS WITH MEN

Apollo men usually get along very well with other men. They look up to and value relationships with older men in authority, and often have mentors who help advance their careers. They are most comfortable in give-and-take relationships. They negotiate well and deliver what they promise.

Their competitiveness makes them assess where they are relative to everyone else; their most comfortable position is that of first among peers, or favored elder brother, and they strive to achieve this position. An Apollo man likes to be the star on a team, rather than a loner. He readily makes room for others, and accepts and enjoys the company of men who are less impeccable than he is. He usually is nobody's regular drinking buddy, however.

SEXUALITY

An Apollo man isn't much of a lover. He doesn't fall in love easily and is so single-minded in his focus that he is not easily distracted by attractive women. In his everyday life, the Apollo man doesn't spend much time having erotic thoughts. He doesn't mentally undress women he sees or spend much time in masturbatory fantasies. His instinctual, sexual, and sensual dimension is often his least consciously developed aspect, and as such it is usually out of mind.

Episodically, the sexuality he gives little thought to may arise. For a time, he may be in ardent pursuit, as his capacity to focus on goals combines with sexual desire. If the woman has not herself fallen under the spell of love, the intensity of his feelings often feels unrelated to her, since it very likely hadn't been preceded either by the intimacy of shared deep communication, nor by a nonverbal sensual dialogue. She may feel very much like a pursued Daphne, and she may run from him, feeling more like an object he wants to possess than a woman being wooed.

Living in his head, rather than in his body or his imagination, the Apollo man is a stranger in the realm of Eros. He knows little experientially of the ebb and flow of sexual attraction, or the ongoing need to be touched and communicated with on a body-to-body level (or of intimate verbal communication either). Thus, if he wins the woman who roused him and then "goes away" as a lover (which is typical of an Apollo man), she may be unfaithful in his "absence." This pattern recalls the raven's report to Apollo of Coronis's infidelity.

Apollo the god also was enamored by Hyacinth, the young man who so attracted him that he abandoned Delphi to spend all his time with him. They were inseparable companions and lovers who did everything together, which is typical of a relationship in which the couple "mirrors" each other—in which one sees oneself in the lover and loves him. Narcissus also fell in love with his own image reflected in the pool, but whereas Narcissus could not get close to the image, and so pined away, Apollo and Hyacinth did have a close relationship. Their relationship ended when Apollo accidentally killed Hyacinth in a competition; when the discus Apollo was throwing ricocheted and hit Hyacinth in the head.

When Eros draws Apollo men into same-sex relationships, the initial relationship is often an Apollo-Hyacinth one. The mirrored self in the other is then the first expression of self-acceptance. There is a narcissism in the feeling of merged sameness and often an effort to limit the other person to being the desired reflection. "Hyacinth" may be killed (the relationship may die) because of competitiveness, growth of one beyond the other, or if Apollo's need to win and show his superiority kills off feelings in the other man.

MARRIAGE

The Apollo man is clearly a "good catch" in any matrimonial sweepstakes. When men, on graduating from college, routinely married younger women who were inexperienced sexually and unambitious for themselves, the Apollo man usually succeeded in winning the bride of his choice. Marriage was a step made with the same consideration as the choice of the college and the initial job offer. Passion and impulse were not decisive; the promise of a good match was.

In a traditional marriage, supported by stereotyping of roles, Apollo may for a period of marriage or for a lifetime have a well-functioning, stable marriage—especially if he marries a woman whose own needs are for an enduring relationship with personal fulfillment for her possible through being a mother (archetypally Demeter). Such might be the case with Supreme Court Justice Scalia, whose appointment to the bench required hard work, political connections, determination to rise through the judiciary, and impressive accomplishments, leaving little time to be involved in the day-to-day raising of nine children.

Apollo men also are highly visible in young urban professional dual-career marriages, in which his wife resembles the logical, intellectual Athena, as out of touch with her instinctual life as he is. Their marriage "works" very well for both of them: each keeps in touch with the other's schedule; they run the household as smoothly as an office; have healthy, regular sex (often with the same intensity and satisfaction as in having a successful dinner party or a good workout at the gym).

However, the marriage will be far from smooth if an Apollo man marries a woman who wants substance rather than form, who needs emotional depth rather than the security of an enduring relationship; or whose Aphrodite nature is passionate, intense, and in the moment, and who thus little values long-term goals that require her to live in the future. Such a marriage leads either to growth or unhappiness. The Apollo man tries (often successfully) to "rise above" the difficulty, which he doesn't see as being his problem. The Apollo man can stay quite comfortably in a marriage marked by emotional distance and lacking in passion. If this makes his wife unhappy, whether the marriage endures depends on the wife and on her real or perceived options to do anything else.

CHILDREN

Apollo men are usually either good or neutral fathers in their children's lives. They are consistent and even-handed in their behavior. They set standards that are fair, and they may even like mottos to live by, which they impart to their children.

Distance is the most common difficulty, as the Apollo man is likely to be absorbed in his career, and will leave the realm of household and children to his wife unless she demands his participation. He doesn't cuddle his children, either, and if he ends up holding his baby (and finds he likes it), that will be because his wife put the baby in his arms until he and the baby bonded.

If his children are like him in their interests, and as they grow older and can engage him in conversations about their plans or his, or do things together, such as share a professional interest or play in a chamber music group together, then they may have a very comfortable, good relationship with him. If his children have deep and hidden feelings that are not observable on the surface, he won't know. And if they expect him to understand their yearnings and passions, they are likely to be disappointed. On the other hand, they may be gratified by his ability to see what they are doing and by the fact that he does keep track of them.

MIDDLE YEARS

The Apollo man may be a midlife crisis waiting to happen. Cultural and family expectations that he succeed nicely dovetail with his own goal-oriented focus, so he very likely devoted himself to his work at considerable psychological cost of which he probably was unaware. He has great unlived-out parts of himself that he has pushed away and a family he has kept at an emotional distance.

In midlife, the pressure and the pace of work may lessen, and the dominance of Apollo as an archetype often lessens as well. And for the first time, other neglected, rejected, and undeveloped aspects of his psyche can emerge.

This is the time when the Apollo man faces his limits. He may find that he will not make it to the top. He is no longer the fair-haired boy. And depression can be a consequence.

Also his children may now react to an absent Apollo father by rejecting him or his values and living out what he never did: they may be rebellious, sexually active, disruptive, or depressed. He may face the reality that he has been a failure as a parent.

His apparently, well-functioning marriage may unravel when his wife reacts to his emotional distance by having an affair or leaving him for someone else. One oft-repeated statement made about George Bush, that he reminds women of their first husbands, is really about Apollo men in general. A resentful maternal wife may precipitate a marriage crisis when she realizes what she sacrificed by having raised their children alone. A well-functioning marriage may come to a standstill when his wife has an empty-nest depression. Finally, a midlife affair on his part may provoke a marital crisis.

Although a major midlife crisis may occur, such as a serious depression or marital discord, chances are that he will get through these years pretty much intact. Somebody may rock the boat, but Apollo is usually in a boat with a very conventional keel. He usually feels internal and external pressures to keep the marriage intact, even if he has an extramarital relationship that touches him very deeply and is sexually more exciting and satisfying than any experience he has ever had.

He may threaten to quit his job, move, or do something radically different when he reaches a plateau. Work ceases to be fulfilling, but the odds are he will stay, dissatisfied and chronically depressed, rather than make what he perceives would be a drastic move. He is a creature of habit and order, who values appearance. Losing the prestige that goes with the job he no longer loves, losing the house in the good neighborhood are too much for him to voluntarily give up to do something that offers the possibility of more personal fulfillment.

LATER YEARS

With his usual far-sightedness, the Apollo man approaches retirement with his economic bases covered. If he's a corporate-level Apollo, his pension plan is augmented by his investments. And if he is a working man, the house is paid up by the time he gets his retirement gold watch.

Once retired, he will find something to do on a regular basis. He may become an active Rotarian or an active member of his church, and be almost as busy as was before retirement.

If he remains true to his Apollo nature, he will probably avoid the introspection that could make him uncomfortable but wiser, and that is a necessary part of psychological growth in the later years.

PSYCHOLOGICAL DIFFICULTIES

Individuals who resemble Apollo have difficulties that are related to emotional distance, such as communication problems, inability to be intimate, and rejection. Problems may also be connected to Apollo's lofty status, which contributes to narcissicism and arrogance, as well as to what he keeps hidden, which is hostile or secretive.

EMOTIONAL DISTANCE

As Sun God, Apollo was "above it all" when he looked down on the earth from a distance. The Apollo man characteristically also maintains a distant stance by avoiding entanglements. When emotions come into conflict, he withdraws: it's "not worth fighting over." This was his attitude when refusing to respond to Poseidon's challenge to fight during the Trojan War.

His indirect communication about emotions is also a characteristic problem. When consulted about something that he did not clearly understand, the god spoke through the Delphic Oracle, whose ambiguous messages required interpretation. People who are close to an Apollo man (or as close as he will let them be) often find themselves having to interpret his few, often cryptic words, which allude to his feelings. Get his meaning wrong, and he withdraws further. Try to draw more out of him, and he becomes more distant. It is paradoxical that the god of clarity, and the man who can speak so precisely and clearly about an impersonal subject (the Apollo lawyer, for example) is so sparing of words about his feelings and so obscure and difficult to interpret when he does say something about himself.

He is as unwilling to merge soulfully with another as he is to get into emotional conflict. Rapport with another person is hard for the Apollo man. He prefers to assess (or judge) the situation or the person from a distance, not knowing that he must "get close up"—be vulnerable and empathic—in order to truly know someone else. As a man, he must expand beyond the archetype to be more than a distant god, to be himself.

THE REJECTED LOVER

Apollo was the most handsome of gods, as well as responsible and dependable: the sun always came up, rose and set when it was supposed to. He emphasized virtue and had precepts to live by carved on his temple walls. Yet he was unsuccessful in love, rejected by Cassandra, Sybil, Daphne, and Marpessa. The women Apollo the god wanted to have and was rejected by were the kind of women who also may reject an Apollo man.

The woman who rejects a handsome, virtuous, dependable Apollo man usually does so because he lacks qualities that are essential for her, such as depth and intensity, or emotional closeness, or sexual spontaneity. Sometimes a woman senses that this particular Apollo man is too attached to appearances and beauty to stay with her as she ages.

Marpessa was loved by a mortal man, Idas, and by Apollo. Zeus allowed her to decide between the two. Marpessa, aware that the god would desert her when she became old and gray, wisely chose Idas over Apollo. Metaphorically, she wisely chose a "human" relationship with the potentiality of growth and change over time, rather than a relationship with unchanging Apollo.

As noted earlier, Apollo taught Cassandra the art of prophecy on the condition that she yield to his amorous embraces, but she didn't keep her word. Sybil (for which the famous Sybilline oracles are named), also accepted Apollo's gifts of prophecy and rejected him as a lover. Apollo mistakenly assumed that love was something that would be given in exchange for what he could provide.

Apollo men are rejected by women who want a deeper bond, with more intensity and emotional expressiveness, than he can provide. The integrity in which an Apollo man may live out his precepts or live up to his agreements draw admiration and respect, rather than love or passion. Women who are aware of these priorities will not choose him to begin with, or, on discovering what is lacking, may reject him as a lover later.

NARCISSISM

The Apollo man prefers to withdraw and think abstractly about ideas, and about the form of things from a distance, rather than concern himself with the realm of feeling, which is least innately present and most in need of developing.

Innate characteristics and culture, as well as his family of origin, shape his personality. The intellectual and unemotional Apollo man lives in a patriarchal culture that doesn't expect men to be nurturing, disapproves of men expressing vulnerable feelings, encourages competition, and rewards acquiring power. If his family also discourages expression and perception of true feelings, as well as enforcing the culture's notion of what a man should be like, then the stage is set for him to become narcissistic, especially if he is intelligent and good-looking.

CRUELTY AND PUNITIVENESS

Apollo was affronted by a flute-playing satyr who made the mistake of challenging him to a musical contest. Apollo was both judge and jury and declared himself the winner because he could play the lyre upside down, and Marsyas the Satyr could not do the same with his flute. The agreement was that the victor could do what he liked to the loser. Apollo flayed Marsyas alive, which was cruel and inhuman.

This streak of cruelty, exercised within his legal rights, can be a nasty side of the Apollo man who has been humiliated and dominated by someone else and who now identifies with the aggressor. When he defeats a rival, he shows no mercy, and instead coolly skins him alive. Similarly, Apollo punished Cassandra, to whom he had given the gift of seeing into the future, by decreeing that she would never be believed. This punishment was both creative and cruel, especially because she could foresee a series of tragedies she was helpless to avert. She suffered doubly, anticipating what she knew was coming, and then living through it.

VENOM

While Apollo exemplies the clarity of the sun and golden moderation, he also had a much less known dark aspect. This Apollo comes like the night and shoots deadly arrows. Homer called these arrows "winged serpents," and Kerényi equated his poisoned arrows with poisonous serpents.[7] A therapist hears of this venom as "poisoned" words, meant to wound. They are often directed toward someone he loved or held in high esteem who hurt him, humiliated him, or did not live up to his expectations.

When a moderate, rational Apollo man lets fly his fury, unleashing emotions he usually represses, what is revealed is primitive (that is, undeveloped) and irrational. He becomes a poisonous snake that strikes out with venom. Although he may harm someone else with his hostility, his own positive self is the major casualty.

ARROGANCE

The Apollo man who has been a golden, fair-haired boy, with a life full of successes, may assume he can take on much more than he is able, with disastrous results. His sense of himself is inflated: he identifies with the god, with the archetype. He forgets he is human. He may enact in his own life the myth of Apollo's son, Phaëthon.

Phaëthon was told by his mother that he was Apollo's son and, on boasting of it, was disbelieved. To confirm the truth, he set forth to find Apollo. Apollo acknowledged his paternity and, to give Phaëthon even more assurance, made an inviolable promise to grant him any favor he wished. Phaëthon asked to drive the sun chariot across the sky for one day.

At daybreak, Phaëthon put on his father's sun crown and climbed into the chariot. The great horses of the sun felt his unfamiliar and inexperienced hand on the reins and left the usual path taken by the sun. Phaëthon lacked the strength or experience to check their flight, and the blazing heat of the sun scorched the earth. It would have done even more damage, except that Zeus struck Phaëthon down with a lightning bolt. Apollo, distraught over the loss of his son, allowed the earth to go without light for one whole day, before once more putting the sun chariot on its regular course.

When I think about Phaëthon, I speculate about the men who think that they can use nuclear power to fight "limited" wars. Such inflation would result in scorched earth; ashes in the atmosphere would blot out the light of the sun and bring the dark of a nuclear winter. People run the risk of such arrogance when success follows on success. It can lead an Apollo man to mistakenly assume that because he is an expert in one field, he can be the authority in others, or to presume that he is entitled and able to do whatever he wants.

In contemporary popular psychological jargon, Phaëthon's assumption that he could drive Apollo's chariot was "an ego trip" that hurt others and caused him to be struck down. Lesser variations on this theme are also common.

DIFFICULTIES FOR OTHERS

Difficulties arise for women who love Apollo men because the form or appearance of the relationship is usually more important to him than depth or intimacy.

DEVALUATION OF THE "NOT WIFE"

It's important for women who get involved with an Apollo man to know that he may put women into two categories: those he considers could be suitable wives, and those who could not. He may even be attracted to women who do not fit into his "suitable wife" category. More than another type, he is often ruled by an idea of what should be.

Since he devalues the emotional and instinctive side of life, even when he is in a relationship that nurtures him, he may not be able to acknowledge the value of it for himself. Consequently he devalues the woman. Although his heart may be involved in his eventual choice, it's never a purely heart choice for a man who lives so much in his head where his values form. In choosing a wife, he doesn't just see the woman, he sees how they will appear as a couple. Marriage for him is an institution that is essential for culture and civilization, part of what brings order to his world and the world.

An Apollo man in midlife may have an extramarital relationship (that often is his first and only affair) that touches him. He may find that he feels more tenderly toward her than toward his wife and is more sexually passionate than he has ever been. Yet he is likely to return to his wife, his home, and his usual life.

It is difficult for a woman who loves an Apollo man, and who knows he loves her more than he has ever loved anyone, to understand how he could walk out of her life to go home to his wife and an empty marriage, once he knows that better exists. Yet unless he grows away from the pattern of Apollo, he will. The woman he leaves grieves for the relationship. But he, being characteristically Apollo, may be able to distance his own feelings of loss and may appear unaffected.

LONELINESS WITHIN THE RELATIONSHIP

Objectively, the woman who is married to an Apollo man may appear to have little to complain about. He's even-tempered, dependable, and faithful, and he probably even pitches in and helps around the house when he's there. People think well of him; he's probably successful in their eyes, and a good man. Many women married to Apollos consider themselves very fortunate indeed.

But if the woman wants a deeper, more personal relationship, then there are difficulties. She may complain of loneliness because he is both emotionally distant and often actually absent because of the demands of work and his devotion to it.

If she wants more spontaneity or passion, this man cannot provide it (for this, a man must also have other archetypes active in his psyche). If she wants communication depth, she is disappointed.

THE RHEOSTAT EFFECT: TURNING INTENSITY DOWN OR UP

A woman married to an Apollo man may find herself becoming more and more like him as she follows his lead, especially if she too values thinking over feeling and is goal oriented. Emotional distance grows, while the form of the relationship continues, as both of them put increasing amounts of time and energy into their separate lives. As she becomes increasingly out of practice at talking about her own feelings, she may become increasingly cut off from knowing what she is feeling.

Just the opposite can occur if she is someone who laughs and cries easily and is often emotional and expressive of her feelings. In a marriage to an inexpressive Apollo, such a woman may find herself becoming a more extreme version of herself over time. She may become increasingly irrational or hysterical as he withdraws further. Her efforts are provocative and usually unsuccessful. She is trying to get him to react emotionally, by her tears or anger, her threats or accusations. But all that results is that he gets more cool and rational and draws farther away, and she becomes increasingly out of control.

WAYS TO GROW

The task for the Apollo man is to grow beyond the confines of the rational and logical mind. For wholeness as a person, he needs to know about matters of the heart and be in his body. Lessons in humility may be needed as well.

MAKING ROOM FOR DIONYSUS

The god Apollo made room for Dionysus at Delphi: for the three winter months, Dionysus was worshiped and celebrated there. Thus Apollo shared his sacred precinct with the god who was his opposite. For a man to grow beyond the Apollo archetype, he too needs to make room for Dionysus, in his psyche.

Clear-thinking, reality-seeing Apollo is a mythic expression of left-brain functioning, while Dionysus, as the god of soulful merging, mystical inebriation, and ecstatic vision, is a right-brain experience. The Apollo man lives consciously only in the left half of his brain, and assumes that this perspective is the only reality that counts. French philosopher René Descartes' precept, "cogito, ergo sum" ("I think, therefore I am") sums up the Apollo man's sense of identity; he is unaware that anything besides his capacity to think might define a man or give him meaning.

As at Delphi, Apollo must leave for Dionysus to be honored. An Apollo man usually must grasp the need cognitively before he allows time and space in his life and psyche for Dionysus. He must seek the opportunity to live in the moment, to be absorbed in sensation, feeling, inner imagery, or outer experience. Then it may be possible for Dionysus to be present.

For many Apollo men, the easiest access to Dionysus is through Dionysian music and dance. Apollo may already have reached spiritual heights through classical music, and he may know of the power music has to move him to a heady ecstatic level. Dionysian music, in contrast, is perceived as a body experience, that invites him to dance without self-consciousness, spontaneously, and to respond instinctively, letting his body do what it wants to do, feeling that the music is dancing him.

Dionysus makes love, as he makes music, differently from Apollo. An Apollo man is as goal oriented and technique minded in making love as he is in every other sphere of his life. When he finds how to bring a particular woman to orgasm, his experience becomes a linear progression from one erogenous zone to the other until the goal of orgasm is reached. As a lover, Apollo may master lovemaking much as a musician masters a particular piece of music on a loved instrument; with practice, there is improvement and even virtuosity. But it is also a performance. Although Apollonian lovemaking can be appreciated (regular orgasms are good to experience), unless Apollo moves aside for Dionysus in this realm, the couple's sexual experience will probably not become a soulful communion or an emotional merger.

Apollo cannot leave lovemaking to Dionysus if he needs to stay aware of the clock or is inhibited in making noise, or is self-conscious in other ways. Apollo remains dominant if the man observes and criticizes how he makes love.

This is why sex therapists emphasize "pleasuring," the slow discovery of what feels good sensually in and of itself.

LIBERATING THE INNER WOMAN

One of Apollo's precepts, "Keep the woman under rule," describes what an Apollo man does to his own "inner woman." This is called the *anima* in Jungian psychology—the archetype of the feminine in a man's psyche—that may also be personified as a goddess. William Sloane Coffin, former college chaplain at Yale University (a bastion of Apollo men) once commented, "the woman who most needs to be liberated is the woman inside every man."

The anima or inner woman is the largely unconscious feminine aspect in men that for Jung was the same as the realm of feeling and relatedness. The anima is linked to the man's emotionality and capacity for closeness and receptivity, which Jung considered undeveloped in men. I find this is true for a significant majority of men, but not of men whose feeling function is more developed than their thinking.)

Liberating the anima, by having a positive regard for "feminine" feeling values, allows the Apollo man to honor his own feelings and the feelings of others. It opens him up to feel connected to the earth and to all living things. It takes the far-distant Apollo man out of his head and into his heart or his body.

For most Apollo men, the woman in himself—his anima—develops gradually through loving women who do not live in their heads and who can speak for their feeling values. They may include mother, sister, friend, lover, or wife. An Apollo man often offends or hurts other people's feelings by being unconscious or self-centered. But if he cares enough about them not to want to cause them pain or make them angry, he will listen and learn about feelings and thus liberate his own inner woman, who speaks for these same values.

LEARNING HUMILITY

When a man is a sun-blessed Apollo, he begins life with a favored-son status within his family and with the distinct advantage of having the personality most likely to succeed in a patriarchal world. The successful Apollo man characteristically takes credit for his accomplishments and assumes that his success is well deserved. His hubris, or pride, involves this taking full credit for his achievements. He can also blame others for not succeeding, without considering their circumstances, sex, personality, or intelligence—typical of Apollo men, who find it difficult to imagine themselves in another person's shoes. For example, U.S. Supreme Court Chief Justice William Rehnquist and Justice Antonin Scalia, who fit the Apollo mold, are described as "self-made men, who tend to be impatient with the complaints of those who have failed to match their own achievements."[8]

An Apollo man may need to actually feel the fit of a different pair of shoes, to suffer loss and feel grief, before he knows how arrogant he was before and how much he didn't know or appreciate. He may need to make a terrible mistake and be forgiven to experience humility. He may need to grow older in order to grow wiser, and then only because life gives him humbling experiences, that teach him about his own and others' humanity. Only then may an Apollo man be able to think, "There but for undeserved circumstances, or for the grace that I received, go I," or to wonder, "If that had happened to me, I wonder if I could have done as well?"

LOVE AS MOTIVATION

The Apollo man has a marked tendency to always do what's expected of him, without questioning whether he really wants to do what he is doing. From the time he was a little boy, he gained love and approval for conforming to the rules, which by his archetypal nature he found no difficulty accepting. It often takes half or more of his lifetime, as well as a midlife depression, before an Apollo man questions if he is doing work he wants to do, is where he wants to be, or loves his wife.

An Apollo man grows beyond his identification with the archetype that limits him when he makes decisions based on love. He then moves beyond Apollo, whose every decision is made by logic. Now he heads into unknown terrain. However, Apollo's ability to discriminate and evaluate, and to take time, can help him distinguish infatuation from love.

When he follows his heart, the Apollo man becomes human; he knows he is fallible and vulnerable, but can step beyond the boundaries of his "known" (rational) world. He can take risks. He gives up the emotional distance that both protected him and kept him isolated.

7.

Hermes, Messenger God and Guide of Souls— Communicator, Trickster, Traveler

He is the god of the unexpected, of luck, of coincidences, of synchronicity. "Hermes has entered our midst," the ancient Greeks would say when a sudden silence entered the room, descended on conversation, introduced into the gathering another dimension. Whenever things seem fixed, rigid, "stuck," Hermes introduces fluidity, motion, new beginnings—and the confusion that almost inevitably precedes new beginnings.

Arianna Stassinopoulos, *The Gods of Greece*

Here we have the master of ingenuity, the guide of the flocks, the friend and lover of the Nymphs and Graces, the spirit of night, sleep, and dreams. Nothing can give better expression to the gay and at the same time darkly mysterious, enchanting, and tender elements in Hermes than the magically sweet tones of lyre or flute.

Walter W. F. Otto, *The Homeric Gods*

Hermes as god, archetype, and man personifies quickness of movement, agility of mind, and facileness of word; moving swiftly, as a male image or as a metaphor, he crosses boundaries, and shifts levels with ease.

HERMES THE GOD

Hermes (better known by his Roman name, Mercury) is the messenger of the gods, the eloquent god of speech, and the guide of souls to the underworld; the protector of athletes, travelers, thieves, and businessmen; reputed inventor of the lyre, numbers, and the alphabet. He was known as "the friendliest of the gods to men" and the god who brought luck.

Hermes was usually portrayed as a youthful man. Homer described him as looking like a young prince at the age when his beard starts to grow. On his missions as messenger of the gods, he wore a traveling hat with a broad brim, which sometimes was given two little wings. He had winged sandals or shoes, and carried a caduceus. Usually the caduceus was represented as a simple staff wound about with two white ribbons (or snakes), a kind of magic wand that was a symbol of the authority and inviolability of the herald of the gods.

Hermes, whose name means "he of the stone heap," is named for the cairns that were landmarks for travelers, to which each passer-by added a stone. Sometimes these mounds of stones also marked graves, which were commonly by roadsides in ancient times. Later, stone pillars called "herms" stood in front of Greek houses or marked property boundaries.

GENEALOGY AND MYTHOLOGY

Hermes was the son of Zeus and Maia. Maia was a shy goddess, who lived in a mountain cave, where she was visited by Zeus in the night (while Hera slept and was, for a change, unaware of Zeus's philandering.) Maia was the daughter of Atlas, the Titan who carried the heavens on his shoulders. She was one of the Pleiades, the constellation of sister stars in the night sky.

Always on the go from the moment of his birth, Hermes was born in the morning, invented and played the lyre at noon, stole the cows of Apollo in the evening, and was back in his cradle at night playing innocent. This first day of his life was an opening prelude in which the major themes that characterized Hermes were evident. Just born, he ventured boldly out of his cradle and into the world, spying a slowly moving tortoise just outside his mother's cave. Inspired by what he could do with the tortoise, and quick to act on his idea, he cut up the tortoise, took the shell, fastened two reed pipes to it, and strung seven strings, thereby inventing the lyre. Hermes played the lyre and sang, making music that evoked joy, love, and sweet sleep.

Putting the lyre in his cradle, the infant Hermes now craved meat. Once more he set out of the cave, this time to prowl and steal some oxen from his half-brother Apollo. The young cattle rustler found Apollo's herd grazing, cut out fifty cows from the herd, and drove them away backward, so that their hind hooves were in front and their forehooves behind. He made himself footwear of branches that disguised his own tracks. When he got the cattle where he could hide them, Hermes lit a mighty fire (generating it from rubbing sticks together with tinder, thus inventing fire starting) and barbecued two cows. When he was finished, he threw his footwear in the river, scattered the ashes, and noiselessly returned to his mother's cave. There he laid himself in his cradle, putting the lyre under his arm, and drew his swaddling clothes around himself.

Apollo discovered his cattle were stolen, noted tracks that seemed to lead in the opposite direction, and was not fooled. He angrily made his way to Maia's cave and demanded that Hermes tell him where his cows were hidden. The infant Hermes guilelessly denied any knowledge of the missing cattle, and asked, "Do I seem like a strong man who steals cows? I am far otherwise employed, in sleeping, drinking my mother's milk, lying in my swaddling clothes or in my warm bath. Yesterday, I was born, my feet are tender and the ground is hard." And Hermes swore on the head of his father that he knew nothing about the cows."

Apollo smiled at this show of innocence, and called Hermes a "'cunning deceiver,' who spoke like a trained thief." Later, in the presence of Zeus, Apollo and Hermes repeated their stories, amusing Zeus who discerned the truth and made Hermes show Apollo where he had hidden the cows.

Apollo yearned for the lyre and promised anything in exchange. For this crafty Hermes received the fifty cows, a herdsman's crook and status, and either a golden staff topped by three leaves that bestows wealth, dominion over the beasts, minor soothsaying, and/or the caduceus, a winged staff circled by two white ribbons or snakes that identified him as messenger and escort of souls to the underworld.

Hermes is known best as Messenger God, and as the god who performed many useful services for the other Olympians. At Zeus's bidding, he went to the underworld to bring Persephone back to her mother. He also rescued Ares from his imprisonment in a bronze jar, helped Zeus give birth to Dionysus from his thigh, and escorted Aphrodite, Athena, and Hera to the Judgment of Paris (at which Paris chose Aphrodite as most beautiful).

HERMES' SONS

Hermes' many sons were the offspring of his own nature. In Autolycus and Myrtilus, his worst traits became intensified. Thus Autolycus was an archthief and perjurer, without the charm of a young Hermes. Myrtilus's inventiveness and sociopathy caused the death of his master in a chariot race. Bribed by a competitor, he put wax linchpins in the chariot axles.

Amoral Pan was another of Hermes' reputed sons, a goat from the waist down, with goat horns and a beard, frisky, short-tempered, and lustful. Pan was god of the forests, pastures, flocks, and shepherds. His son, Eudorus ("goodly giver"), took after Hermes' kindly aspect, as the faithful, uncomplicated shepherd who guides his flocks and is an extension or expression of the caretaking and nurturing aspect that Hermes also had. His most notable son, Hermaphroditus, reflects Hermes' androgynous and bisexual nature and bore the names and sexual characteristics of both his parents, Aphrodite and Hermes.

Hermes had a number of love affairs. With the exception of his liaison with Aphrodite, none are told in any detail, and none of the mothers of sons other than Hermaphroditus are noteworthy in their myths. Hermes can be considered a bachelor god.

HERMES AND ALCHEMY

In alchemy, Hermes-Mercurius was "quicksilver," the spirit concealed in matter. He was the symbol that united all the opposites: metallic yet liquid, matter yet spirit, cold yet fiery, poison yet healing draught.[1] As a substance, mercury adheres only to a precious metal; metaphorically, Hermes can show you the way to find spiritual gold.

Alchemy flourished during the medieval Inquisition, when efforts to seek spiritual truths and mystical experience outside of the Roman Catholic Church were branded and punished as heresy. Some said Hermes invented alchemy; and he was also the subject of alchemical sexual metaphors, as was the hermaphrodite. Hidden in alchemical treatises, as C. G. Jung described in *Psychology and Alchemy,* Hermes was the communicator: through metaphor, he was the guide of souls on a mystical and psychological journey that sought to unite male and female elements.

THE CADUCEUS: STAFF OF HERMES

Hermes carried the caduceus, a rod topped by wings, and encirled by two serpents that identified him as the messenger god and guide of souls. The twin serpents on Hermes' caduceus have carried many meanings; the alchemists considered the snakes male and female; through Hermetic mysticism, male spirit and female soul united. The dual snakes have also represented the twin threads of death and rebirth; most recently they have been seen as symbolizing the DNA chain, through which coded genetic information is communicated in living matter. Whether as new symbolism or ancient metaphor, however, Hermes is firmly cast in the role of messenger between realms.

Hermes' caduceus differed from the rod of Asclepius, God of healing, which had a single coiled serpent.

HERMES THE ARCHETYPE

Like the god Hermes, the Hermes archetype has positive and negative potentialities. Inventiveness, the capacity to communicate well, and the ability to think and act quickly are traits that can be used creatively to achieve or deceive. Hermes is also an unequivocally positive archetype as communicator of meaning and rescuer of the child.

THE MESSENGER

Hermes traveled frequently and swiftly between Olympus and the underworld, between Olympus and earth, between earth and the underworld. He moved smoothly from one level to another, crossing borders with ease.

Men (and women) who share this mobility may be at home in the worlds of diplomacy, public media, and commerce. They are the traders and communicators of the world, carrying goods, information, and culture from one place to another. For

Hermes, it's all in a day's work to go from one city or one country to another, to penetrate the Iron Curtain, or to be the first visitor to some out-of-the-way place. Hermes may travel in person or via radio, television, or writing. Making deals, making money, and making allies are engaging challenges for Hermes people.

Those famous travelers of old, Marco Polo (who opened trade routes from Europe to China and India), and Sir Richard Burton (a man of many disguises whose adventures in Islamic countries culminated in his entry to Mecca), needed to be like Hermes to take pleasure in their adventures and be successful at what they did as travelers and writers. This was true of Alexandra David-Neel, who ventured into Tibet and wrote of her travels into the mysteries there as well. The best-known explorers of nonordinary realities currently are authors Carlos Castaneda and Lynn Andrews, each of whom has written a series of books telling of the adventures, risks, and knowledge gained through their respective apprenticeships to Native American medicine men and women. Like Hermes, Castaneda and Andrews move from one level to another, as they cross over from the ordinary world into the world of spirits and powers.

A modern-day Hermes may be in the foreign service, a representative of a multinational corporation, a peripatetic, internationally known lecturer, or a tour guide. Whether negotiating a treaty or bargaining for a trinket, the more like Hermes a man is the more likely he is to excel at being persuasive and coming up with "creative financing."

Worrying if something is illegal or wrong is not a main concern to a Hermes' mind. He rarely loses sleep over right and wrongs. Thus he might be a legal advisor to the Mafia and, Hermes-like, easily cross boundaries from the legitimate world into the criminal underworld. He is only concerned with whether a ploy or a negotiation will work; thinking creatively makes him an ace problem solver.

THE TRICKSTER

On the first day of his birth, Hermes was engaged in stealing his brother Apollo's cows, cleverly hiding his tracks by tying branches to his feet and laying down a false trail by having the cows walk backward. Next he tried to pass himself off as an innocent newborn, guilefully lying about himself. This Hermes is the Trickster, an archetype known the world over, character-ized by cleverness, cunning, and ability to change his shape or form.

The Trickster is known as Coyote to the Native American Indian. To the Eskimo, he is Raven; to the Japanese, the wily Badger. He is inventive and takes what he wants by trickery or theft. Often he is admired rather than condemned for his clev-erness, depending on what he steals and from whom. When he is Robin Hood, stealing from the oppressing rich to give to the poor, or Prometheus stealing fire from the gods to give to hu-mankind, Trickster is appreciated as a hero. For example, the popular television series *To Catch a Thief* features Robert Wagner as a modern Hermes. His character follows the principle "It takes one to know one." Wagner plays a charming former thief, who now uses for good causes his mastery at making quick and quiet illegal entries and chameleonlike ability to disguise himself.

However, a real-life trickster may turn out to be a "con man," rather than an unlikely hero. He may be an unscrupulous salesman whose clever sales pitch traps people into unneeded purchases, or an out-and-out confidence man who bilks people. Hermes as trickster is the archetype embodied as a charming sociopath, who feels no qualms about lying or taking whatever he wants.

The trickster aspect of Hermes does not have to be lived out in a negative way, however. The ability to think like a trick-ster might help a therapist understand what may be going on in another person's mind, or may make a detective outstanding at his job, or help a man solve problems in a unique or creative fashion.

THE YOUNGER SIBLING RIVAL

Birth order can contribute to the development of the Hermes archetype. The god Hermes' relationship to his older brother Apollo is a key to understanding a competitive and ac-quisitive aspect of the archetype. Hermes arrives in the world acutely aware of his "have-not" status and promptly steals from his older brother. In response to Hermes, Apollo was in turn victimized, angry, placated, and charmed. Although both broth-ers eventually gain skills or power from the other through bart-ering, it is Hermes who began with nothing and acquired much.

Arriving on the scene later than an older sibling, the younger brother initially competes using his baby charm. As he grows older yet remains smaller in size and younger in experience, he finds that he must use his wits. As a youngster, he cannot overpower an older brother. With Hermes as an archetype, a younger brother learns how to use words to get out of physical fights where he is at a disadvantage. He uses strategy to get what he wants, whether he wants a material object or a prerogative that belongs to the older brother.

The "younger brother" sees himself as an underdog, who must struggle for position. Until Joseph Kennedy, Jr., the oldest son of the dynasty, was killed in his plane during World War II, the role of the Hermes underdog belonged to the next youngest brother, John F. Kennedy. Jack's frailer health and lesser physical stamina put him at a disadvantage, for which he compensated by striving for verbal excellence, and by carefully choosing the arenas in which he would compete.

THE GUIDE

In his mythology, Hermes often guided others from one realm to another. As Hermes Psychopompos, he accompanied the souls of the dead to the underworld. He also escorted Persephone out of the underworld, returning her to her mother Demeter.

Hermes was represented by the "herm," a short pillar or pile of stones that marked property boundaries, roads, graves, and the entrance to every home. Thus Hermes was the god who marked the boundary as well as the god that crossed all boundaries.

Murray Stein, a Jungian analyst, calls Hermes the God of Significant Passage. Hermes is the archetype present "betwixt and between" psychological phases—especially during midlife transitions. He is a liminal god, present in the transitional space (from the Greek word *limen,* the space under the door frame or the threshold).[2]

Often a psychotherapist plays the role of Hermes as guide of souls between significant passages. People seek help during periods of depression that follow the loss of a significant person or role, or in periods of uncertainty and anxiety when faced with something new, or in transitions between one phase of life and the next. For a time, a therapist accompanies the person on the journey, much as Hermes did travelers. Sometimes a therapist helps a person see the dangers in a situation and survive, as Hermes did for Odysseus, appearing just as Odysseus was about to meet Circe, the sorceress who had turned his men into swine. Hermes gave Odysseus insight and protection against Circe's power.

The Hermes pattern also guides the individual who seeks meaning and integration of the realms of spirit (Olympus), human life (earth), and soul (underworld), and then communicates or teaches what he (or she) now knows. As the traveler between levels, Hermes seeks to understand, integrate, and communicate between the conscious mental world of mind and intellect (Olympus), the realm in which the ego decides and acts (earth), and the collective unconscious (underworld).

THE ALCHEMIST

Hermes has been considered the father of alchemy, that arcane science that focused on trying to turn lead into gold, and that was also a spiritual and psychological quest to transform what is base in the psyche into gold. The "alchemist" seeks to find the meaning (or "gold") in experience, and seeks transformational experiences. Jung talks about this aspect of the Hermes archetype as the Spirit Mercurius, after the god's Roman name Mercury.

RESCUER OF THE CHILD

Hermes descended into the underworld to bring back Demeter's abducted daughter Persephone. He rescued the infant god Dionysus at least twice, saving his life and protecting him from harm. The young boy Ares also owed his life to Hermes. Hermes is the archetype or metaphor that saves what is innocent and vulnerable, or divine and sacred, by providing meaning for an otherwise terrible experience.

I have felt the saving presence of Hermes when my adult patients have spoken of their abusive childhoods or when I've read of children who did not give up in panic or despair when they were lost in the wilderness, or struggling to stay afloat for hours. A message of explanation came to them that gave them heart to continue. For the abused child, it was some explanation—for example, "these are not my parents, I am being tested." For the child who doesn't give up, the message might be "someone will come," or "I can't die, I matter to someone." Through the ordeal, the child clings to the message, which saves his soul from giving up.

Hermes also rescues the child in the depressed adult. Here Hermes may be part of someone else (as well as an inner figure) who provides the liberating experience or insight that frees the playful or trusting or vulnerable part of the adult held captive in the underworld (another metaphor is the imprisoning jar: Ares's bronze jar, or poet and novelist Sylvia Plath's glass bell jar). And finally, Hermes activates or saves the archetype of the divine child (represented by the child Dionysus), who is latent in each of us (discussed more fully in the chapter on Dionysus).

CULTIVATING HERMES

We invite Hermes to be with us whenever we are willing to venture into new territory with an attitude of exploration and openness, an attitude that can have as much to do with reading as with foreign travel. This archetype makes spontaneity possible between us and who and what we meet—places, material, people. Hermes opens up moments of discovery and synchronistic events—those "coincidences" that turn out to be meaningful, unforeseen "accidental" happenings that lead us somewhere we couldn't have known we would go and that yet turn out uncannily right. People miss Hermes if their minds are set on a particular itinerary and schedule, who set out and know ahead of time just what they will see and when. Thus when we go on vacation or even spend an unstructured day on a lark, with an attitude of adventure, not knowing what we will find, letting each day shape itself, we invite Hermes to accompany us—to be part of us.

We also come in touch with Hermes the communicator and messenger when we have an opportunity to speak and are willing to "wing it." Hermes is the unplanned eloquence, the rapport that happens in the moment, that can offer a deep or a soaring experience for both speaker and audience, that takes people from one level to another. We trust that winged Hermes will be with us when, rather than write out a well-organized, annotated speech, we speak spontaneously, with just a sketchy outline in mind. In winging it, we can tap our Hermes inventiveness, guide the material in a fluid way that doesn't come through in a planned and polished Apollo presentation; we speak about what we know, out of our own experience. This often takes courage at first, but with practice at being spontaneous our trust in Hermes grows.

HERMES THE MAN

The Hermes man has a quick mind. He grasps the significance of an idea or a situation and is quick to act on his intuitions. He often has an "always on the move" physical quality as well, as he gracefully and actively makes shifts from one person to another, from one place to another, or from one idea to another. Trying to pin him down can be as difficult as trying to grasp quicksilver.

EARLY YEARS

The god Hermes was the most precocious of the gods. From the first day of his birth, he was active, creative, and deceptive. Similar traits are typical of the young Hermes child, who often talks early, walks early, and is into things early. It's over the bars of his crib or playpen and out into the world for him. He explores everything, touches and takes apart anything he can get his hands on, and goes through every unlatched gate. Caught "with his hand in the cookie jar," he's probably all innocence and charm. He's inquisitive and friendly, and has a genuine interest in everything and everyone, so he gets along with all kinds of people of all ages and types. Being the curious child that he is, he finds the world fascinating.

Preschool and the first years of grade school are usually easy for a young Hermes. In school, he learns easily and finds school compatible until he is expected to sit quietly in his seat and have good study habits.

Some of his potential problems start innocently enough in childhood. He may make up stories, and invent excuses, and cross the line into habitually lying, even when the truth would be acceptable. He may not learn about "other people's property," have "sticky fingers," and take what attracts him. This innocent childhood behavior may shade into being a petty thief. Since what he does usually lacks malicious intent, his misdemeanors are often not taken seriously, and his excuses found amusing, which may detrimentally affect his character. Conversely, he may also be too harshly judged, and from an early age be unfairly labeled as bad.

HIS PARENTS

How the parents of a Hermes boy react to his made-up-in-the-moment stories, and his unaccountable acquisitions is crucial. He needs to be caught in the lie or the act and taught the difference between truth and make believe, (because he can move from reality to imagination readily, not examining the boundaries) rather than be allowed to get away with behavior that will later reflect badly on him or get him into trouble. Respect for the property and privacy of others are also lessons he needs to learn.

When the mother of a Hermes son is a single parent, the mythic story of Hermes and his mother Maia may be enacted in real life. A bright and underprivileged boy may early in life see that if he and his mother are to have anything, he must figure out a way to get it.

In the "Homeric Hymn to Hermes," Hermes and his mother have a conversation in which he clearly tells her that he will not accept their lowly situation, nor will he accept her definition of how he should act. The dialogue between them captures the essence of the relationship between a bright, ambitious son who does not intend to live by his mother's adherence to conventional rules, and yet who will strive to provide her with the better things of life. After his night out stealing Apollo's cows, Hermes tiptoed back into Maia's cave, and quietly got into his cradle, the picture of an innocent baby:

> But the god
> couldn't fool his mother,
> the goddess,
> who said this:
> "just what are you up to, smartie?
> Where were you that you come in

at this hour of the night,
impudence written all over you?. . .
Hermes answered her shrewdly:
"Mother, why do you aim these things at me,
as if I were a little kid
who knew a lot of rules
in his head, and could be scared,
a kid who could be scared
by his mother's words?
Why, I shall be engaged
—in the greatest art of all—
always concerned for you,
of course, and for myself.
We're not going to stick around here,
as you want, the only two
among all the immortal gods
without any gifts,
without even prayers!"[3]

A Hermes son may take on making his mother's life (and his own) better. He has confidence in himself and the ability to see how he will manage to get where he wants to go in life, often via an unconventional route.

Since Hermes doesn't like to be tied down, he often doesn't settle down. So home is where his mother is. The situation he finds most compatible gives him freedom to come and go. The introverted, nonpossessive, self-sufficient homemaker like Maia (a woman who is archetypally the Hearthkeeper goddess, Hestia) is the easiest mother for a Hermes son to have. A possessive or hovering mother of a Hermes son will cause herself much difficulty. Efforts to tie him to her, especially through guilt, are usually not successful. A Hermes man often is a devoted son in his way, and his mother may remain the most important woman in his life—especially if he does not marry, but even if he does.

Hermes the god, who started out as a little thief, and became greatly honored as a god, had parents who helped him to grow up well. Maia and Zeus both provided positive maternal and paternal attitudes.

Zeus was loving and unjudgmental toward Hermes, even though he could see right through Hermes' deception and show of innocence about Apollo's stolen cows. After hearing Hermes' swear he was not guilty, Zeus merely ordered Hermes "to point out the place—without any further mischief—where he had hid that powerful herd of cattle." And without another word Hermes obeyed.

This firm, no-nonsense, Zeus-like attitude is what most young Hermes sons need. The lucky and cared-for Hermes boys are, for example, the ones who have had to apologize and make restitution to the manager of the store from which they shoplifted something. (This paternal Zeus attitude, like Maia's maternal unpossessive love, can be expressed by parents of either sex, since both men and women can be "maternal" or "paternal".)

Parents of juvenile delinquent Hermes sons may be unaware that they have encouraged their sons' potential for antisocial behavior, by giving them a "double message," as Zeus himself initially gave Hermes. On hearing Hermes lie about stealing the cows,

> Zeus let out a great big laugh
> as he looked at this kid,
> who was up to no good,
> denying so well,
> so smoothly,
> that he knew anything
> about the cows.[4]

Zeus's amused laughter was approving, his reaction to Hermes' outrageous lies and false oath taking was as if he had done something that pleased him. Later, Zeus was more firm.

When a parent gives a child a "double message," that child receives a covert message that differs from the overt message. In studies of the parents of delinquents by child psychoanalyst, Adelaide M. Johnson, this was often the case.[5] The parent may label behavior as bad, and even be very punitive (the overt message), yet an incongruent smile or obvious fascination in the details of what was done, covertly conveys that the parent is pleased. The disobedient child thus obediently "acts out" for the parent, who vicariously experiences the excitement, or perhaps the sexual promiscuity or the antisocial acts that the parent hasn't dared to do but secretly applauds.

ADOLESCENCE AND EARLY ADULTHOOD

The proverb "as the twig is bent, so bends the bough" certainly applies to the growth and development of a Hermes boy.

In adolescence and early adulthood, a Hermes man questions the conventional rules of success. He is interested in getting what he wants from life, but he may not be interested in what it usually takes to get where he wants to go. Moreover, the diversity of his interests makes his path likely to be a zig-zag one.

He "tests limits," an appropriate tendency for a young man whose personality pattern follows Hermes, the god of boundaries, who crossed them all with ease. Those limits may be "the way things are done around here," or curfew hours, or the challenge of figuring out how to use a computer to get into a particular "off-limits" file.

He may drop out of high school or college to have more time to focus on an innovative business or a new invention, or in managing as well as playing in a rock music group, or being a professional ball player or golf pro. A Hermes man doesn't usually work for grades or the approval of others (for this he needs Apollo or Zeus qualities); when he succeeds, it's because the work itself fascinates him and draws out his inventiveness. The problem he solves is often not a purely intellectual or esthetic one; instead, it usually has commercial possibilities as well. The career of college dropout Steve Wozniak, inventor of the Apple computer, has many of these Hermes qualities. When his young, innovative company grew, and corporate-mentality management moved in, Wozniak took his inventiveness and new fortune into another field, and developed a universal remote control apparatus he called Core. Talent, luck, and the ability to make enterprising shifts is typical of a successful Hermes.

In adolescence and young adulthood, another Hermes man may begin his pattern of wandering from one place to another, or one job to another. If his interest is not held, and his potential talents or abilities do not develop into skills, he may remain marginally employed and be a perpetual wanderer.

During this same period, a Hermes man may become firmly identified with Hermes the Thief and Liar, treading a criminal path, usually as a confidence man or white-collar criminal of some sort.

In contrast to the commerical or criminal bent that a Hermes man might take in his young adult years, some Hermes men delve deeply into spiritual, philosophical, or psychological interests during this time. This was the path taken by Richard

Alpert, the bright young Harvard psychology professor, who left a brilliant career to find a guru in India. Now known as Ram Dass, he is a spiritual teacher, a Hermes man who can be identified with Hermes as Guide of Souls.

WORK

Hermes was the messenger of the gods; the guide of souls to the underworld and the guide of travelers; the god of speech, thieves, businessmen, and athletes; the inventor of numbers, the alphabet, and two musical instruments, the lyre and the syrinx. In his choice of work and in his attitude toward work, a Hermes man reveals his similarities to the god: A Hermes man is not likely to be a narrow specialist or a happy cog in a large corporation. His individuality and a diversity of interests make both unlikely. He doesn't like to do anything "by the book." His quick mind finds alternative routes and solutions or shortcuts. Whatever field he is in, he is likely to be an inventive generalist with an entrepreneurial attitude. He's an opportunist, in the most neutral meaning of the word: a person who is able to grasp the significance of a person or an idea and seize the opportunity that the moment presents. This plus his ability as a communicator makes him often a very good salesman or negotiator. He's a willing innovator, who cross-fertilizes ideas from different fields, and he may go beyond usual limitations to accomplish what he wants.

Gordon Sumner, known as Sting, is a contemporary Hermes who very successfully has managed several career crossovers: from schoolteacher to rock star, composer, and lead singer for the Police, whose albums have sold in the millions (*Synchronicity* was named from the writings of psychologist Carl Jung and *The Ghost in the Machine* was named from writings by philosopher Arthur Koestler). Sting has moved from rock star to film star; from group performance with the Police to solo performance in his album *The Dream of the Blue Turtles*.

Sting is described by a journalist as a man who "is in a hurry. He travels light, and alights only briefly . . . meet up with him over three months in three different countries."[6] Typically Hermes, he doesn't like being pigeonholed, values his freedom to move in all the psychological and physical realms in which he readily travels, including the "light and dark" aspects of his personality. In this, he sounds very Jungian, appropriately so for a man who has thoughts of becoming a Jungian analyst when he's much older.

Quoted in *Record* magazine, Sting said,

> If you look at my history in the press in England, at first I was heralded as the golden boy, blond hair, talented, handsome. Here was a chap who was a school teacher, who had a beautiful, talented wife, and a kid. I was athletic and I didn't take drugs. Then the press found out that I did screw people, and, yes, I had taken drugs. And then I started to play these evil characters and suddenly I became the bad boy in the English press. This was great for me because it meant I was free to do what I pleased. So the British press is now totally confused as to what I am, which suits me fine. Sometimes I'm a good boy and sometime's I'm bad. That's me.[7]

That "good boy, bad boy" designation is also obviously Hermes.

The Hermes archetype provides qualities that contribute to being a good psychotherapist. Like Hermes, who was the companion and guide of the traveler, a psychotherapist also accompanies people on their psychological journeys, going with them through the dark areas and the light, through difficult transitions such as midlife crises, through psychoses or borderline conditions. When Hermes is present in a person, that man or woman can see the dark, hostile, psychotic, instinctual, sexual, or aggressive as well as the altruistic, mystical, or illuminated, or the ordinary in people, including themselves, without judgmental comment. This ability is an expression of the "friendly" aspect of Hermes. In *Hermes and His Children,* analyst and author Rafael Lopez-Pedraza comments, "If we internalize Hermes' friendly side, then it is Hermes in us who befriends our psychological complexes centered by the other Gods."[8]

Most characteristically, Hermes' presence in a man's psyche provides him with an ability to communicate persuasively, a friendly attitude that facilitates the ease with which a Hermes man makes his way in the world, a potential for spontaneous, appropriate reactions that stand him in good stead. Hermes was God of Commerce; being like Hermes contributes to being an excellent salesman, an innovative businessman, a superb public relations expert, and—appropriately—a fine travel guide.

RELATIONSHIPS WITH WOMEN

Charming Hermes men seem to suddenly appear in a woman's life: he is sitting next to her on an airplane; he's an out-of-town old friend of the host at an otherwise predictable-faces party; he comes to the rescue when she pulls over to the side of the road with a flat tire. He's helpful and friendly. His conversation fascinates her: he has been to places she has just read about; there's an air of adventure and bad-boyness about him. She thinks she has finally met the right man—but he's elusive.

Typically Hermes, as unexpected as his arrival may have been in her life, he may as suddenly disappear. For example, he leaves on a business trip, and calls to let her know that one thing has led to another, and he's going to be away longer, with his time of return now indefinite. Maybe she gets a postcard. And then he disappears with no further word, until he reappears without apology. With Hermes men, it is usually "out of sight, out of mind."

Maybe he's not a jet-setting Hermes, but a hometown one. The pattern is the same. The adventure that calls him away may be his involvement in a project, or the amateur league baseball season with its evening and weekend game schedule. Without a thought for how it affects her, a Hermes man wants to come and go in a woman's life, without being responsible for her feelings, and without being faithful to her.

A Hermes man enters the realm of love when he finds himself at the threshold being invited in by the woman who has found him fascinating. For him, it may be like visiting a new country: a new woman is new territory to explore and enjoy, after which he feels an urge to travel on. It is this quality that makes many Hermes men behave like Don Juans, seeing themselves like bees going from one flower to another. Warren Beatty, actor and renowned lover of beautiful women, seems to embody this aspect of Hermes.

A Hermes man may get along very well with women who do not have unrealistic expectations of him or needs he can't fill. He may have women friends who are delighted to see him when he's around, and who don't expect to hear from him until he shows up next. They may stay "lightly in touch" in between: an occasional phone call, a note, an open invitation keeps the door open for Hermes to reenter. The friendship often has gone through a going-to-bed-together phase, which may from time to time be replayed.

There is also a darker, exploitive potential in the Hermes man. Acting on impulse and taking what he wants when he wants it are negative Hermes characteristics. If it's a woman he wants, he can become actively seductive and manipulative. Caring only to get his way, he lies, charms, does whatever he thinks will work, with no thought about the consequence to her, or to her marriage if she is married, and no intentions of fulfilling any promises he made in pursuit of her.

RELATIONSHIPS WITH MEN

Hermes was the friendliest god and the protector-patron of athletes, merchants, travelers, thieves, and musicians. He spent a lot of time in the company of a variety of men. This is true for the Hermes man, as well. He does things with a number of men friends and probably has more acquaintances who consider him a friend than any other type of man. He drops in on many men friends: he may join them for a game of cards or golf game; if he's a musician, from time to time he'll show up with his instrument to be part of a jam session. In business, he may get in touch about "a deal" that he wants to "cut his friends in on." He's often generous with his tips—when he has an inside track on something, he will share it with friends, who appreciate the unexpected boon that it may represent.

Hermes is at heart a gregarious loner. He has a gift of friendliness, which makes it easy for him to get acquainted with many people and do things with them. Since most male friendships are based on sharing an activity, rather than on self-revelation with its increased vulnerability and intimacy, a Hermes man has a wider circle of men friends than any other. Typically they cut across class lines and represent the diversity of interests that a Hermes man is likely to have.

SEXUALITY

In the realm of sexuality as in other areas, a Hermes man usually favors the personal and experiential. He ventures across borders in his explorations. As a result, it is possible to probable that he has had a variety of sexual experience, with a variety of people in a variety of circumstances. Again, whether he impulsively does what occurs to him without concern for consequences or the feelings and needs of others, depends on the strength of other archetypal influences, and the influence of family, church, and his social milieu.

Beginning as a youngster with "Let's play doctor" or "I'll show you mine, if you show me yours," he may have sexually experimented. He's persuasive in getting his playmates to do what he wants: at eight years old, he may have gotten the neighbor girl to take her panties off and let him see and touch. At thirteen, perhaps he got several other boys to sit in a secret circle to "jack off" (masturbate until ejaculation together), or to see how far each could direct his stream of urine. He may have been the first in his age group to get a girl to let him touch her breasts or "go all the way." With his intuition, strategy and powers of persuasion, often along with having friendly, "nice guy" qualities, a Hermes young man finds he has a way with women and often gets his way sexually.

Some of the most familiar sexual jokes are about the traveling salesman and the farmer's daughter. They are vignettes about a contemporary representation of Hermes, god of travelers and commerce, wanderer god and thief, who steals the virginity of the daughter and thereby takes something of value from the irate farmer, whose daughter is now (in a patriarchal context) worthless because of the deed.

He may be a heterosexual or a homosexual. In either case, he is more likely to have tried (or at least fantasized) sex with a man or men if he is heterosexual, or with women if he is homosexual, than any other type of man. Regardless of his sexual orientation, a Hermes man is likely to have a bisexual attitude—isn't judgmental or threatened by any tendencies in himself. This attitude is mythologically fitting, as Hermes fathered Hermaphroditus, the bisexual god.

MARRIAGE

If the Hermes man stays an eternal adolescent emotionally, which is one potentiality of the archetype, then he will be the most elusive of bachelors. His on-the-go, never-commit-yourself attitude shows in his relationships with women. He dances away once the first bloom is off the romance. Possessiveness or dependency in a woman puts this Hermes to flight.

A mature Hermes can make serious commitments to work and a significant relationship. Still, in both areas he is likely to stay a loner. If he marries, he expects his wife to manage in his absence, to keep the home fires burning until he returns. He comes and goes, and doesn't share the details of his work with his wife or expect that she will be involved in helping him to get ahead.

With a Hermes man, the marriage of two independent souls can work. In Greek households, the "herm"—a pillar symbolizing Hermes—stood just outside the front door, and inside a round hearth with a fire at the center represented Hestia, Goddess of the Hearth. It was Hestia's fire that made a house a home. Women who embody this archetype are independent, inwardly centered women, who enjoy solitude. A Hermes-Hestia marriage can work harmoniously for both. She may look very much like a traditional wife, but being a wife is not her source of meaning, and jealousy is not a problem.

Hestia was a virgin goddess. Any woman who is involved with a Hermes man does well to have Hestia or another virgin goddess pattern as a part of her psyche, because he will come and go. For example, Jacqueline Kennedy's independence and apparent ability to live with JFK's numerous affairs with women and the importance of his male friends, as well as his absorption in politics and the presidency, was probably due to having the virgin goddess Athena as a major archetypal pattern in her.

Aphrodite and Hermes were mythologically linked, and this combination can also work in real life. Rather than being compatible opposites, as with Hermes and Hestia, women who resemble Aphrodite, Goddess of Love and Beauty, share characteristics with Hermes men. In the realm of love, both are nonpossessive and open to many experiences. Both also can become intensely involved in whatever they are currently doing:

usually in the realm of creative work for her, and the latest challenging project for him. Neither like schedules anyway, so the irregularity of their life together works for them. They often prefer living together to getting married.

CHILDREN

Hermes the god had several sons whose behavior went beyond usual acceptable boundaries. Autolycus was the most accomplished liar and thief of his day; but he was considerably less reprehensible than Myrtilus, who made a wax linchpin that caused the death of his charioteer master. Pan (god of the forests, pastures, flocks, and shepherds) liked to have his afternoon nap and would terrify anyone who disturbed his siesta. He could induce panic, a state of unreasoning terror, named after him, in which people stampeded; especially susceptible were fearful travelers in lonely or desolate places. Pan was goatish in appearance and in lust. Although the children of a god can be metaphors for qualities that the archetype "fathers," myth can parallel real life as well. The sons of a Hermes man may in fact (like father like son), have difficulties with antisocial or sexual impulses.

When acting impulsively without thinking of the consequences is an innate quality—the "go now, pay later" mentality that has to do with living in the present, then learning to consider consequences, to consider the effect on others, to learn what the limits are, is an essential part of growing up, if a Hermes boy is to mature and adapt to the expectations of the world. These lessons are equated with "good fathering" in that it is the father who traditionally intercedes with the outer world. Unfortunately, Hermes men father children but aren't psychologically suited to be good fathers to their children (unless some patriarchal archetypes are also present, or they have themselves been well fathered).

As a parent, a Hermes man usually doesn't set limits and hold to them. His children know that they can get their way, especially if they can present a persuasive case: whether at delaying bedtime or at taking time off from school. They may also find that they can make excuses or lie to cover impulsive behavior, and not be held accountable by a Hermes father. Consequently, the children of Hermes all too often learn that rules are disregardable, that the tasks they are expected to do can be put off with an excuse, that they can get away with things. They fail to learn to respect authority, and often have a blurred sense of right and wrong as a result.

The children of Hermes are then ill prepared for the world of school or of work. They know very little about discipline. They expect that they can get away with not performing up to expected standards without penalty and usually find out later that they cannot.

On the positive side, the Hermes father knows how to play with his children, enjoys taking them on adventures, appreciates and stimulates the imagination, and is often like a kid himself with them. Hermes fathers were very evident in the hippie generation—or flower children—of the 1960s. Unlike traditional fathers who prepare children to adapt to the world, to perform and achieve, to produce, a Hermes father influences his children to look at life as a series of adventures.

Besides not setting limits and being inconsistent, a Hermes father may also be absent. He may have actually abandoned them and moved on. Or he may be "on the road" a lot, as a salesman or deal maker, coming and going, not alighting for long. Either because of his nonpaternal, playmate attitude toward his children when he is home, or because he rarely is home, he often leaves child rearing to the mother.

MIDDLE YEARS

If a man is a mature Hermes whose work is both challenging and materially rewarding, the Hermes man finds that the middle years of life offer more options than ever before. He finds opportunities for growth, for travel, for diversity. More so than most types of men, this Hermes may not only find outer life rewarding, but he may also begin exploring the inner world, adapting with ease to this phase of life.

However, if at midlife the Hermes man is still an eternal adolescent flitting from place to place, job to job, and woman to woman, the middle years are unexpectedly harsh. Charm no longer works to cover his lack of substance. It's evident that he is a failure. This is a time when some Hermes men have fatal accidents, and others become significantly depressed.

The fate of the antisocial or sociopathic Hermes at midlife varies. He may be successful economically and quite unreformed, or he may be in disgrace or in jail or on the run as a result of his actions having caught up with him.

LATER YEARS

The Hermes man in his later years may be an unusual man, not a run-of-the-mill, out-to-pasture retiree. If he stayed the eternal adolescent even into old age or kept an identity as a marginal thief, he could end up a homeless wanderer who travels from place to place with the weather or the opportunities, picking up some cash here and there, surviving by his wits and conversation. A contemporary variation of this version of Hermes is seen by psychiatrists in Veterans Administration hospitals; such Hermes patients have learned how to get admitted, find shelter, and then move on.

In contrast, the positively evolved Hermes may be a wise guide for other "travelers" along whatever path he has traveled, through which he acquired a depth of experience and an overview of its meaning. He may be an astute businessman with lessons to teach, an explorer of psychological terrain who can map the way for others, or a politician who may deserve to be called a senior statesman. Whatever the area, he may be a successful lecturer or author, who now communicates what he learned in his "travels." Typically Hermes, until the day he dies he still is exploring new terrain, meeting new people or being intrigued with new ideas. And he probably views death as the next adventure.

PSYCHOLOGICAL DIFFICULTIES

When Hermes is the major archetypal influence in a man's personality, how he behaves—what he does, how impulsively he acts, whether he has any thought about the consequences—is the issue. The shadow aspects of Hermes are character defects.

IMPULSIVENESS AND LACK OF LIMITS

On the first day of his birth, Hermes the God proved himself a clever thief and a convincing liar. Not nearly so early, but soon enough, similar problems may arise in the Hermes boy. Whether or not he learns to respect other people's possessions, feelings, and rights, and not just take what he wants and do what he likes, and reap the consequences, is crucial for his development. A Hermes boy needs to be taught about limits—what is acceptable behavior and what is unacceptable, and why—in order to develop a sense of right and wrong that will modify what he might think of doing. Otherwise, the typical Hermes will act immediately on impulse, focusing his inventive mind on how to get what he wants. His lessons may still be learned when he is an adult through important relationships, because he is imaginative. He most naturally uses this gift with thinking, but he can also use it in the development of empathy and understanding if significant others, hurt by his negative behavior, express how they feel and state their limits.

SOCIOPATHIC HERMES: THE TRICKSTER

When a Hermes boy grows up in an abusive situation where the significant adults act both impulsively and aggressively toward him, he will neither learn to tell right from wrong, nor will he learn restraint. Sneaking, stealing, and lying easily follow, leading to antisocial behavior and a sociopathic personality pattern.

Conflicts then arise between himself and others who disapprove or are affected by his behavior. As he grows older, if what he does is illegal he may get caught, although his mental agility and persuasive speech give him an advantage. He doesn't use force or violence; as with Hermes' theft of Apollo's cattle, he takes what doesn't belong to him, often in a clever way. As a trickster, he is a "con artist" who gains the confidence of his victim and then fleeces them, or a selective and imaginative thief, or the imposter. For example, we read of Hermes men who have posed as doctors, fooling hospital staff for a long time before being exposed.

Hermes men do sometimes get caught, however. And being jailed is especially hard for such a man. He is out of his element, with his wings clipped, experiencing what he finds most difficult: confinement, routine, and lack of freedom.

THE ETERNAL YOUTH: THE MAN WHO NEVER GROWS UP

A Hermes man finds settling down difficult. He likes to explore possibilities and new options. But this openness gets in the way of staying with something until it develops and until he matures. He finds new grass always greener, which invites him to flit from one situation or person to another.

Beginnings come easy for him. With his charm, he makes friends easily. With his quick mental grasp of a situation, he can impress others. Unless he or the situation makes him stay until he learns something in depth, he will have only a superficial understanding or skill: "Jack of all trades, master of none." This superficiality is an aspect of the *Puer Eternus,* the eternal adolescent boy.

The eternal adolescent lives in a realm of possibility, unwilling to make a commitment to any one thing or person, because he does not want to give up the next possibility that comes along. Until it is often too late, he thinks himself immortal as if he had all the time in the world—and he doesn't. While other men are establishing careers and families, he may be pursuing adventure or merely going from one thing to another, only to find at midlife that life is passing him by and that he is getting old. He has been a Peter Pan living in Never-Never Land until he is around forty, and then, as he looks in the mirror and at his life, the realization dawns, that it is—or may be—too late for him, and a midlife depression results.

LACK OF EMOTIONAL COMMITMENT AND INTIMACY

Hermes men seem more immune than most men to intense infatuations. In his many sexual encounters, his taste for variety and newness rather than passion lures him both into relationships and out of them. If he falls in love, he may stay long enough for infatuation to lead the way to love and depth; if he yearns for a home fire that he can come back to, and feels that he will be able to come and go freely, he may marry and find that over time the relationship deepens. But commitment and intimacy do not come easily. He's too busy to settle down, too actively thinking about other matters to give much thought to a relationship once he's in one, and too likely to leave as soon as he feels fenced in.

PSYCHOLOGICAL DIFFICULTIES FOR OTHERS

Hermes men adversely affect others who love them by avoiding commitments, by leaving, or by not growing up.

THE ELUSIVE LOVER

Hermes men can cause a great deal of grief for the women who fall in love with them. Typically, a Hermes man is charming, verbal, and persuasive. He finds resistance a challenge and may move on once he has managed to steal his way into her heart and bedroom.

It's often hard for a woman to see a Hermes man clearly. He may turn out not to be what she thought because she only saw or was shown one aspect of a man with many facets to his personality, a way with words, and a trickster element. A Hermes man often takes on different guises as he embellishes a part of himself and doesn't touch on others—which makes him seem chameleon-like.

His elusiveness and avoidance of commitment present problems for the woman who wants marriage and security. For him, commitment often feels like the proverbial ball and chain, and the more a woman expects or depends on him to fulfill her needs, the more likely he is to flee. He likes to come and go, prefers to act on impulse rather than plan ahead, and likes to play the field. For many women, a Hermes man is the archetypal rat, a charming man who cons her, first into believing she's very important to him, and then (until she finally sees through him or he disappears from her life) there are the many let-downs when he doesn't do whatever she expected of him, and each time he has a story to explain it.

THE INADEQUATE FATHER

Parenting is not something most Hermes men do at all well. If he is unreliable and inconsistent, his children grow up mistrustful and resentful of him, and these feelings contaminate other relationships. Especially affected are his daughter's relationships with men. If he fails at work because he lacks self-discipline and authority, his children are usually at a disadvantage when they go into the world; his sons, especially, fear that his inadequacies are their own. For a Hermes man to serve as a positive role model for his children, as well as an adequate, consistent parent, he must grow beyond his identification with Hermes the eternal adolescent.

WAYS TO GROW

In mythology, two other gods were important to Hermes and helped him grow up: his brother Apollo and his father Zeus. These archetypes are also the two that are most important for the Hermes man. In order to function effectively in the outer world, he must grow beyond Hermes by developing the characteristics Apollo and Zeus represent. Like both Apollo and Zeus, Hermes functions in the realm of the mind; like them, he needs to develop his emotional and sensual life.

SAYING NO TO HERMES

The man who grows beyond his identification with Hermes does so by knowing the assets and limitations of this archetype. He especially needs to be aware of the negative trickster potential of Hermes; he needs to act from awareness of the consequences to others and himself, and say no to this side of himself.

HELP FROM APOLLO

Apollo, God of the Sun, sees clearly and thus is not fooled. He immediately saw through Hermes' lies. If a man develops Apollo's clear-sightedness and reasoning, he cannot get away with Hermes' tendency to rationalize to himself as well as to others. Apollo also represents linear thinking and the ability to focus on a far target. He has a clear sense of the progress of time and the step-by-step approach needed to accomplish disciplined work. Apollo is also concerned with ethical precepts and with right and wrong. These traits are sorely needed by Hermes men if they are to achieve something in the world.

Fortunately for most Hermes men, especially middle-class American ones, the Apollo pattern is unavoidable. This pattern dominates the culture. Every important institution—church, school, Boy Scouts—works on teaching him what he needs to know.

As an adult, a Hermes may himself realize that he needs to find a way to become, at least partially, a self-made Apollo, and must make his success possible by completing projects. He can succeed when he grasps the need to finish what he starts, to learn what the requirements are, and to make himself stay with it.

SEEKING ZEUS THE FATHER AND MENTOR

Zeus clearly had the authority to tell Hermes to stop the lies and restore the stolen cows. He left no ambiguity, no place for an excuse. Hermes recognized this authority, and without another word did as Zeus told him. The Hermes man usually needs to recognize and respect authority, and to do what he is expected to do. Usually such intervention occurs because an outer figure acts as a father figure, someone who carries the Zeus authority and makes an impression on Hermes. If he has a positive relationship with a Zeus man who mentors him in the world, Hermes also benefits from the old-boy network. In this mentor relationship, a Hermes man apprentices himself and is encouraged both to use his communicative and mental gifts and to rise in the ranks. The patriarchal values are Zeus and Apollo ones, and usually they rub off on Hermes the apprentice. In a patriarchy, a Hermes man more than any other type other than Zeus and Apollo is supported, rewarded, and encouraged to develop further. The three share an affinity for the mental realm, and Zeus and Apollo men admire Hermes' resourcefulness and communication skills.

A Hermes man who finds that the eternal boy in him has too long directed his life, can sometimes change course by actively seeking a mentor and by deciding to take work seriously. When he struggles to control his own eternal youth, who would prefer that he quit and play, he is calling on the Zeus in himself.

FINDING HIS APHRODITE

Hermes did not marry or have a consort. His principal love was Aphrodite, who was married to Hephaestus and who had other lovers to whom she was passionately attracted. Hermes yearned for her, and she initially would have nothing to do with him. Zeus took pity on him and sent his eagle to steal one of her golden sandals while she was bathing. Hermes then offered her the sandal back in return for her favors, and she was willing.

A major way for Hermes to grow is through falling in love with a woman who thus becomes his Aphrodite. Typically, she needs to be a challenge, a woman he yearns for and cannot immediately have, someone who moves him deeper into his emotional life by making him aware of his vulnerability to her as well as who moves him out of his mental outlook and into the sensuality of his body. (Apollo's way to grow, by developing Dionysus, also applies to Hermes. Also like Apollo, growth may come through relating to his anima or inner woman.)

SPIRITUAL EVOLUTION

Hermes has an innate potential to become a guide of souls and a seeker of meaning. Inspired and centered on the soul, he seeks access to spiritual truths and ventures down into Hades depths. The man (or woman) who is in touch with this aspect of Hermes is drawn to what is sacred, to the mysteries of death and the afterlife, and is not content to follow only one path. And as Hermes the communicator, whatever he learns he is then likely to teach and pass on.

In the myth of the rape of Persephone, which is contained in the "Homeric Hymn to Demeter," Hermes goes down to the underworld to bring the maiden Persephone back to the upper world and to her mother. This myth was the background for the Eleusinian mysteries, whose initiates "no longer feared death." The Eleusinian mysteries predated Christianity and celebrated the return of Persephone from the underworld; like Jesus, Persephone returned from the realm of the dead. In the mythology of Dionysus, Hermes plays a similar crucial role, this time in saving the child Dionysus. Persephone can symbolize the soul, which in most men and also in many women is personified as feminine, while Dionysus symbolizes the divine child. Hermes as an archetype is present in people who are in touch with these aspects in themselves and in those who seek spiritual meaning in their lives.

8.

Ares, God of War—
Warrior, Dancer, Lover

Ares as the embodiment of aggression, has been one of the strongest forces working through human history. He is Olympos' "Action Man," the god of war and strife, the restless and turbulent lover, thriving on conflict and rejoicing in the delight of battle. In Ares we see our own aggression raw and bloody, before civilization tempered or repressed it.

Arianna Stassinopoulos, *The Gods of Greece*

In literature and art Ares is known to us in the two roles which Homer assigned to him, warrior and lover. Under his Roman name of Mars, he is virtually a synonym for war and for anyone taking pleasure in its bloody aspects.

Philip Mayerson, *Classical Mythology in Literature, Art, and Music*

Ares as god, archetype, and man is an image of masculine physical power, intensity, and immediate action. His heart and instincts literally move him to act and react with his body, unmindful of the consequences. His father Zeus disliked him and sided against him, just as the patriarchy devalues his attributes.

ARES THE GOD

Ares, whom the Romans called Mars, was God of War. Least respected and honored of the twelve Olympians by the Greeks, because of his irrationality and battle frenzy, Ares represented the uncontrolled lust for battle and bloodshed. In contrast, as Mars, the Romans held him in high regard, second only to Jupiter (Zeus) in importance. For them, he was protector of the community and the father of Romulus and Remus, the twin founders of Rome.

He is portrayed as a vigorous and virile man, often but not always bearded, usually with a helmet and a shield, sword and spear, sometimes with a breastplate, seldom in full armor.

GENEALOGY AND MYTHOLOGY

Ares was the only son of Hera and Zeus. However, like Hephaestus, Hera's other Olympian son, in one Roman version (Ovid's) she conceived Ares parthenogenically, through an herb whose touch could make the most sterile being fruitful. We have no details of his birth.

Giant twins called the Aloadai almost succeeded in killing Ares, probably when he was still a boy as were they. They captured him and shut him up in a bronze jar. Ares was imprisoned for thirteen months and would have perished (even though he was a god and thus immortal, which is peculiar) if their stepmother had not told Hermes. When Hermes freed him, he was nearly dead of torment.

Hera's choice of a tutor for Ares was Priapus, the deformed phallic god. Priapus first trained the boy to be a perfect dancer and only later to be a warrior.

ON THE BATTLEFIELD

Homer's view of Ares in the *Iliad* has prevailed. Ares was on the side of the Trojans against the Greeks and was portrayed by Homer as a bloodthirsty, contemptible, whining braggart who repeatedly was defeated, wounded, insulted, or shamed by his half-sister Athena. When a son of his was killed, and he charged onto the battlefield against Zeus's orders, Athena berated him, calling him "Blockhead!" and "Maniac!" for losing reason and restraint (her virtues, and the Greek ideals). He was described as not knowing "what is right," for lacking character because he turns "now to one and now to another." Ares reacted emotionally; his feelings drew him into battles on the side of men he felt related to, often by blood. Loyalty or retaliation motivated him, and overrode other considerations. For other Olympians, the Trojan War often seemed to be a spectator sport, with half favoring the Greek side, half the Trojans. The Olympians themselves entered the battle from time to time, but then according to Zeus's rules. Ares, in contrast, definitely did not see this as a "game."

When the gods and men fought among themselves at another battle, Athena guided one of her favorite heroes, Diomedes, to wound the god with a spear. Ares let out a bellow and complained to Zeus about what Athena had done. Zeus sided with Athena, and rejected and humiliated him further by saying, "Don't come to me and whine. There is nothing you enjoy so much as quarreling and fighting, which is why I hate you more than any god on Olympus."

Yet Homer acknowledged that Ares spurred on the Trojan forces, as he repeatedly came to their aid, accompanied by his sons, Fear and Panic.

LOVER OF APHRODITE

Ares and Aphrodite, Goddess of Love, were noted lovers. She had several children by Ares: the sons Deimos (Fear) and Phobos (Panic), who accompanied their father on the battlefield; a daughter Harmonia, whose name suggests potential harmony between the two great passions, Love and War; and perhaps Eros, God of Love. Eros has two mythological origins, as the son of Ares and Aphrodite and as a primal, generative force present at from beginning of time.

These two lovers shared much history between them in what was the most committed affair between Olympians. In the *Iliad*, when Athena knocked Ares down with a stone, Aphrodite tried to help him off the field, and was struck by Athena's fist. Both of them also had many other lovers. When Aphrodite was enamored of Adonis, Ares turned himself into an avenging boar, who killed the handsome youth.

When Aphrodite's husband Hephaestus, God of the Forge, was told of the affair, he devised a way to trap the lovers in the very act of committing adultery. He constructed an invisible and unbreakable net, which he draped over the bedposts and hung from the rafters. Then he pretended to leave for his forge, which was the signal for Ares to enter his house and his bed. Hephaestus sprung his trap on the lovers, and then summoned the gods to witness their perfidy. Instead of being outraged for Hephaestus, however, the gods roared with laughter at the sight.

FATHER OF MANY CHILDREN

Ares fathered at least three or four of Aphrodite's children (and, as the Roman god Mars, also fathered Romulus and Remus). Besides these noted children, he had close to twenty other offspring from his liaisons with numerous women, several of whom bore more than one child of his. At least three of his sons were Argonauts, and one of his daughters was the Amazon queen Penthesileia.

Ares was a father who felt strongly and took action on behalf of his children. When one of Poseidon's sons raped Alcippe, one of his daughters, Ares struck him dead on the spot. Poseidon then summoned him for murder before a council of the gods, and he was tried at the same place and acquitted—on a hill in Athens close to the acropolis, which was thereafter called the Areopagus (Ares' hill) after this event. A son's death similarly provoked Ares during the Trojan War: when he heard that his son Ascalaphus, had been killed in battle, Ares impetuously entered the fray to avenge him, even though Zeus had forbidden the gods to take part.

When Heracles was challenged by Cycnus, a highwayman who waylaid travelers bringing gifts to Delphi, and another of Ares' sons, Ares fought at Cycnus's side. Athena came to Heracles' aid, and with her help Heracles wounded Ares and killed Cycnus.

Yet another of his offspring was a sacred snake who guarded the spring at Thebes. When the man Cadmus killed it, he had to serve Ares for eight years, after which he married Harmonia, Ares and Aphrodite's daughter, and founded the city of Thebes.

MIXED REVIEWS

The prevailing negative view of Ares is the Greek poet Homer's. Ares was the most formidable of the deities arrayed on the side of the Trojans, who lost the war and the right to write its history. As mythologist Walter Otto notes of Ares, "Against this grim spirit of slaughter and bloodshed, the bright form of Athena stands in admirable contrast, and this contrast is intentional on the part of the poet."[1]

In the Homeric "Hymn to Ares," however, Ares' virtues are extolled, with lines such as "Ares has a mighty heart," "Ares, father of Victory," "Ares, helper of Justice," "Ares, leader of most just men, Ares carries staff of manhood." He is called "helper of mankind, dispenser of youth's sweet courage."[2] This view of Ares, which is also part of the Greek tradition, is consistent with the Romans' positive view of the God of War, whom they called Mars.

When contrasted with rationality and Athena, Ares is seen in a hostile, negative light as maddened carnage. When he is viewed positively, it is for his qualities of heart and courage (from French *coeur,* meaning "heart"); he is a god who reacts emotionally. In a family headed by Zeus, the offspring who found favor were, in contrast, noted for emotional distance.

ARES THE ARCHETYPE

The Ares archetype, like the god, is present in passionate, intense reactions. With Ares, a surge of emotion is likely to evoke an immediate physical action. This is a reactive, here-and-now archetype. The Ares archetype unquestionably predisposes a man (or woman) to be in touch with his feelings and in his body, which can be very positive when it comes to lovemaking. However, when rage and anger arise he reacts instinctively and often gets into situations that are detrimental to him and damaging to others. In either case, not considering to whom he is responding, and what the consequences will be, leads to trouble.

THE WARRIOR AS HERO OR BRAWLER

Ares is an embodiment of aggression, the impetuous response to battle, that instinct that makes some men wade into the middle of a conflict and strike out with weapon or fist, without thinking. If that man is a soldier, he may become a much decorated hero, with citations reading, "with no concern for the consequences to himself, he. . . ."

Movies and television dramatize that moment when the Ares archetype is provoked, and the man becomes an enraged and unstoppable powerful force. In a television series, we watched a mild-mannered scientist provoked to anger, transformed by rage into the muscle-bound, giant, green-skinned Hulk, who had superhuman strength and was unstoppable and unreasonable. In Sylvester Stallone's movie *Rocky* and its sequels, a point comes when the boxer is exhausted and bloodied, when he fights with pure instinct and wins. He personifies a much less dramatic Ares than the Hulk, but is likewise taken over by mindless aggression.

The *Rambo* films also feature an Ares hero, who like the god is motivated by loyalty, outrage, and retaliation.

In mythology, Ares represented the uncontrolled, irrational frenzy of battle. He was intoxicated by the tumult. In real life, intoxication too often plays a part in unleashing Ares: barroom brawling results when Ares is provoked. Ares doesn't get into fights as a competitive contest or for strategic reasons; his is a reactive emotional response to some provocation.

The Ares archetype represents battle lust. Homer portrayed Ares as the god who loved war for its own sake, who delighted in the din and roar of battles, and in the slaughter and destruction. This aspect of Ares can make fighting exhilarating to the barroom brawler and decorated war hero.

For the Olympians, who were immortal, battles such as those of the Trojan War were games. At this war—while the deities were mostly spectators, some on the side of the Greeks, others for the Trojans—from time to time individual deities would join the fray. A contemporary Ares delights in being on the playing field amid the din and roar, not in the stands or in betting on the outcome, but expressing raw aggression himself. A football lineman or a hockey player moved by the Ares archetype is likely to be penalized for being too rough, or for an illegal move, or for brawling when passions run high. These are the contact sports in which Ares finds recognition, where he may be penalized but is not denigrated for his temperament. In the gentlemanly sport of tennis, however, where form and gamesmanship are stressed, reacting in anger is definitely bad form. A tennis champion is expected to behave like Apollo, and as John McEnroe has found, he will be booed and hissed from the stands for reacting like Ares.

THE LOVER

Ares and Aphrodite were lovers who were caught together by her husband Hephaestus, who suspected that Ares entered his bed as soon as he left for work. This was a reciprocal and long-standing relationship between equals. Ares fathered four children with Aphrodite. Other women lovers of his also bore him more than one child. In contrast, most Olympian affairs were one-time seductions, usually between a god and a mortal. Even between two deities, seduction or rape was usual; the woman was commonly overpowered, tricked, or abducted. Rarely was she made love with.

Ares' passionate nature, his physicality, and the totality in which he is caught up in the emotion of the moment are the qualities of the Ares lover. This lover doesn't worry about comparisons with others as he makes love to the most sexually experienced goddess. His is a lusty personal sexuality without the ecstatic transpersonal Dionysian dimension. In *Lady Chatterley's Lover,* D. H. Lawrence created Mellors, a fictional personification of an Ares lover, who like Ares in his earthiness and occupation was considered an inferior.

THE DANCER

In Greek mythology, Ares first learned to be a dancer, from his tutor Priapus, before he learned to be a warrior. Although this side of Ares has not been described much at all, it fits the archetypal pattern of a physical rather than mental man, whose emotions and body act together. He could very well be a dancer, and predictably, known for passion and intensity more than technique. When audiences watch Mikhail Baryshinikov dance, for example, the experience is not cool appreciation for beauty and form, though he has both. The charismatic Bolshoi ballet star, who defected to the West and has a reputation as a lover, has a strong emotional and physical impact on his audiences.

Young Cassius Clay who became the heavyweight boxing champion of the world (and later changed his name to Muhammad Ali), also had the grace and form of Ares the dancer as well as his aggressive instincts.

In tribal cultures, warriors are dancers: before battle, the men dance. The drums and music encourage the warrior to become Ares.

THE REJECTED SON OF A SKY FATHER

The Ares archetype, like the god, is disparaged by men who exert power from a distance, who are cool strategists and sometimes deceptive tricksters (as power brokers and lovers). While Ares would get down to the level of the soldier on the field, Zeus preferred to fire a thunderbolt from on high, and Hermes stole Apollo's cattle rather than more directly express his sibling rivalry. The Greeks idealized thinking and rationality, and, from that historical point on, these have been the values of the patriarchy. Zeus hated Ares. Psychologically, Ares represents Zeus's shadow, that part of himself that he disparaged because it was undeveloped and/or was contrary to the ideal image he had of himself.

In our culture, Ares is equally devalued and rejected. The black man has become the carrier of Ares attributes and the recipient of the denigration and contempt Ares received from his father. Sexuality, violence, even the dancer aspects of Ares (in racist stereotypes), are attributes of the "inferior" son.

In white families, these same values and judgments are perpetuated. I often hear from men analysands how unseen and unvalued they have felt because their idealized or successful fathers favored their more verbal, more mentally facile brothers or sisters. One felt tongue-tied and stupid when, to include him in the conversation, he was quizzed in front of guests by his father, who never went to a single game or even inquired about the sport in which he excelled. For all the lack of support, however, he at least had the deep satisfaction of living out this aspect of the Ares archetype. Many men accept the devaluation or give up the innately meaningful aspects of Ares in order to conform or be successful, and they never know the joy of doing well what is archetypally theirs.

ARES THE PROTECTOR

A prudent person would not attack anyone related to Ares, for to do so invited immediate retribution. He looked after his own, his daughter as well as his sons. In fact, Ares was the only god to do so. As Mars, he later protected the citizens of Rome in the same fierce way.

As U.S. Attorney General, Bobby Kennedy had an Ares streak that both Mafia and corrupt labor unions feared because getting back at them was not a legal game, but a passionate battle. Known for his loyalty and partisanship, for his visceral reactions, and as father of many children, he was the most Ares of the Kennedy brothers.

Ares joins the battle when someone he cares about is attacked, especially if he or she is getting the worst of it. Ares (as contrasted to wrathful Poseidon) isn't a grudge carrier who will even a score even if it takes years of pursuit. Even if he is humiliated, Ares can lick his wounds and go on.

CULTIVATING ARES

Today, in a patriarchal world that still follows Zeus's lead, Ares is still an unappreciated archetype, one that is more likely to be repressed than cultivated, especially in men who seek success.

But if the Ares archetype is repressed in a man's psyche, embodied feelings are not accessible to him. This whole aspect remains undeveloped and bottled up: the image is of the boy Ares locked away in the bronze jar.

Rescue is possible, but only when the man feels the stirrings of the boy in him who once was spontaneous and physically expressive. The boy Ares locked up in the jar is his yearning for physical contact with the father who never wrestled with him playfully or hugged him strongly; it's the impulse he can't act on to fling an arm over a friend, to be a buddy; it's the kid in him who gyrated to music or wanted to, the boy who once played stickball on a city street; it's lustiness and earthiness, and sweatiness. It's not being self-conscious. Moments or opportunities will come when a man feels he wants to express Ares: Will he free the boy in that moment or keep him in the jar?

When Ares has been so long bottled up, physical reactivity to people and events—the embodied emotional responses—can be totally outside of conscious awareness. A man (or woman) may appear to live only in his head, and yet his body still reacts with physical tension or release. For example, he may not feel anger and fear, but his muscles may tense or hands may become clenched fists. He usually doesn't notice this physical reaction until someone else comments. Even further from consciousness and expression is an Ares who makes himself known only in an elevated blood pressure, or through the bowels, as constipation or diarrhea.

When Ares is detested, as Zeus detested him, this archetype may stay undeveloped or repressed, especially when Ares is not the major archetype. Before the locked-in Ares can be rescued or freed, the person must become aware of the situation. Help can come through other people: if significant others really care what a man (or woman) feels and can read his body language or intuit the feelings of which he himself is not aware, and if he heeds and values their comments, he begins to learn. He can also note his own body language. These are just beginnings; he must next have earthy experience through physical contact with others or through activities in which he is in his body to cultivate and free Ares, and allow him to grow.

ARES THE MAN

The Ares man is an assertive, active, intensely emotional and embodied person who does not think before he reacts. His innate traits get him into difficulties, and the reactions of others to him are of great importance in shaping his life.

EARLY YEARS

An Ares boy is active, emotional, and expressive from the moment he arrives. Most likely he first gave notice of his personality with his first loud howl of protest. That same lusty cry soon becomes familiar, for if something is wrong and he's hungry or wet or hurts somewhere, there's no mistaking the intensity of his scream: "Do something now!" When he wails, his whole body is involved in the protest, from the redness of his face to the tension in his little limbs, the unmistakable message is either "I'm in pain" or "I'm enraged!" And when the bottle or the breast comes, or the burp relieves the air bubble, the totality of the change is equally dramatic. If he's typically Ares, he's a hearty eater and has an engaging, responsive personality when all is well. He likes stimulation, and from infancy on laughs with glee at the physical joy of play or throws himself heartily into rough and tumble. If he's hurt or unexpectedly startled, his protest will be equally hearty.

As he gets older, if something attracts him and is within reach, there's hardly a second between his admiring eye and his reaching hand. Baby proofing the house is now especially important, for he is the kid that takes the tumble down the stairs, or gets a shock when he puts his finger in the socket, or knocks over the vase, or gets scratched or bitten by a startled pet. He is dauntless in his approach to whatever catches his interest. He needs more Band Aids than the average kid, because he always seems to learn by firsthand experience, which leads to bumps and bruises, skinned knees, and scratches.

His budding self-esteem also gets bumps and bruises because his impulsive behavior gets him into scrapes and invites criticism and punishment. Much depends on his parents and teachers, on their patience, consistency, and ability to appreciate that he is a spontaneous, impulsive, emotional boy—an intense child who overreacts.

HIS PARENTS

Since an Ares child is such an energetic and often demanding handful who lacks caution and doesn't think before he acts, he is often not an easy baby or youngster. Thus he is especially in need of firm, loving, and often patient parents. Although he needs more guidance than other children, often he gets just the opposite. Since it is natural for him to be caught up in the moment and thus forget whatever he has been told, he provokes parents, especially authoritarian or legalistic ones, by his forgetfulness. They define it as disobedience or failure to live up to his agreements. He is not cautious enough about many things, including holding his tongue, and he may say things in the heat of anger that can provoke a physically abusive father.

Conversely, mothers with a compliant personality sometimes find that they have trouble asserting themselves against a demanding, angry Ares son who intimidates them, even when he's little more than a toddler: an angry four-year-old Ares boy can tyrannize some mothers. Ideally, his mother should be a strong and loving physical woman, who is constant in setting limits that give him enough room to be himself. She hugs him often and knows how to channel his energy into physical activity that increases his sense of mastery and helps him learn patience and discipline.

Sometimes life imitates myth, and an Ares boy has an angry Hera and a rejecting Zeus for parents. In contemporary versions, the father may be a high-powered successful man who is a distant father at best even for sons he approves of, who rejects his Ares son for being emotional, reactive, and physical rather than intellectual. Or if he is an angry man, whose rage is disproportionate to what instigates it, an impulsive son finds himself the target of physical and verbal abuse, which in turn makes it even harder for him to learn restraint, and the typical pattern follows where the abused boy grows up to be the abusing man.

Having Hera for a mother means that his mother's major bond is with her husband; she is emotionally and archetypally "the wife" rather than "the mother." Her Ares son often is un-mothered—she resents his sensitivity and vulnerability, and expects him to be a "little man." Often it is the angry mother of an Ares son who is the verbal or physical abuser. The boy receives her rage at her husband if she feels humiliated and powerless and yet so strongly bonded to her husband, as she can be. A more introverted boy might be able to stay out of trouble and raise himself with the same set of parents that are disastrous for an Ares boy. How he will turn out greatly depends on the quality of parenting.

ADOLESCENCE AND EARLY ADULTHOOD

Adolescence is a crucial period: the surge of male hormones at puberty magnifies qualities such as impulsiveness, aggressiveness, physicality, emotionality, and sexuality. Peer groups are especially important for Ares: Will he go out for football, soccer, or rugby, and learn discipline, channel, his aggressiveness in competitive sports, and receive recognition and admiration as a result? Or will he resort to gangs and gang warfare? Will he cut school, or drop out? Will he disregard authority, become anti-social, and get into real trouble? Or will his assertive, engrossed-in-the-moment energy become absorbed by an interest in racing cars or rock climbing? Will music and dance and romance be major discoveries and sources of pleasure? Or will his sexuality be a channel for his aggression?

High school and college offer Ares the possibility of early failure or potential success. If he does not think ahead and responds to some opportunity or to an emotional situation in the immediate present, he may leave school early. Although what beckons a change or provokes a move may turn out well, an Ares man may hurt his chances by cutting short his academic, music, or sports life.

WORK

Temperamentally, Ares is drawn to action and intensity, likes using tools, and enjoys moving on. He's bored and restless with paperwork and long-term goals, and does not fit into the corporate hierarchy. Occupations that present some risks interest him, and his skills can grow in the process of taking on one project at a time. He likes working with other people and offers fraternal loyalty to other men.

Like Ares the Warrior, he may join the army or the marines, and may well have a spotty disciplinary record. He may become a noncommissioned officer or receive a battlefield promotion. If other archetypes are also present and active, he may become an officer with a reputation for seeking action. Soldiers of fortune, mercenaries who hire out to fight, who in the past might have joined the French Foreign Legion, also are likely to be living out roles consistent with Ares the Warrior.

If he becomes a professional athlete, he may give it his all and may have trouble containing his aggression in the middle of a heated situation. Learning to restrain his immediate responses to a disputed call or a provocation (which may lead to the penalty box or the dugout) will hold him in good stead in all other areas of his life. As a hockey or football player who cannot contain his impulses, he'll hurt his team and himself through penalties—for unnecessary roughness, unsportsmanlike behavior, or disputes with umpires or referees. (He may also be a performer—an actor, dancer, or musician, known for emotionality and sometimes erratic performance on and off the stage.)

The construction trades and oil fields attract a number of men with Ares personalities, who are drawn to the action and the risks. Paid well, they are apt to be impulsive spenders when they have the money.

His success depends greatly on luck, because Ares does not follow a long-term plan. His success may also come through one thing just leading to an other. It may also depend on having developed innate abilities, skills he honed not by deliberate practice but because he kept on doing something he loved to do.

When he succeeds, it often surprises everyone, including himself. Along the way, he undoubtedly ran into problems with authority and got fired for having lost his temper or for not showing up. If his work life goes well, that results from having learned some lessons, ability, and serendipity.

RELATIONSHIPS WITH WOMEN

In mythology, Ares and Aphrodite were lovers and their relationship is the most compatible pattern for a man with an Ares nature. He and women who resemble the Goddess of Love and Beauty are similar temperamentally in their intensity and sensual natures. Both are here-and-now people. The likelihood of fireworks, due both to erotic flames and flashing anger, may make their relationship stormy, full of fights and making up. Yet for all the expressiveness, their relationship is sometimes quite harmonious, with more mutual tolerance and acceptance than they can find elsewhere. However, when an emotionally wounded, angry Ares man who is physically abusive, combines with a woman who has low self-esteem and had a childhood in which she was abused, the combination can be one of the most destructive possible for both these people.

Women who resemble Athena, the goddess with the mind of a fine strategist, who scorned Ares' emotionality and impulsive reactiveness, judge Ares men similarly. And women who assess a man's future earning power, are attracted to status, and want stability and security, avoid Ares men as potential mates. Some women are even put off by what they perceive as too personal a manner. Thus Ares men often find themselves judged and found wanting by women, and in turn they harbor resentment until they express it in anger—which is further alienating.

Ares men often are friendly with many women toward whom they are warm in their gestures and comments whatever their age, but usually they don't count women among their best friends. They don't usually share interests or work concerns with women.

An Ares man gravitates to women he genuinely likes to be with and with whom he can be spontaneous and physical in his affections and actions. Whether making love or dancing, enjoying food or playing games, he's totally involved and most comfortable with women who also can be this involved.

RELATIONSHIPS WITH MEN

An Ares man likes to spend time with men friends, doing things, playing, mock challenging, watching or playing a sport. He's not interested in deep conversation or talking philosophically; his talk focuses on women, sports, whatever he and his friends are doing. He bonds with his friends, and physically comes to their defense.

Often his deepest connections have been made with other men in uniform in combat or conflict—as a soldier, or on a team, or even in a gang, where he has been physically aggressive, fighting with others to win. In these settings, his aggressiveness is valued and so is his expressiveness. Here he can also cry without being called a sissy, or give a rough hug without stirring up homophobic feelings.

Being shunned or scapegoated by his peers—which can happen to an Ares boy or man—is enormously painful and intolerable. Not only is he hurt, but he also feels deprived of the camaraderie he especially wants.

SEXUALITY

Whether an Ares man loves women or beats them up depends on what happened in his childhood. If that childhood was good enough for the lover in him to develop, he will be a man who loves to make love, a man who loves women's bodies, a man who can spend hours making love, a man who prefers a grown-up, sexually liberated woman who enjoys sex as much as he. He isn't a mystically oriented, ecstasy-seeking Dionysian lover, nor is he conquest minded; he makes love for the physical joy of it, exuberantly. In the movie *Tom Jones,* based on the English novel by Henry Fielding, Albert Finney played the title role with the earthiness, amorality, enjoyment, and appetite of Ares the Lover.

An Ares man doesn't fare well in a culture that is both puritanical and hypocritical. He may judge his own lustiness as sinful and feel it is a part of him to condemn and suppress, especially if he marries a woman who is inhibited and puritanical and if he thinks about or acts on his adulterous feelings. If he acts on these feelings, he usually isn't a good enough strategist to cover his tracks or anticipate problems. So, like Ares the god, he gets caught and exposed.

A homosexual Ares had a much easier time of it, as a lover—at least until the AIDS epidemic—because of his impulsiveness, total absorption in the moment, amorality, and ready availability of partners in bars and bathhouses. Also, the gay culture's acceptance of nonmonogamous relationships allows for the kind of relationship that Aphrodite and Ares had, where both had other lovers and yet themselves had a long-term significant sexual relationship. A gay Ares may dress in leather, a contemporary version of warrior armor as well as build up his muscles to look like Ares.

MARRIAGE

An Ares man neither plans on marriage nor avoids it. He gets intensely involved and doesn't think about the long haul: He doesn't wonder, "Will this woman make be a good partner?" "Will she be a good mother?" "Will she enhance my career?" "Shall I marry her?"

If others—the woman, her family or his—have marriage in mind, marriage may follow. He may marry right out of high school, especially in blue-collar communities, where this pattern is expected. Given his earthy, sensual nature, his marriage may follow getting a woman pregnant. If he loves her and they have a satisfying sexual relationship, if he has a job and can play baseball or basketball with his buddies, and if his wife is content with the life they have together, life is good for him. He is grounded in his family and in the stability of his life, has self-esteem and the esteem of others.

When matters are more complex, problems arise. On the one hand, his reactive, impulsive nature may lead to job instability and infidelity, which strains the marriage or ends it. On the other hand, influenced by non-Ares aspects of his personality, an Ares who marries young and then develops ambition or discovers his intellect, or meets men and women who make him aspire for more, may now find the woman who once attracted his physical nature too limited for him. If the initial physical chemistry between them is lost, or his wife's response to his ardor in courtship was not genuine or not strong, and fades, or she is more ambitious or jealous, the stress that results, compounded by whatever he does, may lead to battles between them.

CHILDREN

Ares men often father children unintentionally, the result of his "in the moment, don't think of consequences" nature, coupled with his sensuality. If the woman does not look out for birth control, fatherhood is then likely to be a matter of roulette.

If he is a presence in his children's lives, he usually looms large. If life has turned out well for him, and his family is the center of a rewarding life, he spends time doing things with his children. He teaches his sons baseball and football, takes them to games, wrestles with them, likes having them around him. He dances with his little daughter and picks her up and takes her on his shoulder with him on his rounds to see friends. He can give young children a basic sense of being fathered. Conflicts often arise as his children grow older, if they are introverted or intellectual, and cannot share his interests, or feel his personality is intrusive. If the family is working class and the children aspire to climb, conflicts and hurt feelings also arise.

His children may also suffer from abuse if he is a rejected, angry Ares man, who is unstable in his work and relationships. His children may react with fear and terror to the rage he carries around in him, which is set off by minor provocations. He can be physically abusive, especially if he drinks.

Other children of Ares men are neglected, especially if he fathered them when he was an emotional adolescent. The Ares man may have sown many wild oats. He may not be temperamentally or financially able to look after children he fathered, both within marriage or outside of it. And he may be an absent father. However, if he can look after his children, he usually will. It's his nature to be generous when he has something to give.

MIDDLE YEARS

The Ares man's life status in his middle years is tied closely to the social class in which he was born. For example, it is the tragedy of many Ares men to have been born into upwardly striving ambitious families and the upper middle class, which values emotional distance or coolness, intellect, the ability to manipulate others and to acquire power and money. The fate of such men mimics that of the god Ares, who as the target of Zeus's contempt, was found unworthy and rejected. Many Ares men who have fathers like Zeus, and are born into the contemporary equivalent of the Olympian social class follow the god Ares' fate, humiliated and denigrated as a failure on the corporate battlefields.

For an Ares man from a business or professional family to feel good about himself at midlife, he must have been able, early in his life, to recognize that he stepped to a different drummer from his father or his social class. He must have received emotional support to pursue his own interests and talents, as well as to feel fine about his temperament, which is warm to hot rather than cool. Emotional support to be himself was essential. Sometimes psychotherapy, at other times a significant person, most often parents who loved him and saw him as he was made this success possible. Still, to have established himself by midlife, he has had to stuggle to find a place for himself in the world. His success is highly individualistic and thus hardwon.

It is easier for an Ares man to reach a stable and satisfying situation by midlife, if he was born into a working-class family in a closely knit community. Avenues of acceptable expression for his temperament and physical nature, both occupationally and as pastimes are more available. Male camaraderie, sports, and even an occasional fight serve as outlets for his aggression, and he needs others to make allowances and even appreciate his lustiness—all outlets that are just not available to upwardly mobile urban men. In the working class, occupations that engage a man physically are respected, so acceptance and with it self-esteem are more readily available.

More so than some other archetypes, the fate of the Ares man seems sealed by midlife. It is more predetermined by outside factors such as social class and family, because the culture itself does not naturally support who he is.

LATER YEARS

By midlife, the pattern is largely set for how life will turn out for the Ares man. The stability and self-esteem (or lack thereof) he has achieved by then makes all the difference when it comes to later years.

Many Ares men do not live out their later years. Death may claim them early through violence or accidents or war. By temperament and occupation, their lives is are more physically dangerous. And if the country is at war, the possibility of an early death is even greater. Ares men were overrepresented as soldiers and casualties in the Vietnam War, with its exemptions and alternatives. Stress-related physical conditions also claim Ares lives when anger and powerlessness exist together, as is often the case. When recession hits and mills and factories shut down, security can end, and family violence and instability results.

However, some Ares men in their later years are contented—perhaps more so than at any other time in their lives. The working-class family man is fortunate who now enters a happily anticipated retirement, with family around, sports events to take an interest in, pastimes and old buddies to occupy him, kids to coach, perhaps a house he built at the lake, and an innate capacity to live in the moment.

A harder-won satisfaction comes to Ares men who had to struggle against the tide. Their lives are often unsupported by community fabric and highly individualistic solutions. Where they live, and with whom, and what they do is then a result of personal choice based on deeply held and authentic responses in themselves. They have learned how to adapt and stay true to themselves, and are among the most individuated and evolved men: old age is a rich harvest time.

PSYCHOLOGICAL DIFFICULTIES

Just as the god Ares was the most beaten-upon of the Olympians, and suffered humiliation and wounds, so also many Ares men are abused and rejected as children and adolescents. As a result of these personality traits and ill treatment, a range of difficulties trouble Ares men.

IDENTIFICATION WITH THE GOD OF WAR

A man who is "only Ares" identifies with this archetype and never develops the ability to observe himself and reflect on his actions. He lacks choice and is a bundle of impulsive reactions. An extreme example is the street fighter who cannot pass up a provocation. Occasionally Hollywood personalities get in the headlines for this kind of behavior. A photographer takes an unwanted, uncomplimentary picture, or a verbal taunt is thrown, and—in spite of the headlines, arrest, and suits for damage that will result when someone "pushes his buttons" by doing something provocative—the run-amok god of war explodes, and he wades into a fight with his fists, flashbulbs popping all around.

ABUSED ABUSER

When his fists and anger are directed against women and children, the Ares man is usually an abused abuser, who as a child was himself beaten and humiliated. His emotions trigger a physical response. An abused, terrified, or humiliated child inhabits the body of such a man, who now lashes out or beats up someone else when he feels inadequate. In this way, the sins of the fathers are perpetuated for generations. Sit in an abusive men's group—which are modeled after Alcholics Anonymous—and you usually find that these men were all abused children.

To survive his childhood as best he could, this man repressed his own feelings of terror and helplessness. As a result, he cannot put himself in his victim's place. Better than anyone else, he ought to be able to imagine what it is like to be beaten by someone who is out of control and physically able to inflict great harm, because it happened to him. But he cannot empathize until he risks uncovering the victim in himself.

Home thus becomes the battlefield for Ares, where he can fling abuse at family members when he feels inadequate. The raging god archetype acts on behalf of his own inner child, the humiliated and abused boy in himself who is now powerful enough to strike out.

SCAPEGOAT

As a child and adolescent, Ares may be the kid who is provoked on the school yard by a group and who reacts with hurt and rage when it would be better to be "cool" and unruffled. Life can parallel myth if he is physically ganged up on and injured (as when the huge twins held Ares captive in a jar). He may also be emotionally hurt if he is rejected and left outside the group. This rejection does happen to an Ares, because he acts without thinking and wears his emotions for all to see. Also, if he is already a victim of abuse or denigration at home, he's all the more vulnerable to ostracism at school.

In the family, he may encounter difficulties not just with parents, but also as the sibling who loses out in the sibling rivalry (as Ares repeatedly did to Athena). Often he gets in trouble and looks bad, either on his own, or because he's teased, prodded, or egged on and then is caught and "catches it" from an authoritarian parent—who already disparages this particular child for his unacceptable qualities.

In the classroom, an Ares boy may find himself cast in the same scapegoat role. On acting up, he may be cast out and sent to the principal. He is also the scapegoat when the teacher is biased against him. Other children, knowing his role, let him take the blame.

Once his pattern of being the scapegoat is established, it often continues into adulthood, where he still is the one who gets provoked into acting badly and then is ostracized. The likelihood then is that he will inflict on his family what was done to him.

WORK AND UNEMPLOYMENT BLUES

A man who is quick to react with anger has problems at work. He flares up and is fired. Ares also has real difficulties "going by the book" and following rules and regulations or principles, instead of what he feels is called for right now. He may get in difficulties for speaking the truth, when it wasn't either diplomatic or prudent. Or maybe he followed his heart, and made an exception when the rules said not to. Thus even when anger is not the issue, Ares often does not last long in a bureaucracy or in business.

Advancement is also an issue. Ares is not a strategist and does not take a long-range view, which has negative effects on his work life. He may have dropped out of school too early or may not have done well because he couldn't think about tomorrow.

ALCOHOL AND ARES

Ares is discouraged and repressed as the here-and-now lover, dancer, warrior, and abuser, and is opposed by other archetypes and by a culture that wants men to live in their heads, not in their bodies. Often alcohol liberates Ares, again in both positive and negative ways. Sometimes alcohol dissolves inhibitions to spontaneity and affection: witness the comradeship among men who are teammates or soldiers, who fight together and then drink together. It can also unleash the abusive man, whose violence is triggered much easier when he is drinking.

UNMET EXPECTATIONS

The god Ares was a lover, not a husband. His father Zeus (a chief executive type) hated the way Ares behaved. As an archetype, Ares lacks the qualities and drive that lead easily to either a responsible married life or a successful career. Often an Ares man finds himself not meeting someone else's expectations; and falling short, feels badly about himself. If this happens too often, he becomes permanently defeated and sees himself as a loser. This problem can arise when he is loved for who he is initially and is then expected to be someone totally different. For example, a woman may be drawn to his sensuality and aliveness, or to his intensity and sex appeal. Or her heart may have gone out to the wounded, rejected boy that she perceived in him. Once in a relationship with him, however, she may try to remake him into an upwardly mobile, urban professional married man, and become angry at him for not succeeding.

PROBLEMS FOR OTHERS

If jealousy is a problem for the partner of an Ares man, their relationship will be very turbulent. For an Ares man, fidelity is usually a hard-won achievement that grows out of his love and loyalty, not something that comes easily. He has to learn to say no to an attraction that exists in the moment and say no to his amoral, purely instinctive sexuality; otherwise his penis decides what he will do. Later consequences are vague to him, compared to the immediate situation, even when a situation is repeated. His partner may be hurt—"How could you!"—and accusations are flung. Characteristically, Ares must learn from experience and may not get the lesson until it is repeated, many times over.

When unfounded jealousy is the woman's issue, Ares will arouse it because he doesn't account well for his time. Maybe he stopped by a bar and got engrossed in a conversation or a game, or maybe he was absorbed and lost track of time. If jealousy is an issue, a woman cannot count on her Ares partner to solve it for her. Yet in struggling with her and the pain she experiences, he can learn to say no or to call her if he is going to be late. Another type of man behaving the same way may be indirectly expressing hostility or resentment because he does remember and decides he won't reassure her; but usually Ares is just being his in-the-moment self.

OUT-OF-WEDLOCK CHILDREN

Just as the god Ares fathered many children with many women, so might an Ares man repeat this pattern. Living in the here-and-now of sensuality and eroticism, Ares does not think of birth control, plus he likes children and the idea of having them, while he may not like the idea of marriage. A woman involved sexually with an Ares man has to make responsible and realistic decisions about birth control and the possibility of being a single parent. It would be a mistake to assume that having his baby will necessarily lead to marriage. On the other hand, often the only reason he can see for getting married is for the children's sake.

ABUSIVE ARES

Physical abuse is the worst-case situation for women and children living with an Ares man who gets angry and takes his rage out on them. Such a woman needs to know that the physical abuse will not stop if she allows it to happen, and that staying in a situation where she and her children are physically abused will perpetuate it, not only now but most likely in the next generation as well. She must leave or call the police when the threat or actuality of abuse occurs, both to protect herself and her children and to help him stop. If she doesn't act the very first time by leaving and/or calling the police, chances are good that she will become a battered woman, who will soon need outside help herself.

WAYS TO GROW

Psychological growth happens when the Ares man can choose if and how he will respond to a provocation, when he ceases to be a purely reactive person. For this, he needs to develop self-control as well as other archetypes.

LEARNING SELF-CONTROL

Quick to respond emotionally, the Ares personality flares up and reacts aggressively to provocation, so that learning self-control is a more difficult lesson for Ares than others. Best learned early from consistent, patient, and loving parents, it's a lesson that will keep coming up until it is learned.

Several years ago, for example, Hollywood actor Sean Penn, who has been repeatedly hauled into courts after violent fights, at twenty-eight stood before a judge and was sentenced to sixty days in jail. Noting his need to learn self-control, his attorney Howard Weitzman presented his situation: "He has to learn that people are going to attempt to goad him into situations where he may react inappropriately. He needs to and does understand that incidents like this (he beat a man he thought was trying to kiss Madonna, Penn's rock-star wife) are inescapable."[3]

Former tennis champion, John McEnroe, with his Ares temperament, flunked the same lesson. Noted for his outbursts on and off the court, McEnroe was portrayed by the press as a poor sport who behaved like a child.

To learn this crucial lesson, a man (or woman) has to be motivated to change, and then with practice, hold back the impulse to retaliate or react. The explosiveness of a held-in Ares can then be defused if the ego can choose a different response at this point; if help from another archetype can be enlisted.

HERMES TO THE RESCUE; APOLLO AS ALLY

Fortunately, all the archetypes are potentially present, and even if one predominates—especially if it is Ares—others can be developed. In mythology, Hermes came to the rescue when Ares as a child was hidden and imprisoned in a huge jar. Similarly, the Hermes archetype can also come to the rescue of a person who would otherwise react as Ares and instinctively retaliate when provoked, and then becomes scapegoated, labeled, and rejected, as John McEnroe was.

Hermes represents the capacity to communicate and think on his feet, usually in an inventive or clever way. Hermes can get Ares out of a destructive situation. An adult Ares being goaded by freelance photographers who want to get a picture of him acting badly, or an Ares child on the schoolyard being deliberately pushed by another boy who is trying to provoke a fight, will get in trouble if he retaliates. Already labeled as a troublemaker, he'll get the blame as well and becomes the scapegoat. But this pattern changes when Hermes helps him learn to speak up instead, to say something that deflects or defuses the fight.

Sometimes his family helps him to develop restraint, to think before acting, to use verbal skills instead of physical action. If his family doesn't help, the opportunity to learn later in life may come from a coach or a therapist, or from anyone who cares about him and sees him as needing to learn self-control and an effective means of expression, rather than needing to be blamed or feared.

Academic work and going out for a sport enlists the Apollo archetype, another major potential ally for Ares. Apollo is the archetype of discipline, emotional distance, self-control, and long-range targets. He shares with Hermes the ability to get the situation into perspective and be mindful of consequences, and in addition represents the ability to use will and intellect effectively.

Bobby Kennedy, whose Ares nature made him the passionate fighter he was, might have been elected president of the United States had he not been assassinated. Kennedy was a loved son in a political family where the communication of ideas was an essential part of dinner, sports competitions were practically an everyday occurrence, and college and law school were preparation for a public career. From his earliest years, Kennedy's Ares emotional intensity was thus tempered by Hermes and Apollo, so that he could be effective and positively regarded.

PAUSING FOR REFLECTION AND CHOICE MAKING: ATHENA'S INFLUENCE

The Greek hero of the Trojan War, Achilles, was a favorite of Athena, although he was temperamentally more like Ares than Athena. When Agamemnon, commander of the Greek forces, exerted his authority off the battlefield and took Achilles' mistress away from him, Achilles put his hand on his sword and was drawing it from his scabbard. He would have committed mutiny and murder but for Athena's calming intervention. Invisible to others, she descended from the sky, caught him by his fair hair, and told him,

> I have come to stay your anger—but will you obey me? . . . Come then, do not take your sword in your hand, keep clear of fighting, though with words you may abuse him. . . . Some day three times over such shining gifts shall be given you.[4]

Athena represented the moment of reflection, the inner voice, the pause that changes an emotional reaction into a choice of action. Thinking that may feel to an Ares man like an "other" within himself, a counselor on whom he learns to call. For some men, it is a feminine voice, inspired by a rational, loving mother, rather than another male aspect of himself.

ACTIVE IMAGINATION: CALLING ON THE ARCHETYPES

Active imagination can be called on to help. Once he understands the problem of reacting without thinking, a boy or a man can mentally "call on" Athena. Imaging or intuiting her, he can then imagine a dialogue. She counsels him to be cool in an emotional situation, to think through the consequences before doing anything. (If Achilles had not listened to Athena, the Greeks would have lost the Trojan War; the *Iliad* would have had one chapter instead of twenty-two). Similarly, Apollo or Hermes can be activated by the imagination and called on.

RECOVERING THE MEMORY AND PAIN OF CHILDHOOD

If a man was much abused in childhood and, as is often the case, has "forgotten" or repressed the experience because of its emotional pain, then psychotherapy or taking part in a supportive men's group may help him. Gradually he can retrieve the memory and the long-buried rage, grief, and helplessness, which otherwise may stay unconscious, yet powerfully influence his behavior. With abuse, the sins of the parent often color successive generations, until the pattern is stopped by someone who not only retrieves what has been repressed but in the process also discovers his capacity for trust and compassion. This task is presented to Ares men who find themselves behaving in the same abusive way as themselves were once treated.

EVOLVING FROM ARES INTO MARS

Just as the Ares, the battle-lusting Greek God of War, evolved with time and a different culture into the Roman Mars and in the transition became the protector of the community, so can the Ares aspect of a man change and evolve. The young male Ares may have played rough and dirty at football or hockey, and loved lustily; he may not have thought of himself as a man who would settle down—but most Ares men do. And if he has not been an abused child and was not rejected, when he does become a family man he can be an involved Earth Father who enjoys the company of his children and is very much involved with them. He is a natural protector: anyone who hassles his kids finds themselves facing an Ares father who will physically do battle if necessary. This kind of man helps his children feel emotionally secure. As he grows older, he may become a community leader who is willing to battle for the safety and rights of others.

9.

Hephaestus, God of the Forge—Craftsman, Inventor, Loner

Hephaistos' creative gift is solidly grounded on the earth, and there is magic as well as magnificence in what he produces. In his workshop he is supreme, unrivalled, but like the modern man who identifies himself exclusively with his work, he is at a total loss outside it.

Arianna Stassinopoulos, *The Gods of Greece*

A Hephaistian fantasy: the rejected of the earth, by whose labor and sweat civilization has grown; class-conscious and seething with pyromaniacal resentments and grudges; endlessly creative and the source of most of the world's supply of genius; restless, volcanically explosive and ready to take up arms against tyrannical masters, yet not lovers of war and strife but rather peacemakers and natural humanitarians; simple as fire itself and equally energetic.

Murray Stein, "Hephaistos: A Pattern of Introversion"

Hephaestus as god, archetype, and man, personifies a deep human urge to make things, to create objects that are functional and beautiful. Rejected and thrown off Mt. Olympus, Hephaestus was not appreciated in the lofty realm of Zeus, where power and appearance mattered. Instead, he worked alone in his forge under the earth. His attributes are similarly devalued in a patriarchy, and men who resemble this god have difficulties achieving success.

HEPHAESTUS THE GOD

Hephaestus (called Vulcan by the Romans) was the God of the Forge, the craftsman and metalsmith of the Olympians,

219

whose smithy used volcanic fires. Worshipers appealed to Hephaestus to control the destructive forces of the volcano. He was considered the god of subterranean fire, and his Greek name also meant "fire" in a general sense.

He was portrayed as a big robust muscular man with a sturdy neck and a hairy chest whose clubfoot caused his rolling gait. The least blessed and probably the least happy of the gods, he was deformed, unsure of his parentage, rejected, and unlucky in love. But he also was a creative genius, and the only god who worked.

GENEALOGY AND MYTHOLOGY

In the most widely known version of his origin, a resentful Hera gave birth to Hephaestus parthenogenetically, in a tit-for-tat, "I can do it, too" retaliation, after Zeus had birthed Athena from his head and was acknowledged as her sole parent. However, although Athena was perfectly formed, Hephaestus emerged with a clubfoot. This defect humiliated Hera; on seeing it, she rejected her newborn son and flung him down from Olympus. In another version, an angry Zeus—furious because young Hephaestus had sided with Hera in one of their domestic quarrels—hurled Hephaestus from Olympus, crippling him as he hit the ground on the island of Lemnos. The outcast son was rescued by two sea nymphs, Thetis and Eurynome, who nurtured him for nine years. In their company, Hephaestus learned to be a craftsman, making beautiful jewelry for his adoptive mothers.

HEPHAESTUS THE CRAFTSMAN

Hephaestus is the inventive artisan of Olympus. For example, Hephaestus created a beautiful golden throne and gave it to Hera, who sat on it with delight. But the chair was an exquisitely wrought trap, for once she sat on it she was tied by invisible bonds and then levitated. Hera found herself mortified and helpless, unable to move and suspended on this throne in mid air for all to see. According to one myth, Hephaestus made the golden throne to bind Hera because he had been kept in ignorance of his parentage. He devised this trap as a means of extracting the information from her. In other versions, Hephaestus demanded Aphrodite or Athena for a bride before he would release Hera.

No one except Hephaestus could free her, and he refused to leave the depths of the sea where he was living with his two surrogate mothers. His brother Ares the God of War came down to drag Hephaestus back by force, but Hephaestus drove him away by throwing fire at him. Then, Dionysus the God of Wine and Ecstasy succeeded by getting him drunk. Hephaestus had never seen or tasted wine before and, urged to imbibe, soon found himself, with Dionysus, returning to Olympus drunkenly draped over a donkey.

Moreover, in Hesiod's *Theogony* Hephaestus is credited with having created Pandora, the first human woman, as an instrument of Zeus's revenge. In this Greek patriarchal version, humanity was originally made up only of men, from whom Zeus withheld fire. Then Prometheus stole a spark of fire and gave it to them. This infuriated Zeus, who had Hephaestus create a beautiful woman, modeled after the immortal goddesses, to bring misery and confusion to men. She was clothed finely, taught shamelessness and deceitfulness, endowed with sex appeal, and given a jar or box to open, which released suffering, evil, and disease into the world.

Hephaestus also built palaces for the Olympians, created Zeus's thunderbolts and scepter, built the winged chariot for Apollo, god of the sun, to travel across the sky, made arrows for Apollo and Artemis, a sickle for Demeter, weapons for Athena, armor for Achilles, and a necklace for Harmonia to wear at her wedding. He also made himself golden maidservants, marvels of his ingenuity who looked like beautiful women, could speak, and skillfully do what he ordered.

THE BETRAYED AND REJECTED LOVER

Hephaestus was the cuckolded husband of Aphrodite, Goddess of Love and Beauty, known for her many liaisons with gods and mortal men. Suspecting that her lover visited Aphrodite when he left for work, Hephaestus laid a trap of invisible nets draped over the bedposts and suspended from the rafters. He thus caught Aphrodite in bed with Ares. When Hephaestus summoned the gods to witness this infidelity, however, rather than be outraged for him, they roared with laughter at the sight.

Hephaestus once fell in love with the virgin goddess of wisdom, Athena; filled with passion, he tried to make love to her. She pushed him aside as he sought to impregnate her, and his semen fell to the earth to fertilize Gaia (Mother Earth) instead. The child who resulted was Erichthonius, the founder of the royal house of Athens, who was raised by Athena.

HEPHAESTUS THE ARCHETYPE

As the god Hephaestus was thrown out of Olympus, so is this archetype an unvalued and rejected one in a culture that values the heroic, the intellect, lofty spiritual values, power, and the ability to adapt to what is expected and to anticipate the next move. In a sky god culture, such as patriarchies are, what is "earthy" is devalued or oppressed: Mother Earth, passionate feelings, instinct, bodies, women, and men who are like Hephaestus.

As an infant, Hephaestus was rejected by his father Zeus, who ruled from Mt. Olympus with his thunderbolts, and by his mother Hera, who was Queen of the Heavens. Olympus was inimical to Hephaestus as an adult as well. In myths, when he ventured there he was the ridiculed buffoon, the drunk, or the cuckolded husband. In his own element, however, at work at his forge, Hephaestus the master craftsman used the fire of his forge and tools to transform raw material into beautiful objects.

This life pattern is the archetype of creative work, work that emerges out of the metaphors of volcanic fire and forge, work that comes from being cast from Olympus and falling to earth, work that redeems and expresses the wounded creator. The Hephaestus archetype is at the heart of a deep instinct to work and create out of "the smithy of the soul"—the metaphor that James Joyce used in *Portrait of an Artist as a Young Man.*

When this archetype is present, beauty and expressiveness that otherwise would remain buried inside a man (or a woman) can be liberated through work that gives tangible form to these aspects of himself. This way of becoming conscious is the opposite of insight in which outside experience is translated into meaning inside. Instead, something inwardly present becomes literally visible, after which awareness of what it means can follow.

Michelangelo saw himself as freeing his magnificent statues from the blocks of marble in which they had been "imprisoned." I wonder if he ever stepped back to contemplate a newly finished work and realized that he had made visible something in himself. When the archetype of Hephaestus is a part of a man (or woman), what is deeply felt and inarticulate in his psyche is given form as he creates and makes something.

SUBTERRANEAN FIRE AND THE FORGE

The fire associated with Hephaestus is fire under the earth, that molten core that rises from the depths as the lava of volcanoes. Subterranean fire is a metaphor for passionate feelings: intense sexual and erotic fire contained within the body until it is expressed, or rage and anger that is held in and dampened down, or a passion for beauty that is stirring and felt in the body (or earth of the person).

These feelings, which lie beneath the surface in a deeply introverted person, may suddenly and unexpectedly erupt. When revealed to another person in a moment of intimate conversation, almost invariably that person is surprised: "I had no idea that you felt this strongly."

The Hephaestus archetype predisposes a man (or woman) to *not* talk about or address his feelings. He prefers to go to his personal version of the forge and work in solitude. There he either sublimates his feelings or expresses them through his work. For example, the architect who longs for a peaceful and orderly home may put these feelings into the house plans he creates (rather than express to his family how strongly he feels about the disorder): The abstract expressionist painter creates on his canvas the atmosphere he longs for, or he may express the anger and pain of feeling that his (unstated or, at best, understated) needs are so disregarded.

The forge is wherever he does the work of transforming or translating what he feels deeply into something outside himself. Many artists' studios or basement workshops are really places where men go to be alone with the Hephaestus archetype, a place to be Hephaestus in his underground forge.

Unconsummated love, an unobtainable woman, or unrequited love can fuel the fire of the transforming forge when

Hephaestus is an active archetype. The fire of the forge is the unexpressed passion that inspires the creative work.

THE CRIPPLED CRAFTSMAN

As noted, Hephaestus was the only physically marred Olympian, the only imperfect major deity. He was rejected from Olympus either because he was born with a clubfoot, which offended his mother Hera, or because he angered Zeus, who threw him off the mountain and crippled him.

Hephaestus's physical deformity cannot be separated from the emotional wounding caused by his parents. As a result of his crippling and rejection, Hephaestus became God of the Forge— the archetype of the instinct to work as a means to evolve and to heal emotional wounds. Hephaestus is the archetype of the crippled craftsman (or wounded artist, writer, healer, inventor, manufacturer) whose creativity is inseparable from his (or her) emotional wounds.

Hephaestus the craftsman is very much like the wounded healer whose motivation to heal comes from himself having been wounded, and whose wound heals as he heals others. Hephaestus had a deformed foot and he walked with a rolling gait that amused the other Olympians, who ridiculed him. He couldn't be beautiful, so he made beauty; his foot didn't work as it should, but what he made worked perfectly. Through his work, Hephaestus and men (and women) like him can see themselves reflected intact and functioning; through this reflection flows self-esteem and self-respect as well as the respect and esteem of others. Thus are healed the wounds that motivated the work.

As Jungian writer James Hillman comments, "Our parents are our wounders. Everyone carries a parental wound and has a wounded parent. The mythical image of the wounding or wounded parent becomes the psychological statement that *the parent is the wound*."[1] Literally, we hold our parents responsible; but the same statement, "the parent is the wound," can metaphorically mean that our wounds can also parent us. Our wounds can become the fathers and mothers of our destinies.

When the Hephaestus archetype is a major component of a man's personality, then he may follow the pattern of the crippled craftsman—his rejection and wounding can "parent" his creativity. But this can occur only if, like Hephaestus (who had two foster mothers), he is fortunate enough to have received nurturing and had the opportunity to find a medium and develop skills that let him express his creativity.

Being thrown off Mt. Olympus and coming "down to earth" is like Adam and Eve being thrown out of the Garden of Eden. In both myths, suffering and the need to work results from "the fall."

FAMILY PEACEKEEPER

Hephaestus was abused as a child when he was thrown off of Olympus by a parent and thus permanently crippled. In conflict-ridden families, one child often takes on the role of peacekeeper. Often it's a vulnerable child who is exceedingly sensitive to the first signs of impending conflict: in Olympus, this child was Hephaestus.

A description of events at the beginning of the *Iliad* is that of dinner table conflict between parents that threatens to escalate, except for the quick intervention of Hephaestus, the family peacekeeper. This experience is all too common in many households. "Don't make Daddy angry, because he'll take it out on all of us!" is the tack Hephaestus takes:

> The rulers have disagreed; the lord of heaven has promised Thetis to bestow honor upon her son and to humble those who affronted him. Thereupon strife begins in heaven; Hera reproaches her husband vigorously, and is sharply rebuked by him. With ill-repressed anger she sits silent, and rebellion moves through the ranks of the gods. Thereupon her son Hephaestus rises to make peace. He calls it intolerable for gods to wrangle for the sake of men and spoil the pleasure of the Olympian banquet; all would be well if only his mother would be reconciled and speak amiably to his father, so that he should not grow angry and make them all feel his superior might. And Hera smiles. Gladly she accepts the goblet which her son hands her.[2]

HEPHAESTUS AND APHRODITE: UNITING WORK WITH LOVE AND BEAUTY

In the *Odyssey*, Aphrodite the Goddess of Love and Beauty was married to Hephaestus, and had many affairs. Every affair resulted in children. Only with Hephaestus were there no offspring; instead their marriage was seen as a personification of the union of craft and beauty, which gives birth to beautiful things. In Homer's *Iliad*, Hephaestus was married to Charis or Grace; in Hesiod's *Theogony*, his wife was Aglaea, youngest of the Graces, a handmaiden (or lesser version) of Aphrodite. Each is a version of the wedding of beauty or grace to craftsmanship.

Hephaestus seeks union with Aphrodite on many levels: in personal relationships as well as in work, the Hephaestus archetype is drawn to beauty and love—that which he was denied, yet seeks to have. Deep and passionate feelings in a Hephaestus can be stirred up by a beautiful woman who is like Aphrodite in her intensity and sensuality. She can inspire his work and set his feelings afire.

In this process, male-female roles are reversed, for she psychologically "impregnates" him, fertilizing his creativity from which new work will grow in him.

HEPHAESTUS AND ATHENA: UNITING CREATIVE WORK AND INTELLIGENCE

As noted earlier, Hephaestus once pursued Athena, Goddess of Wisdom and Handicrafts, and overtook her. She resisted his unwanted embrace, and his semen fell on the ground and impregnated the earth, Gaia. In due time, Erichthonius, whose name meant "child of the earth" was born and was given to Athena to raise. Later he fathered the line of legendary kings of Athens.

Athena, who fostered the child whom Hephaestus fathered, represents the intellect that knows how to get something done. Her wisdom was that of the field general whose strategy is successful, or of the weaver who can envision a tapestry, design it, and line by line bring it into being. Contemporary Athenas may talk business plans instead of battle plans, and they score victories in the marketplace.

The union of Hephaestus with Athena within a man's psyche enables him to know how to bring his work into the world. The Hephaestus archetype's pursuit of Athena may draw a man to mate with a woman who has these qualities. The task of fostering her creative husband's work, or finding a way for him to make money at it (if he doesn't develop this side of himself), by default then falls on her. Athena-type fostering of Hephaestian creativity is also done by same-sex partners.

CULTIVATING HEPHAESTUS

The only way to cultivate this archetype is to take the time to do it. Withdraw from the company of others and let yourself be absorbed in making something with your hands or doing something that is manual, something that you may intuitively know, shifts, expresses, transforms something in you that has been pent up, in the process of the doing.

Developing Hephaestian introversion is something that is valuable to teach children who are extraverted and who potentially depend on people to do things with them all the time. Parents can cultivate Hephaestus in children by stressing the importance of quiet periods, of learning how to entertain themselves, (without television, which is a passive pastime). Building block toys and clay are beginnings: there are any number of possibilities where imagination and handwork come together. Allowing children the privilege of joining them in a parallel quiet creative activity, while the parent is being an Hephaestus at work at the forge, conveys the value of this kind of time to the child. It's important to stress the value of being absorbed in creative time. Adults who want to develop this aspect of Hephaestus need to go about encouraging themselves in the same way as they would their child.

When Jung was rejected by Freud for differing with him, thrown off the psychoanalytic summit where he once had held a crown prince position among Freud's followers, he went through his darkest period. He was isolated and suffered through a period of inner uncertainty and constant inner pressure—a Hephaestian figure of ridicule and rejection. Yet he found a way to his own creative sources as Hephaestus would do.

Jung wrote,

The first thing that came to the surface was a childhood memory from perhaps my tenth or eleventh year. At that time I had had a spell of playing passionately with building blocks. I distinctly recalled how I had built little houses and castles, using bottles to form the sides of gates and vaults. Somewhat later I had used ordinary stones, with mud for mortar. These structures had fascinated me for a long time. To my astonishment, this memory was accompanied by a good deal of emotion. "Aha," I said to myself, "there is still life in these things. The small boy is still around, and possesses a creative life which I lack. But how can I make my way to it?" For as a grown man it seemed impossible to me that I should be able to bridge the distance from the present back to my eleventh year. Yet if I wanted to establish contact with that period, I had no choice but to return to it and take up once more that child's life with his childish games. This moment was a turning point in my fate, but I gave in only after endless resistances and with a sense of resignation. For it was a painfully humiliating experiene to realize that there was nothing to be done except play childish games.

Nevertheless, I began accumulating suitable stones, gathering them partly from the lake shore and partly from the water. And I started building: cottages, a castle, a whole village. . . .

"I went on with my building game after the noon meal every day. . . .[I] in the course of this activity my thoughts clarified, and I was able to grasp the fantasies whose presence in myself I dimly felt.

Naturally, I thought about the significance of what I was doing, and asked myself, "Now, really, what are you about? You are building a small town, and doing it as if it were a rite!" I had no answer to my question, only the inner certainty that I was on the way to discovering my own myth. For the building game was only a beginning. It released a stream of fantasies which I later carefully wrote down.

This sort of thing has been consistent with me, and at any time in my later life when I came up against a blank wall, I painted a picture or hewed stone. Each such experience proved to be a *rite d'entrée* for the ideas and works that followed hard upon it.[3]

HEPHAESTUS THE MAN

A Hephaestus man is an intense, introverted person. It's difficult for others to know what is going on in his depths or for him to express his feelings directly. He can become an emotional cripple, a smoldering volcano, or a highly creative productive man.

EARLY YEARS

A Hephaestus infant may not be easy to mother, because he has intense energy and sensitivity to what is physically going on inside of him. He has a coiled-spring quietness that may erupt suddenly into thrashing with pain and outrage, even if it's only a gas bubble or colic. He's usually not a placid, cuddly infant entranced by what is going on around him and easily diverted. Sometimes his little body even feels as if it's more dense than another child who has a lighter personality. He has a mind of his own, and he becomes absorbed in what engages him, not in what someone else wants him to pay attention to.

If early life is difficult, and he—like the god Hephaestus— is rejected by his mother for not living up to her expectations of what a baby should be, or if he has the misfortune to be born into an abusive household, then these personality traits intensify. He isn't a baby with a naturally sunny personality who can win people over. Thus if he is not accepted and loved as he is, he can become a withdrawn, brooding child.

In school, he may be a loner, a child who observes from the periphery, the one who doesn't fit in and never seems to be in the center of activities. More interested in things and machines than he is in people, he needs others to relate to him through what he is making or doing, often in solitary play. The teacher or mother who draws him out usually does so by being attuned to what has engaged his interest, often through being attentive when he shows her what he has made and explains how it works or how he made it.

He can win self-esteem if he is appreciated for his individuality, loved just for being himself and actively encouraged to follow his own interests (rather than forced to be the one who is out of step in the crowd). This support allows him to live unencumbered and to develop his creative abilities later in life.

HIS PARENTS

The mythological Hephaestus was a rejected son, and rejection can be the fate of an Hephaestus boy as well. If his mother is like Hera in wanting a baby to enhance her own esteem—as an accomplishment, or a competitive act, a "look what I can do" feat—and if she births a baby who doesn't live up to her expectations (which is almost always the case for this type of nonmaternal, narcissistic woman), she will reject him for not being perfect.

If life imitates myth in that the newborn is in some way deformed, then total rejection is a possibility. For a mother who needs the child as a means of self-enhancement, a defective child deals her ego a severe blow and becomes a source of humiliation. She may overreact to whatever is deformed, and resent and reject him totally, thus creating an emotional cripple. If institutionalization is possible, she will immediately rid herself of him, and then forget him there.

His father's rejection and abuse also may cause crippling (as in the alternate myth). Since a Hephaestus boy doesn't naturally cue into what other people want of him, isn't diplomatic, and has intense feelings, he may trigger rage in an authoritarian father (especially one who is also an alcoholic). Such a father may beat him, perhaps even for siding with his mother, which was what provoked Zeus. This abuse can result in permanent physical damage as well as emotional scars.

Even in ordinary families, a Hephaestus son may be the least favored child, the one who differs by being "too serious," "too intense and touchy," "too withdrawn," or "too unsociable." He is often criticized for his lack of success and ambition, and compared unfavorably with others. A Hephaestus boy suffers twice over from this rejection and slights, first from the negative experience and then from taking it in and brooding about it.

In an ideal situation for growth, however, a Hephaestus boy has parents who are pleased with the way his hands and mind works. They value him and encourage him to grow as he is naturally bent, and help him become more at ease socially while validating his introverted nature.

ADOLESCENCE AND EARLY ADULTHOOD

If the young man Hephaestus has been fortunate enough to discover a means to be creative and has embarked on developing his skills and his artist's eye, then adolescence and young adulthood mark the beginning of coming into his own through creative work. He may achieve this initial success through having his talent nurtured by craftspeople who recognize his talents and provide the tools and the skills for him to develop. He may enter a different world: a big city arts and crafts school, for example, where he has a niche for once in a school situation, and through his work has a means of expressing himself and of becoming friends with others.

As a child, introspective Hephaestus may have had a strong feeling that he didn't belong in his own family. Now as a young man, he may leave home to seek his "true" parentage: people more like himself, who work with their hands on the land, artisans or artists. If he has been rejected and abused, he may be a brooding, angry and depressed teen, who fantasizes revenge. Hephaestus doesn't strike back with his fists; instead, he devises elaborate plans to humiliate his persecutors. Or he may become a graffiti artist on the sides of subways and buildings. As a loner, he doesn't usually become a gang member.

If the youthful Hephaestus goes through a growth spurt, and if he is unhappy and angry, he may begin to intimidate people (especially if he towers over them), though usually not intentionally. Since he bottles up his intense feelings, he can be sullen and full of smoldering rage. People who sense this rage may be wary of him, but it's more characteristic of him to hold his anger in or turn it against himself than to lash out at someone else.

What initially saves most rejected Hephaestus young men from serious depressions, whatever degree of alienation and rage they may harbor; is hard, physical work. They may discover this relief by working on a car or finding an absorbing craft. Thereafter, rewarding work helps them grow—work that uses their creativity and psychological energy—including their anger.

WORK

Hephaestus was the only god who worked. At his forge that is the equivalent of a studio, a workshop, and a testing laboratory, he worked prodigiously, to make beautiful and functional objects, weapons and armor, vehicles, and lifelike golden maidservants, and even Pandora.

No man is so absorbed and dedicated to work as an Hephaestian man who has found his life work. In the years I spent in medical centers training to become a doctor, I met many men whose passion for work and particular skills made them like Hephaestus. Some were surgeons held in awe by their residents for their surgical abilities and research, as well as for their stamina, which exhausted interns and residents who were twenty or more years younger.

As medical students, we wondered how these men led even a semblance of ordinary mortal life. One neurosurgeon routinely took on six-hour operations, and once, we were told, did an operation that took twenty hours, wearing out whole shifts of assistants. Some heart surgeons, especially in the early years of perfecting procedures that are now fairly commonplace, seemed to live at the hospital. When not operating or making rounds on patients, they were in animal surgery trying new techniques, or at postmortems learning what had happened when a patient died. They had a passionate intensity for the work that could easily be inferred but otherwise was not expressed.

Like the god who made Pandora and the lifelike golden maidservants, the surgeon works on making a human body function. He (or she) is a skilled craftsman, a highly developed artisan: to assist at an operation of an Hephaestian surgeon is to watch an artist. If such a man resembles Hephaestus in his personality, he is also an inwardly intense man, with few social or political skills: he receives recognition solely for his work. (Apollo is the other medical center god, who dwells in the articulate physician who has star-quality gifts of diagnosis and theory, which he can communicate well. Apollo is the enabling archetype that facilitates rising within the medical hierarchical system, without which Hephaestian skill and passion may not have the opportunity to be expressed fully in work.)

A more typical setting for Hephaestus is in a creative field, where many men think of themselves as "outsiders," have an intense passion for work, and do work that provides a means of expressing their intense feelings. A painter, an architect, and a metal sculptor come to mind as exemplars of the Hephaestian men I have worked with as a psychiatrist. All were in my office due to their distress and a drive to be more conscious of what they so strongly felt but could not articulate. Like Hephaestus surgeons, they were intensely engaged in their work, working schedules equally heroic—but unheralded as such. How to do what they thought possible engaged them also, and as with the surgeon who spent hours in the animal laboratory, these men spent hours constructing and experimenting, doing "hands on" work that evolved from images.

For a Hephaestus man, work is more than a job, or a source of status, or a livelihood. It is a means to fulfill the instinct that presses him to go beyond whatever was the last creative solution to a new effort that totally absorbs him. Work gives his life depth and meaning; what he knows about the god within himself he experiences in moments of creativity.

The Hephaestus man who knows he is doing his life work, work that continues to challenge him and give him pleasure each time he finishes a significant piece of it, is doing work he loves: This work often feels to him intimately related to his own evolution, an expression of his psyche made tangible. If in addition, it provides the means to live well and receive recognition, then he is fortunate indeed.

A significant proportion of Hephaestus men are not so fortunate. To fulfill a deeply held work instinct, a man must first discover work he loves, have the opportunity to develop the skills needed, and then have the opportunity to do it. Also, he works best as a loner, motivated neither by profit nor influenced by competition. The corporate world is foreign and meaningless to him. He cannot sell himself or his products. When he is successful, that is because his work speaks for itself and for him, and because someone else, or some other archetype in him, has a business sense. Given all these prerequisites that need to be met to find fulfilling work, no wonder lack of significant work demoralizes Hephaestian men, who suffer deeply from job-related depression or unemployment.

RELATIONSHIPS WITH WOMEN

Women are enormously important to a Hephaestus man: they may have the power to "make or break" him. He may need a woman to look after his personal well-being, be the source of his creative inspiration, mentor his social skills, and represent his work to others. The significant people with power in his life often have been women: mother, teachers, principals, gallery owners, bosses. Given his genuine admiration for women with intelligence, assertiveness, or beauty, he is drawn to women with these qualities and then may give them power over him.

If a woman can perceive his depth and sensitivity, and in turn evoke his imagination, she can become a major event in his life. However long or short in duration, the relationship will live for years (perhaps forever) in his inner world. For most Hephaestus men, significant relationships are few and far between.

His intensity and introverted nature make him ill at ease. His behavior may even be inappropriate, and he's no good at initiating cocktail party sociability. The dating game is one he avoids.

The Hephaestus man (or the Hephaestus part of the person) is capable of doing inspired work that comes out of the depth of his inner life, through which he draws images and emotions from the collective unconsious of humanity. The intensity of his feelings, especially for a woman he cannot have an everyday relationship with, and thus cannot ever make her into an ordinary woman, may move him into creative work from the depths of his soul. Such seemed to be the case when the noted painter Andrew Wyeth, a man of studied reclusiveness revealed in 1986 what *Time* magazine described as his "stunning secret"[4]: 246 works, all of the same woman, whom he identified only as Helga, done over fifteen years. She clearly inspired his best as well as most prolific work.

RELATIONSHIPS WITH MEN

A Hephaestus man is not a fraternity brother sort of person: he is repelled by the superficial extraverted camaraderie, and fraternity men (who later become members of corporations and professional organizations) find him too unlike themselves. If he also has other archetypes, such as Apollo or Hermes that make it possible for him to join, his Hephaestus nature makes it impossible for him to ever feel that he belongs.

Relationships with men who are with one another for business reasons do not work for him. The same difficulty he has with superficial meetings at cocktail parties carries over here. Thus he feels—or is—the outsider. Usually he has been rejected by the "old boy network," so the outsider role is one often put on him as well as chosen.

Often he has specific difficulties with men in authority. The man may be his father, a teacher, or a supervisor. Whoever tries to shape him up—in the way that U.S. Marines "make men" out of recruits—usually fails at it, and then in anger may throw him out. Hephaestus is not motivated by outer demands to conform and live up to other people's standards, partly because he is so inner directed, and partly because the judgment and anger directed at him to make him shape up evokes intense anger in him, which he then bottles up. This anger makes it even more difficult for him to perform whatever is demanded of him. Authoritarian personalities overreact to anything that seems insubordinate or disrespectful, making matters even worse.

Ares, God of War, once tried unsuccessfully to drag Hephaestus up to Olympus by force. Hephaestus threw burning brands at him and drove him away. Like the god, the Hephaestus man resists force, which when directed at him makes him "burn" with hostility. Even the god known for his uncontrolled power and battle frenzy could not budge Hephaestus to do something he did not want to do, nor does this approach usually work with a Hephaestus man, even a young one.

In contrast, Dionysus plied him with wine and persuaded Hephaestus to accompany him on a mule. Dionysus did not resort to power, softened Hephaestus's stubborn position, and succeeded where Ares failed. He related to him in his own territory, altering his hard position with alcohol, which made Hephaestus more pliable rather than bellicose.

Life resembles myth in the Hephaestus-Dionysus friendship department. Often only another intense outsider who makes an effort to know a Hephaestus man, succeeds. Drinking together can be a male-bonding ritual: with Hephaestus, it does not work as a group initiation, but it can work with a another man who appreciates beauty and knows pain, and is not afraid to show his feelings, as a Dionysus man can do. The more extraverted and expressive Dionysus can articulate, emote, or act out what lies hidden inarticulately in Hephaestus. This complementarity provides a common basis for the few deep and lasting friendships that an Hephaestus man may have.

SEXUALITY

Intensity and privacy characterize all aspects of the Hephaestus man's life, especially his sexuality. He is monogamous and faithful, and he expects his partner to reciprocate. Too often he suffers the same fate as the god, discovering that the woman in his life has betrayed him. He contributes to her infidelity by neglecting her, even though he may all the while keep her image before him in his inner world. A typical Hephaestus becomes overinvolved in his work, doesn't spend much time with her, is not communicative, and may also go through long periods without sex.

He can sublimate sexual fire into work and have long periods of celibacy even in a relationship. His work becomes like a mistress who claims his time and sexuality.

When a Hephaestus man makes love, more may be going on for him as an inner experience than he feels sensually in the act itself. He may well not share the experience with his partner as a communication or a communion between them. Yet his partner is the source of the inner experience, and he may truly treasure her.

He often does not see in her true context the Aphrodite woman who is drawn to his intensity and fascinated by his creativity, as an attractive woman with many relationships. When he finds that she has other lovers, he often feels grossly betrayed by her, although he made a typically introverted assumption. Sometimes, too, such a woman may simply seduce and then betray him.

A homosexual Dionysus may similarly seduce and betray a homosexual Hephaestus, and alcohol can play a part in the situation. Hephaestus, however, is not well represented in the gay social culture: he is turned off by the superficial bonding and group identification that make fraternities and corporate life unattractive to him. And in turn he is rejected by gay groups for not fitting in.

MARRIAGE

For the Hephaestus man, marriage is both exceptionally important and problematical: his well-being in the outer world as well as in his intimate world may depend on whom he marries and how the marriage fares. Otherwise he may be emotionally isolated. Traditionally (and stereotypically) for most men, but especially for the introverted Hephaestus, relationships are something his wife takes care of. She invites friends in, makes holiday and vacation plans, keeps in touch with relatives, and remembers important dates.

The Hephaestus man's wife may also be crucial for establishing and maintaining his work in the world. The artist or craftsman Hephaestus who creates his work in solitude usually needs someone to be his agent. Often his wife either sells his work, or finds the agent, gallery, or outlet who will do it.

In his mythology, Hephaestus married Aphrodite and was cuckolded by her. He also unsuccessfully attempted to impregnate Athena, who resisted him, and he created Pandora (as well as the golden maid servants). These three mythical relationships reflect three types of Hephaestus marriages.

Hephaestus and Aphrodite

Women who resemble the goddess of love are drawn to intensity in relationships, which Hephaestus can provide. If he creates beautiful objects or art, her esthetic sensuality is attracted to his work as well. Besides, he sees her as his personal Aphrodite and projects this image on her; she feels like a goddess in his presence.

Both of them have a here-and-now intensity; he can withdraw and take the relationship with him as an inner experience, which she usually cannot do. Typically, a Hephaestus man will "go away" in this fashion, and focus that intensity on his work, expecting her to stay monogamous meanwhile. Unless she either channels her energy into creative work, or has the archetype of Hera the wife as a major aspect of her psyche, however, she may have an affair while he is working.

Hephaestus and Athena

Of all the Olympian deities, Athena, Goddess of Wisdom and Handicrafts, had the clearest mind. She could design a plan to besiege a city or design a tapestry, with equal ease. Athena women assess situations very well, favoring men who are successful, or will succeed with their help. Jealousy is not a problem for them. Hephaestus men admire and appreciate and even find mysterious how Athena women manage to take care of the finances and alliances that they need to succeed.

Andrew and Betsy Wyeth seem to have this kind of union. Betsy is Andrew's business manager. When Wyeth's secret and apparent obsession in painting Helga was revealed, Betsy's response was typically that of a secure Athena: "He's a very secret person. He doesn't pry into my life and I don't pry in his. And it's worth it. Look at the paintings. Oh God! The paintings are remarkable! And how many there were."[5]

She sold the collection for over $10 million, according to reports.

Hephaestus and Pandora

Hephaestus was the ultimate creator when, at Zeus's behest, he made Pandora, the first mortal woman. She was not the only woman Hephaestus created. Homer noted that Hephaestus had solved the household help problem by creating golden maidservants who looked like real women and could not only speak and use their limbs but were endowed with intelligence and trained in handwork.

Similarly, when an older, intimidating Hephaestus marries a younger woman resembling the maiden goddess Persephone, who is receptive and compliant, he may mold her into a wife who behaves like a golden maidservant.

Or she may be less intentionally shaped. Her lack of definition (typical of a Persephone) and her appearance provide the "screen" on which his "projected" image falls. Her receptivity to be what he wants her to be is both conscious (she wants to please him, and so will heed his preferences) and unconscious (with her psychic receptivity, she turns the aspect of herself toward him that is most closely attuned to his image of her).

She may also be an "invention" of his own mind and heart, which will lead to the unleashing of all kinds of woe on him. Introverted as he is, often with very little practice at assessing women, he may fall in love with the image he has of her, as well as assuming that she feels as strongly for him as he does for her. Given his intensity and his monogamy, which may be coupled with a yearning for intimacy and acceptance he has never had, his mistaken assumption that she was identical to his image of her results in personal disaster. She may turn into a Pandora for him, endowed with the features with which Pandora was designed: feminine skills, sex appeal, and shamelessness, cunning words, lies, and deceitfulness.

CHILDREN

Hephaestus the God had no children, and many Hephaestus men would rather not have them either, especially if their own childhoods were unhappy. The Hephaestus man's response to his own child is not easy to predict. Whether he bonds to the child as an infant is decisive. (Bonding will be more likely if he is present in the delivery room and is involved from the moment of birth.) If he does bond, his attachment is deep, almost visceral. He'll like having the child around even if he doesn't do much playing or talking.

Children may feel him to be a distant, brooding man who is irritable when they interrupt him, angry at the noise they make, and unaware that his expectations are inappropriate for their age. One such daughter relates that when she was only six years old, her father demanded that she make him some coffee and was furious when she didn't know how.

There are some predictable problems between Hephaestus fathers and their children, made worse by his chronic anger and depression and his need to be in control. For example, his communication is rarely direct and explicit. The children often learn to tiptoe around, intuit, and infer what his reactions will be.

Often his children will balk at his authority because his reasons for what he does are subjective and he doesn't communicate well. Also, he often dislikes change, and growing children and adolescents change all the time. Friction results.

Angry, controlling Hephaestus fathers with malleable daughters can mold them into "golden maidservants," who do what they are told. They will stay under his thumb. He stifles their autonomy and requires obedience, constricting them and making later victimization or domination by another man more likely. Sons more often rebel directly against an angry, controlling Hephaestus father; unpliable daughters also often act out in rebellion, usually outside his domain.

Both sons and daughters miss being mentored by their Hephaestus father, who is too individualistic and introverted to help children make their way forward in the world. Hephaestus himself is usually out of step, so that the "old boys' network" rarely serves as a resource for his children, and he is not a role model of how to succeed.

Although many children have difficulties with their Hephaestus fathers, a very special positive relationship is also possible if the father is not an angry man and if he bonded with his children. Like the artisan father whose studio behind the house is a warm sanctuary for his children to develop their own creativity and just be with him, children in positive relationships spend time with their Hephaestus fathers. Their creativity, confidence, and self-esteem grow out of the experience of being with him, making things with him, letting him show them how something is done, and then creating something of their own.

MIDDLE YEARS

The first half of life has usually been difficult because he doesn't conform to what society expects men to be like: he is not a competitive, logical, extraverted man who enjoys the challenge of getting ahead in the world. Although most men do what is expected in establishing a career and a family in the first half of life and leave the inner journey to the second half of life, the Hephaestus man was oriented toward the inner world to begin with, and has needed to express his inarticulate and intense feelings.

If, in spite of being out of step, he was able to establish a career and a family, then the second half of life is usually happier for him than the first half of life. For the first time, compared to his male age peers, an Hephaestus man may approach this new phase of life with an advantage. He has had to struggle to be himself and meet the outer tasks, and has succeeded in doing both. (The more extraverted man adapts without much struggle to doing what is expected in the first half of life. His individuality suffers and makes demands that draw him into conflict and depression in the second half of life.)

However, the angry, chronically depressed Hephaestus man who either antagonizes or intimidates people, or withdraws from them may arrive at the middle of life with neither intimacy nor rewarding work. The pattern may be too set to change, except to worsen. If he takes stock and compares himself to other men, he may enter the throes of a midlife crisis where it is possible to make a major shift. (See later sections on psychological difficulties and on ways to grow).

LATER YEARS

In the later years of life, when "how his life story turned out" is clear, Hephaestus men may end up content and creatively at work at their chosen "forge," craftsmen whose skills have matured and been honed by life. Yet Hephaestus men are also found overrepresented among socially isolated derelicts.

PSYCHOLOGICAL DIFFICULTIES

Most Hephaestus men have had to cope with feeling unacceptable, of failing to fit the stereotype (or expectation) of what he should be like, first as a boy and then as a man. If he has a troubled or abusive home life and is a rejected boy, that experience will usually make him even more of a loner than he might be anyway. With his locked-in, introverted attitude, he usually cannot compensate for lack of love or approval at home by being popular or successful at school (unless other archetypes are also present).

As a man, he will continue to find difficulty fitting in and adapting. Through his work, he may find he is a productive, valued, and creative person. But he lacks political, social, and communicative skills, so this avenue does not easily open up to him, either. Thus psychological problems can be anticipated.

EMOTIONAL CRIPPLING: THE CONSEQUENCE OF REJECTION

Hephaestus was rejected at birth by his unmaternal mother Hera when she saw that he was imperfect. Ashamed at his appearance, she threw him away, a fate literally shared by those newborn babies who are found in trash bins, whose mothers treat them like shameful mistakes to be discarded. This fate is also shared metaphorically by a great many other babies as well, who do not live up to expectations and are rejected emotionally.

Babies who are not held and touched fail to grow, and (as was discovered in wartime England) without human touch (which equals love), a baby will die, even with regular feeding and clean surroundings. Many underweight, apathetic "failure to thrive" babies were brought into the clinic and emergency room of the two county hospitals I trained at; their major problem seemed to be maternal rejection and neglect.

Even if a rejected baby survives physically, the psychological damage still causes emotional crippling. Such a child lacks a basic trust that the world is a good place, and is anxious and mistrustful. He begins life as a loner because he had no one with whom to bond.

In another version of the rejection, Hephaestus was flung from Mt. Olympus and injured by an irate Zeus when he took Hera's side and came between Hera and Zeus. This time it was the child's behavior that was unacceptable and cause of paternal rejection. In this version, Hephaestus became a cripple as a result of child abuse. Again, life literally imitates this myth often enough, when a woman with a small son lives with a man who is not the child's father, who resents the child's presence either as competition or as an irritation, and abuses the boy. Left unprotected by his mother, and abused by a father figure, such a little boy may survive the physical abuse but he will be emotionally crippled, with fear and anger smoldering deep within him.

A Hephaestus boy who becomes emotionally crippled reacts to a range of experience with his parents, from the extremes of maternal abandonment or paternal abuse to the more subtle, psychological effects of maternal distance and paternal judgment. The degree to which he is affected may not be directly related to the degree of difficulty faced, but rather related to his subjective experience. He may even observe much later that objectively, "it was not so bad," but his sensitivity to rejection, coupled with his innate introversion, produced strong reactions and painful feelings. Such a boy may be easily "woundable," which compounds the difficulties.

His traits intensify the effects of painful experiences. A more extraverted or impulsive child who is abused may become a person who strikes out or bullies others, or he may tell someone and draw attention to his plight. Instead of doing either, Hephaestus retreats and does not reveal how hurt, angry, and afraid he is; he doesn't talk to anyone about it and can become emotionally crippled, constricted in expression, and alienated from others. As a man, he may repeat his childhood experiences, rejected by women from whom he seeks affection and negatively judged by men in power.

DISTORTION OF REALITY: PROBLEMS WITH INTROVERTED EMOTION

Harboring hidden feelings and being easy to wound makes him likely to distort of "what really happened" a problem both for Hephaestian men and for others around him. The emotional effect on him, rather than the intent of the other person or the facts of the situation, determines his perspective.

Small hurts that might even go unnoticed by another man can wound him. And when he doesn't mention it, or can't accept another person's version, whatever the incident was for him becomes "what happened." If months or even years later, he finally speaks of it, the other person may not even remember the incident, and be touched, sad, appalled, or angry at him for feeling the way he does.

Positive feelings may also be evoked by small gestures, a tenderness that moves him and warms him for years. And these gestures also may or may not have been as significant an expression from the other person.

With introverted feeling, the inner reaction to the outer event is what is retained. The person's memory is not of facts but of events colored by emotions. Everybody does this to some extent, of course, but Hephaestus much more so.

LACK OF SUCCESS IN THE WORLD

Hephaestus was thrown down from Olympus, which is a symbolic pinnacle of power. And when he visited Olympus, he clearly did not belong among the rich and beautiful people at the top. So too with Hephaestus men. The image of Hephaestus at his forge brings to mind the steelworker, glassblower, or smith at the furnace: the blue-collar aristocrat who no longer has much prestige in a world dominated by moneymakers. Little dignity is accorded men who work with their hands rather than their minds, whether skilled, semiskilled, or manual laborers. The Olympian heights are populated by men who do not make anything tangible themselves: they are the dealmakers and investors.

Rage smolders in many Hephaestus men who realize in their teens that they will never "be anybody." A man may feel the same rage when he realizes that a woman will not look at him as a potential mate because he is working class, or when he cannot give his children something they need that is beyond his means. If he never finds gratifying work and if (true to his Hephaestian nature) his mode of dealing with his rage is to contain it, he becomes depressed and bitter. In this he is unlike Ares and Poseidon, who under similar circumstances explode in rage at others.

ACTING THE BUFFOON: PROBLEMS OF LOW SELF-ESTEEM AND INADEQUACY

Outside his workshop, Hephaestus the God became the buffoon. The gods of Olympus burst out laughing when they saw Hephaestus with his awkward gait bustling up and down the halls of the palace, serving them nectar from a large bowl. And they laughed at the sight rather than take offense for him, when he caught his wife Aphrodite with Ares in his invisible net, and invited them to witness the scene.

In his psychological interpretation of Greek mythology and the Greek family, Philip Slater, author of *The Glory of Hera,* saw in his Hephaestus role as clown his "resignation from manhood":

> Hephaestus conveys the interpersonal message: 'You have nothing to fear from me, nor is there anything about me which should arouse your envy or resentment. I am merely a poor lame clown, ready to serve you, and make you laugh with jokes at my own expense."[6]

The Hephaestus man who follows this pattern usually inadvertently becomes the clown. With his "out of step," introverted personality, he is continually doing something inappropriate, which evokes laughter or ridicule. He is the kid whose school garb leads others to make derogatory humorous comments, or who doesn't know what to say to the most popular girl in the class, and says something quotable and laughable. He is the boy who overreacts when teased, and then gets unmercifully pummeled. Perhaps he learns that his humiliation is always worse if he objects, and discovers that if he acts the buffoon he defuses the situation. In the Deep South when black men were called "niggers" and could be lynched, a black man might save himself from abuse by becoming the shuffling, self-effacing "Festus."

(Hephaestus is pronounced he fes' tus.) The Hephaestus man who does so is often in a similar psychological position as a consequence of feeling like a rejected loner, with no one to back him up.

But this way of coping is usually self-destructive. Each incident occurs at the expense of self-respect and the respect of others. It often invites someone who enjoys humiliating others to pick on him.

A much more subtle, related (to the clown) persona or "public face" that some Hephaestus men put on, is that of affability: the "always Mr. Niceguy," who under this mask harbors anger or depression because he was rejected in some significant way by his parents. A common pattern parallels Hephaestus's relationship with Zeus and Hera: he is an "unfathered son" of an absent or distant father, who was also "unmothered" by a self-centered, narcissistic mother.

RAGE TURNED INWARD: PROBLEMS WITH DEPRESSION

Depression can be a severe and chronic problem for Hephaestian men, whose introverted nature makes bottling up hurt and rage more usual than expressing these feelings outwardly. Rejection, lack of acceptance, lack of success—the susceptibilities of this pattern—are obvious sources of anger as well as grief: he has reasons to rage but he does not. When he holds these feelings in and turns inward himself, depression results.

ADDICTIONS

Hephaestus men may use alcohol to numb their feelings and feel less intense. Alcohol may also make it easier for them to be affable with others, as a means to become more mellow. Many working-class men whose work is physically demanding, and whose sensitive feelings stay inarticulate and buried both by nature and by culture, deliberately get drunk when they're trying to get over something painful. Drinking too much, followed by a hangover serves as an acceptable way to be numb and to suffer: a week out to get over something in this way is also viewed as manly.

End-of-the-day, after-work drinking or drinking when there is no work, done to numb emotional pain that is not shared or expressed, serves as an emotional anesthetic. Used thus as a drug, alcohol can become a problem in itself. Television is used in a similar way by men who numb their feelings and withdraw from intimacy by spending hours in front of the set.

PAYING A HIGH PRICE FOR PEACE

When an abused, emotionally traumatized child becomes family peacemaker—a role that may be lifelong—he usually does something to defuse the situation as soon as he senses that tension is rising in order to avert an angry outburst from the feared parent. Often the child or man is not even consciously aware of the perception, nor consciously choosing to do whatever it is he does next. The explosiveness of the situation simply grows, and he becomes increasingly anxious until he is compelled to do something appeasing.

To appease a feared parent, a traumatized Hephaestus child may sacrifice those parts of himself that put him in danger. He commonly represses what he feels, driving his own anger and hostility deeper inward. The cost he pays to be conciliatory and appeasing is very high: he loses touch with what he really feels and cannot tolerate anger in others either. As an adult, the cost is his own authenticity and a lack of tolerance for expression of feelings by others, which takes its toll on any significant relationship.

DIFFICULTIES FOR OTHERS

Communicating with the Hephaestus man in a woman's life can be problematic if she wants or needs him to talk about what he is feeling or what he plans to do about something. He fits the stereotype of the strong, silent man. Since he feels intensely about matters, the air can get very heavy around him, and yet nothing is forthcoming when she asks him to talk about it.

And when she tells him about herself, she never knows exactly how he'll take it. Years later she may find he was very disturbed or moved about a conversation, to which he seemed to have no response at the time.

Attempts to change him and make him more communicative may or may not work—usually not. A woman who is married to a Hephaestus man must often decide if she can let go of wanting communication from him.

ABUSIVE RELATIONSHIPS

The strong, silent, angry man who feels impotent, drinks too much, and erupts in rage at those closest to him is the father so many adult children of alcoholics had. Although Hephaestus usually bottles up his rage, when he hits the bottle the lid on that rage may come loose. Their daughters often have glimpsed the sensitivity and the pain in their fathers, or known of skills that never were either developed or rewarded. They grow up with a soft spot in their hearts for such men, a hope of making life meaningful for such a man, and a tolerance for abuse. These women are susceptible to being in abusive relationships, as their mothers before them were.

ROLE REVERSALS

If the Hephaestus man has difficulty making money because he is an unpaid artisan, or because those hiring do not need his skills or appreciate his personality, then a woman who loves him may have to be the major breadwinner. Roles also may become reversed when tasks arise in which one of them has to negotiate for something. If she has the more logical mind and more social skills, she often represents them both in the world.

In role reversals, she may take pleasure in her own competence and accept the situation, or she may resent it and him. He, in turn, may be appreciative or resentful. Given the power of "what ought to be," a relationship that goes against tradition is usually stressful for both.

WAYS TO GROW

If the Hephaestus man is rejected or devalued for being "out of step," and as a result feels that there is something fundamentally wrong with him, growth begins when he gets the idea that there was something wrong with how he was treated. Next comes discovering and valuing "who" he is, through what he does when he is being authentically himself, and growing beyond the Hephaestus archetype to develop other aspects of himself. These last two tasks are what every Hephaestus man (or woman) needs to do.

"KNOW THYSELF"

A Hephaestus man needs to take Apollo's dictum—"Know Thyself"—to heart. He can begin by seeing how much like Hephaestus he is, and what that has meant. He must see how he fit or didn't fit into others' expectations, how he felt he was a socially inept buffoon when he tried to act like a verbal, social, and recreational-minded "Olympian," and must remember, in contrast, his absorption and mastery of something he created, usually with his hands. Objective knowledge about the archetype and subjective knowledge about himself can help him to discover what gives him a sense of competence and meaning.

If there are traumatic or abusive situations in his life, then psychotherapy may be essential, because his nature is to keep everything to himself, to withdraw from people, and be depressed, his rage bottled within him. Besides a need for catharsis, he needs the empathy and perspective of another person. In the process, he also develops his ability to communicate and be more verbally expressive.

KNOW OTHERS

Even a very introverted Hephaestus usually has some significant people in his life. Unlike the comfortably reclusive Hades, Hephaestus feels deeply and reacts strongly to people who affect him emotionally. Thus he needs to learn how to be in relationships in a less purely subjective way. He especially needs to know that "This is what I feel" is not necessarily the same as "This is what really happened." The strength and intensity of his subjective reactions distort the reality of what the other person actually did or said to him. Only through dialogue, which he often avoids, can misunderstandings and misperceptions be cleared up. Dialogue provides the means through which to appreciate differences between people who are important to each other. This objectivity is especially important for Hephaestus, who otherwise may misrepresent his own subjective picture as reality. A more extraverted person usually starts out with more information to go on, so the situational context is ordinarily part of his or her picture. The subjectively feeling introvert, however, usually needs to get the picture from the other person, and only dialogue can provide that picture.

DEVELOPING OTHER ARCHETYPES AS HELPERS

If the Hephaestus boy stays in the educational system through college, he will probably develop communication skills (Hermes), objective perspective (Apollo), and strategic thinking (Athena), and perhaps even ambition (Zeus). Developing these aspects in himself greatly aid an innate Hephaestus to be motivated and function effectively in the work world. They enable him to learn and develop the skills through which he can do the work he wants to do, negotiate to be paid adequately, receive recognition, find a position, or sell what he creates. In short, they enable him to do the creative, hands-on work that expresses his Hephaestian nature. Yet the world often doesn't honor Hephaestus, and the other, more rewarded archetypes may not develop. The man (or woman) may then work a lifetime at something that will never be more than just a job, however much he advances, because it isn't deeply satisfying, creative enough, or personally meaningful. For him, being a highly skilled craftman is more fulfilling than being in a downtown office; doing research work in a laboratory is far more satisfying than being in the sales office; doing surgery far more absorbing than chairing the department of surgery.

BECOMING MORE THAN HEPHAESTUS

When a Hephaestus man finds works he loves, the problem arises of becoming so absorbed in work that he does not develop any other facets of himself or make space for others exists. Other potentials in him are kept locked away, and even if he identifies with positive qualities of this archetype, it limits him. Here the man must realize the need to be more than Hephaestus in order to free time and energy, and make choices that will allow him to grow.

BEING CHOSEN BY APHRODITE

Aphrodite, Goddess of Love and Beauty, chose Hephaestus for a husband: he did not vie for her and win her or court her. Analogously, a love for beautiful things can just be present in a workingman's psyche, not there as a result of effort or study or even exposure to beautiful things. This is a gift from the Goddess of Love and Beauty, who thus "chooses" him. Then, when he makes things, however functional the thing may be, his craft is married to beauty and love, and it becomes manifest in the shape, balance, and material. To do otherwise goes against his integrity of craftsmanship and esthetics. To remain faithful to this inner standard, and to have his work grow, he must honor the union. Others may not appreciate either his craftsmanship or the esthetic element in his work, and he may be pressured or tempted to devalue this as well. But if he does, he will miss the joy and satisfaction that could otherwise come to him. When work comes through his Hephaestus-Aphrodite union, he feels touched by divinity as he creates. He is an inspired instrument through which beauty becomes manifest in matter.

REPARENTING HEPHAESTUS

If life imitates myth, the Hephaestus man may need to find "foster parents" or substitute parental figures who can affirm him, value him, and perhaps even teach him or sponsor him as he seeks to make his way in their world. If either natural parent rejected him for not living up to expectations, his wound is deep, but can be healed by relating to maternal and paternal people who value him as he is. Often he needs "earth" parents who show him how to do tangible things that require skill and physical effort to replace his rejecting "sky" parents who stressed achievement and wanted him to climb the ladder of success.

Ultimately, he needs to find and develop attitudes within himself that support and validate him and what he is doing. And then, as he works at developing his creative talents, the promise in the myth of Hephaestus is that he will overcome adversity, humiliations, and handicaps.

10.

Dionysus, God of Wine and Ecstasy—Mystic, Lover, Wanderer

To affirm the Dionysian is to recognize and appreciate the place of pain and death in life, and to tolerate the full range from death to life and from pain to ecstasy, including the wounding in which one is "delivered" from the flat ennui of numbing conformity to cultural and familial expectations.

Tom Moore, in James Hillman, ed., *Puer Papers*

Dionysus was the god of the most blessed ecstasy and the most enraptured love. But he was also the persecuted god, the suffering and dying god, and all whom he loved, all who attended him, had to share his tragic fate.

Walter F. Otto, *Dionysus: Myth and Cult*

Dionysus as god, archetype, and man was close to nature and to women. The mystical realm and the feminine world were familiar to him. He was often an unwelcome and disturbing element, a cause of conflict and madness in mythology, just as Dionysus can be in a man's psyche.

DIONYSUS THE GOD

Dionysus (known to the Romans as Bacchus) was God of Wine, and "the god of ecstasy and terror, of wildness and the most blessed deliverance."[1] He was the youngest of the Olympians, and the only one with a mortal mother. The grape vine, the ivy, the fig, and the pine tree were dear to him. His animal symbols were the bull, goat, panther, fawn, lion, leopard, tiger, ass, dolphin, and snake. His domain "extended to all nature and especially to its life-giving and seminal moisture: the sap rising

251

in a tree, the blood pounding in the veins, the liquid fire of the grape, all the mysterious and uncontrollable tides that flow and ebb in nature."[2]

In his mythology and his rituals, Dionysus was surrounded by women: by mothers and nursemaids of the young Dionysus as the divine child, or by enraptured lovers, the frenzied Maenads or Bacchae, who were possessed by the god Dionysus. He was portrayed either as an infant, or more usually as a youthful man with a wreath of ivy or vine leaves on his head, wearing an animal skin draped around his body, and carrying a staff called the *thyrsus* tipped with a pine cone and often wrapped with vine or ivy leaves.

GENEALOGY AND MYTHOLOGY

Dionysus was the son of Zeus and Semele, a mortal woman who was a daughter of Cadmus, king of Thebes. Semele had attracted the love of Zeus, who impregnated her while in the guise of a mortal man. Jealous Hera found out and was determined to avenge herself on Semele and her unborn child. She appeared to Semele in the form of her aged nurse, Beroe, and persuaded the unwary girl to make sure of her lover's divinity by insisting that he visit her in the same splendor in which he appeared to Hera.

That night, when Zeus came to be with her, Semele begged him for a favor, and Zeus swore by the river Styx—making his oath irrevocable—to do whatever she asked. Semele, who had been tricked by Hera, asked him to appear before her in all his majesty as chief god of Olympus; she did not know that this would result in her death. Bound by his oath, Zeus transformed himself into God of Lightning, in whose presence no mortal could live. The fire of Zeus's thunderbolts killed Semele but made her unborn son immortal. At the very moment of her death, Zeus tore Dionysus from his mother's womb and sewed him into his own thigh, which served as an incubator until Dionysus was ready to be born. ("Dionysus" may mean "Zeus's limp," a name that describes how Zeus walked when he carried him in his thigh.) Hermes acted as a midwife in this unusual birth.

Dionysus was then taken to Semele's sister and brother-in-law to be brought up by them as a girl, but even this disguise did not protect him from Hera. She drove his caretakers mad, and they tried to murder him. Dionysus was again saved from death by Zeus who changed him into a ram and carried him to the nymphs of Mt. Nysa (a divine, mythic mountain country, inhabited by beautiful nymphs). They brought him up in a cave (which accounts for another meaning of his name: Dio-nysus or the "divine Nysus").

There his tutor Silenus taught him the secrets of nature and the making of wine. Silenus is usually portrayed as an aged, kindly, and sometimes tipsy old man who was also part horse.

MADNESS AND VIOLENCE

As a young man, Dionysus traveled through Egypt, and from India to Asia Minor, crossing the Hellespont to Thrace and from there to his birthplace Thebes, in Greece. Wherever he went, he taught the cultivation of the vine. Madness and violence accompanied him. In some myths, he was driven mad by Hera and committed murders; in other myths, people who rejected him became mad and violent. For example, after King Lycurgus rejected Dionysus, Lycurgus went mad and killed his son with an ax, thinking he was cutting down a vine. Women who rejected Dionysus were similarly afflicted: the daughters of King Proetus and King Minyas who had rejected him, were driven mad and in their frenzy killed their own sons by tearing them to pieces.

Upon his return from India, the goddess Cybele or Rhea (both pre-Olympian great mother goddesses) purified him of murders he committed in his madness, and, significantly, taught him her mysteries and rites of initiation. Thus Dionysus was a priest of the great goddess, as well as a god himself.

MARRIAGE TO ARIADNE

Ariadne, daughter of King Minos of Crete, fell in love with the Athenian hero Theseus. With her help, Theseus entered the famous labyrinth, killed the Minotaur, and retraced his steps until he made his way out. Theseus and Ariadne then set sail for Athens, but he callously abandoned her on the island of Naxos, where she would have killed herself in despair if Dionysus had not saved her and made her his wife. For Dionysus's sake, Zeus made Ariadne immortal. She was most closely related to Aphrodite, Goddess of Love and Beauty and was worshiped on Cyprus as Ariadne Aphrodite. In their mythology, the Greeks had made Ariadne, once the Cretan moon goddess, into a victimized mortal, and through Dionysus she was again deified.

RESURRECTION OF HIS MOTHER, SEMELE

Dionysus descended into Hades to bring his mother, Semele, back to life. Together, they then ascended Mt. Olympus, where she became an immortal. Like Ariadne, mortal Semele had in early pre-Hellenic times been worshiped as a goddess associated with the moon and earth. In Greek mythology, Dionysus is the only god who rescues and restores (instead of dominating or raping) women who represent diminished earlier goddesses, whose people and worship had been conquered.

WORSHIP OF DIONYSUS

The worshipers of Dionysus, predominantly the women of ancient Greece, communed with this god in the wildest parts of the mountains. There they also entered the realm of the emotional and irrational, dancing to the compelling power of highly emotional music, and possessed by the god. Alternating states of pandemonium and deathly silence were hallmarks of the worship of Dionysus.

The celebration of Dionysus was called the "Orgia" of the god (from which the word *orgy* is derived). With wine or other sacramental intoxicants and with rhythmic dances accompanied by the frenzied music of reed pipes, drums, and cymbals, the celebrants entered an ecstatic state and felt themselves "one with" the god.

The Orgia came to a climax with the tearing to pieces and eating of the raw flesh of a sacrificial animal, believed to be an incarnation of the god. This was a sacramental act of communion, through which the divinity of Dionysus entered the celebrant.

At Delphi, Apollo turned his sanctuary over to Dionysus for three winter months. The festival of Dionysus at Delphi was orgiastic, but was limited to official women representatives from Greek cities and celebrated biennially. Dionysus was not suppressed there; he was recognized, moderated, and institutionalized. Also at Delphi, women celebrants began an annual sacred dance with the ritual discovery and awakening of the infant Dionysus in a cradle.

At the festival of flowers (Anthesteria) that marked the beginning of spring in the Mediterranean, new wine was brought in and ceremoniously blessed before a large mask of Dionysus. The eyes of the mask stared directly at the worshiper, for whom the god himself was present in the mask.

Dionysus had a significant place in Orphism (sixth century B.C.), which took its name from the mythical poet, Orpheus. In orphic theology, the infant Dionysus was torn to pieces and devoured by two jealous Titans, but his heart was saved by Athena and he was reborn through Zeus, in some versions as the son of Semele. He was worshiped as Zagreus, the Orphic name of the Underworld Dionysus.

THE FATE OF DIONYSUS

Life and death are intertwined in the mythology and worship of Dionysus. His grave was in Apollo's sanctuary at Delphi, where he annually was worshiped as a newly awakened infant. He was an adult god who died, a god who spent time in the underworld, and a god who was a newborn child.

DIONYSUS THE ARCHETYPE

The Dionysus archetype has powerful positive and negative potentialities, stirring up the most ethereal and the basest of feelings, creating conflicts within the psyche and with society. It is an archetype that is present in some men who are mystics, and in others who are murderers. In between, it is the archetype in men (and women) who experience ecstatic moments and intensely contradictory impulses.

THE DIVINE CHILD

One of the images representing Dionysus was that of the divine child. The divine child archetype carries with it a sense of specialness of person and of destiny. In dreams of contemporary people, the archetype is often represented by a precocious infant who talks to the dreamer or who in some other way is obviously not an ordinary child. The personal feeling that "my" life has a sacred meaning, or that there are both human and divine elements in "my" psyche, occurs when a person comes in touch with the divine child archetype, which often heralds the beginning of an adult's spiritual journey or path of individuation.

However, due to the instinctual intensity of the Dionysus archetype, an ego is very susceptible to being overwhelmed by it. If he identifies with the divine child archetype, he (or she) will often find it difficult to adapt to ordinary life. He will expect special treatment or recognition, and will harbor resentments when his specialness is not honored and he is expected to do his share of mundane work. Psychologically speaking, he becomes inflated by an overblown and undeserved sense of importance.

If the Dionysus archetype is repressed and with it the divine child aspect, other difficulties ensue: feeling inauthentic or out of touch with some vague sense of not heeding something important, or leading a meaningless life. The Dionysus archetype is actively repressed in men. From childhood on, boys are discouraged from having any "girlish" traits, or from being "a dreamer" (the mystic aspect of Dionysus), or from being sensual and being told that they "mustn't touch!"

THE ETERNAL ADOLESCENT

Dionysus and Hermes are the two archetypes that most predispose a man to stay an eternal youth (or, as Jung called him, the *Puer Eternus*) regardless of his actual age. The Dionysian version of the archetypal adolescent is an intense and emotional person, who becomes absorbed in whatever is his (or her) current passion, forgetting the obligations, assignments, or appointments that he may have made. Consequently, he cannot seem to commit himself to working steadily toward achieving long-term goals. Nor is he likely to make a commitment to an enduring relationship. Regularity and constancy are foreign to him. Like the god Dionysus, he may wander through many places, attracting women to him, disrupting their normal lives, and then moving on.

He can be very moody: one moment he may be in profound despair, the next, ecstatically transported to a new high by someone or something. He is drawn to whatever intensifies experience for him. Mood-altering or hallucinogenic drugs attract him, as does music.

In the 1960s, the hippie movement was an expression of this aspect of the Dionysian archetype, with its use of LSD and marijuana, the wearing of bright colors and sensual materials, being "flower children," having love-ins and celebrating the sexual revolution, dropping out of school and jobs. This identification with Dionysus may have been a phase for most, but for some, who remained eternal youths, the lifestyle continues. They are now "aging hippies" with gray hairs in their beards; they may have several children, but the pattern continues.

The Dionysian archetype of eternal youth was personified by the rock star and the rock culture. Jim Morrison of The Doors and Mick Jagger of the Rolling Stones embodied the archetype in the 1960s, David Bowie took up the pattern from then through the 1970s into the 1980s, and Prince and Michael Jackson follow it in the 1980s. Most of these stars have cultivated an androgynous appearance as well, and many also have had a darker side, which was emphasized by the punk rockers.

THE MOTHER'S SON

Dionysus's mother died while he was still a fetus. In his mythology and worship, he was surrounded by foster mothers and nursemaids, who were inconsistent and unstable in their nurturing. Later Dionysus descended into Hades to find his mother. Often men who are identified with this archetype also seem to be seeking an idealized woman who is both mother and lover, seeking unsuccessfully to find "her" in a series of relationships. This is especially true when there has been a physical or emotional separation between mother and son.

The archetype may also predispose a man to have an inner psychological relationship with the Great Mother. Then he feels himself associated with the maternal world, possibly drawn toward expression of "maternal instinct" via caretaking occupations and domestic interests that are more traditionally feminine. Or the connection with the Great Mother may be a spiritual one (especially now with the return of the Goddess as a spiritual principle into the culture), perhaps expressed through becoming a follower of a charismatic woman religious leader.

The result may also be a man who feels intimately related to women, who much prefers the company of women, who is a lover of women, merging with them in the ecstasy of lovemaking, and who intuitively understands women's experience. D. H. Lawrence, author of *Lady Chatterley's Lover, Sons and Lovers,* and *Women in Love,* is an example.

Women often are drawn to take care of the Dionysus man, just as he seeks to be mothered by them. In his need, he seems a "motherless boy," which evokes maternal feelings. If this "mother's son" is not married—for example, because he is a priest or a homosexual—then he may surround himself, as Dionysus did, with three or four mothering women.

THE SHAMAN: MEDIATOR BETWEEN TWO WORLDS

In the tribal society of the Native American, the shaman is very important as the mediator and intercessor between the invisible world and the physical world. The man who became a shaman was often marked from childhood as different from his boyhood peers. He often stayed with the women, and later dressed as a woman—an experience shared by Dionysus, who was raised as a girl for a period of his childhood.

The shamanic psyche is very often that of an androgyne— a male-female, as Dionysus was described as "man-womanish," and called "the womanly one."[3] Catholic priests, whose sacramental function is to mediate between the invisible world and the visible world, to this day often wear vestments that are dresses. Apparently psychological androgyny, the inward experience of both masculine and feminine perceptions, is a key to entering this realm.

The shamanic vision is of nonordinary reality, the altered state of consciousness of which Carlos Casteneda and Lynn Andrews write in their books about their own initiations by shamans or medicine women. In Jungian psychology, which values development of the feminine in men, the invisible world is the world of archetypes, dreams, and active imagination.

Dionysus called women out of their ordinary lives to revel in nature and to discover an ecstatic element in themselves. Essentially, he initiated them into a shamanic experience. Dionysus the god was an initiate and priest of the Great Goddess. In the contemporay women's spirituality movement, Dionysus is present in some women who embody the priestess archetype as mediators between two worlds. Metaphorically functioning like Morgaine in Marion Zimmer Bradley's *Mists of Avalon,* a priest or priestess of the Goddess can go through the mists to Avalon, and take others to the spiritual feminine realm, the isle of the Goddess.

To be a man with a shamanic personality in a culture that emphasizes "getting ahead in the real world," is to be out of step. The adolescent religious mystic who has an ecstatic vision of the Madonna feels as unacceptable as the taker of hallucinogenic drugs. Both—like Dionysus—also seem to others, to be courting madness.

If Dionysus is one of several strong archetypes within the man, then he will not totally identify with this shamanic aspect, but will have a predisposition toward altered states of consciousness. The realm of the invisible world feels both familiar and fascinating to him and may lead him to profound insights. He may be a "closet mystic" who, while operating effectively in the world, finds that this Dionysian element provides him with a hidden source of meaning.

THE DUALISTIC PERSONALITY

Of all the masculine archetypes, Dionysus is the archetype of intense opposites. As scholar Walter F. Otto describes him,

> His duality has manifested itself to us in the antitheses of ecstasy and horror, infinite vitality and savage destruction; in the pandemonium in which deathly silence is inherent; in the immediate presence which is at the same time absolute remoteness.[4]

When this aspect of the Dionysian archetype takes over, the person can rapidly cross the borderline between these opposites. Major emotional shifts are precipitated by minimal events. To be in a relationship with a man (or woman) who is crossing back and forth thus is to be treated like an exquisitely precious and valued person one moment, and like a terrible monster the next. At the same time, he may fluctuate between being a passionate lover and a cold stranger. To be in ecstatic communion with a man who then turns on you and tears you into pieces is to meet and suffer from this dualistic aspect of Dionysus.

Women, too, can become possessed by this archetype. The Maenads—the women worshipers who sought the god on mountain tops—could change from loving maternal women to raging Maenads without mercy.

Beauty and fatal danger were hallmarks of this dualism. The panther, leopard, and lynx were sacred to Dionysus, reflecting this aspect of the god. These large cats are the most graceful and fascinating of animals, but also the most savage and bloodthirsty.

Whether or not the Dionysian tendency for extreme and intense feelings repeatedly disrupts his life and is inflicted on others depends on how strong the archetype is and how stable and strong the ego is. A person with a healthy ego can say and mean, for example, "Just because I want to murder you or cut my wrists doesn't mean I'll do it." If the ego is unstable and has experienced severe emotional trauma, a mass murderer can result, such as Charles Manson, who was a mystic, a lover, and a killer. In the presence of a strong and stable ego, however, the Dionysus archetype adds breadth and depth of feelings, increases the possibility of peak emotional experiences, and intensifies erotic spiritual and physical reactions.

THE PERSECUTED WANDERER

The motif of severe persecution and flight is part of the mythology of Dionysus and his women followers. For example, due to the hostility of King Lycurgus, Dionysus was beaten and forced to leap into the sea, while the women who worshiped him were beaten unmercifully in their horror-stricken flight.

In his mythology, Dionysus traveled through the known world of the Greeks, often encountering hostility as he called women away from their household hearths and looms to follow him to remote mountains for ecstatic revels. From his conception, Hera the Goddess of Marriage was his deadly enemy—no wonder, considering the clash of values these two deities represent. Hera honors enduring marriage with its social obligations, continuity, and fidelilty. Dionysus evokes disruptive passion and calls on women to forget their usual roles.

THE DISMEMBERED ARCHETYPE

The motif of dismemberment is woven through the myths of Dionysus who shared the same fate as Osiris, an earlier, Egyptian god. Later, the crucified Jesus Christ had the role of the divine son who suffers death and is resurrected. The Dionysian archetype predisposes a man (or woman) to the possibility of psychological dismemberment or crucifixion, caused by his inability to reconcile powerful opposites within. "Being on the cross" between two opposing tendencies is a common affliction of a Dionysus man. He may, for example, want to both merge with a lover and leave her. "Dismemberment"—metaphorically having difficulty "keeping it together" or feeling split into many pieces—is common for such men.

The dismemberment motif is especially strong when the Dionysian archetype comes together with religions that emphasize guilt, such as the Judeo-Christian religions, which say "If thy left hand offend thee, cut it off." Since mysticism and sensuality are two aspects of Dionysus, a young man may be drawn to Catholic mysticism, for example, yet feel he is a terrible sinner because of his sensual feelings or erotic images. Dismemberment dreams involving swords, knifes, and self-mutilation occur in men (and women) whose inner conflicts are often irreconcilable within their religion.

CULTIVATING DIONYSUS

Many non-Dionysian men suffer from emotional aridness and are out of touch with their deeper emotions. Some lack sensuality (let alone ecstasy) even if they have sex often. For them, cultivating Dionysus could be life-enhancing. The Dionysian focus is on the moment, not on some goal further down the way. There is an openness to be moved by what happens between people or inside oneself in response to events. Dancing and lovemaking are realms in which Dionysus is especially important, to enable intensity, spontaneity, and merging with the music or with the lover. Having a "technique," mentally following a dance diagram, or a sex manual's suggested steps prevents a man from truly "being there." Whenever the man is aware of the clock, Dionysus is not present. Whenever other thoughts crop up that take the man out of the immediacy of the moment, Dionysus has left. Whenever the man is unaware of having a body, he is not attuned to Dionysus.

To invite Dionysus to be present may require getting out of one's usual environment, out of one's usual clothes, out of one's habitual persona or roles: Dionysus's gift of the vine, music that moves the dancer into a spontaneous sensuality, a Mardi Gras or masked fantasy ball—anything that loosens the hold of the mind and the grip of time helps bring Dionysus closer.

If we leave the city and our concern with work and responsibilities behind and seek communion with Mother Nature, we also can connect with Dionysus. Dionysus can come to us when we are in nature and become one with nature. When we leave our usual conscious awareness of time or miles to go and lose ourselves in the experience, we are transported to another subjectively felt ecstatic realm.

DIONYSUS THE MAN

As in each preceding chapter, this section provides a glimpse at what life is like for a man who identifies with the particular god. However, a composite impression does not work quite as well for Dionysus as for the others because this archetype is characterized by opposing tendencies and extremes.

Even though it may be hard to describe with certainty just how Dionysus will manifest, the man usually has some recognizable traits that other men usually mistrust or reject. By "old boy" standards, the Dionysus man is likely to be either too feminine, too mystic, too counterculture, too threatening, or too attractive and too fascinating, for them to be comfortable with him. Dionysus disrupts mundane life, not only by calling others to revel, but by making a mundane life difficult or impossible for him to live.

EARLY YEARS

Dionysus the god had two unusual early experiences that offer some insight into what are psychologically analogous experiences for some men who come to be identified with Dionysus. The god was raised as a girl, and his mother surrogates were driven mad and murderous.

If a parent has stereotyped expectations of what a boy should be interested in—rough-housing, mechanical interests, and sports—then a Dionysus boy who follows his own interests will probably be told, in one way or another, that he's behaving "like a girl." Little Dionysus gravitates toward what the women are doing because he loves to use his five senses—he wants his world to be full of sensual experience. He likes the feel of silk and fur, is interested in colors, can be enraptured by music. The kitchen, with its smells and tastes, is much more interesting to him than the garage. The theater is infinitely more fascinating than the ballpark, clothes are more captivating than computers. This natural interests usually invite others to call him a "sissy," for acting like a sister—a girl.

If his interests don't set him apart from what he "is supposed to care about," his emotionality will. A young Dionysus is rarely able to be a stoic, even when expected to be. Chances are he has been told that "big boys don't cry." Yet he cries easily and laughs gleefully, too. It is harder for him to get his emotions "under control," which for most boys means learning how to squelch them. This again makes him seem "more like a girl."

Having his caretakers go mad and become murderous was another characteristic of Dionysus's childhood. In her book *Prisoners of Childhood*, psychoanalyst Alice Miller describes how a bright, perceptive son learns to keep on the good side of a narcissistic parent, usually his mother, who will turn hostile toward him unless he acts the way she wants him to. He pays attention to emotional cues and learns how to be pleasing (which is one facet of "being raised as a girl"). If his mother's (or his father's) emotional reactions are extreme because of a borderline psychological state of mind, he will be her "precious love" one moment, and be exposed to raw, rejecting hostility—murderous rage—the next.

With a parent who acts like this, most of Alice Miller's patients learned as boys to stifle their emotional responses (which then never developed) and instead to live in their heads. When Dionysus is the major archetype, however, a boy is often not able to do this. Instead, he may run away, become a delinquent, make dramatic threats, or develop physical symptoms.

His Parents

Whether the Dionysus boy has a positive self-image depends more on his parents than with most other types of boys because he doesn't fit into an "all boy" mold and so the world beyond his family is not validating. However, lack of paternal approval is a common experience for a Dionysus boy, who by being himself never seems to please his father. Attempting to be the son his father wants him to be with varied success is a typical experience.

The god Dionysus himself had a powerful father who cared about him. In his mythology, Dionysus—more than other sons of Zeus—was cared for by his father, who began by being both a mother and a father to him, and whose protectiveness continued after his birth. Later Zeus made Ariadne, Dionysus's mortal wife, an immortal. To have a loving and approving Zeus father who accepts him and supports his choices is ideal for a Dionysus boy, whose personality and masculinity are thus affirmed.

Furthermore, Dionysus was the youngest son of Zeus, and regardless of actual birth order, a Dionysus boy behaves like a youngest son. He is playful, can live in the moment, and lacks concern with success.

Most Dionysus boys seem to be "mother's sons": they are more like their mothers than their fathers in interests and in personality. If they have an emotionally distant or rejecting father, or were raised by single mothers, they often overidentify with their mothers and feel alienated from other males and from their own sense of masculinity.

Mother-son alienation can also occur when he does not live up to her expectations of what a boy should be like. This is especially likely when his mother is archetypally Athena, the most logical of the deities and the patron goddess of heroic men. She is a mentoring mother who can help her son in the world, but she is not a particularly maternal woman. She is disappointed and frustrated by his lack of ambition, and he misses having a motherly mother, which he will seek in other women.

ADOLESCENCE AND EARLY ADULTHOOD

Adolescence is usually a crisis period. Everything about this period is intensified for a Dionysus. His emotional moods swing both higher and lower than with other teenagers. His questions about his sexual identity are greater, and he falls in love with girls or boys—or both—with alarming intensity. Use of drugs is a definite risk. Outrageous dressing is likely. He doesn't care about grades, an indifference that increases as everything else intensifies.

His parents typically become alarmed, and school authorities may be equally polarized. His lack of conformity or fitting into the mainstream, which was always present but may not have been so obvious, now may become blatant.

Sometimes the conflict lies within the Dionysus boy, rather than between him and others. His effort to conform and repress the Dionysian part of himself now becomes more difficult. Emotional breakdowns may occur as the boy feels himself at odds with himself—torn up into pieces. Severe mental disturbance can result. When a repressive religion and family condemn even having "impure thoughts," then his feelings of guilt and sin can be profoundly disturbing.

Moving away from home, between adolescence and the early adult years, continues the teenage emotional turmoil and experimentation. Seeking ecstatic experience in spiritual or sexual realms or through intoxicants often interferes with education and career beginnings. This is often a time of experiential brinksmanship, which can be extremely risky.

But it is also possible to explore and express the Dionysian elements of the personality without risky extremes if he was seen and valued for himself while he was growing up and if he also got some helpful guidance. For example, since Dionysus lives in the immediate present, he needs to be patiently taught to consider today what comes due tomorrow, as well as what and how to learn from past experience (lessons he otherwise often fails to apply).

WORK

If seeking the ecstatic moves him toward the mystical and the religious, a young Dionysus may become a priest, drawn to the ritual and the mysticism of the sacraments and the ceremonies. Or he may join an ashram, where drumming or chanting may be used to alter consciousness. Even more Dionysian are the sensual mystic experiences of tantric yoga or the sexual practices of the Bhagwan Shree Rajneesh's followers. In this setting, his work is defined by the religious community, which suits the noncompetitive Dionysus very well.

A Dionysus man is not attracted to a competitive career fueled by personal ambition, nor is he interested in the academic world of ideas. Developing competency at something that takes years of study or practice goes against his grain. And achieving power and prestige is not personally meaningful to him. No wonder, then, that the world of work is a problem area for many Dionysus men.

There are many unemployed underachievers and a few spectacular successes in the work world. Some Dionysus men are successful in the creative spheres where talent and the experience of grappling with their dark side or their Dionysian conflicts can come together in their work. Eugene O'Neill's play *The Iceman Cometh* reflects the author's years of uncontrollable drinking. Another playwright and Pulitzer Prize winner, Sam Shepard, uses pairs of brothers to describe the polarity in his own personality. Dionysian men can likewise be found among rock stars, musicians, and actors, some of whom have had to conquer alcohol or drug addictions.

RELATIONSHIPS WITH WOMEN

The god Dionysus was surrounded by women, and the Dionysus man usually is also. Motherly women often see him as a troubled and vulnerable man to nurture. Whether he is a young adult or a middle-aged man, his boyishness makes some women want to care for him. He may have been harshly treated or rejected, and seeing him lick his emotional wounds draws out the mother in some women.

His sensuality and appreciation of beauty draws women to him, some as friends, others as would-be lovers. When he does make love to a woman, especially if she has up to then never been made love to by a man for whom making love is an ecstatic, merging experience, it deeply affects her. One may be awakened to her own sexuality and be grateful to him; another may become addicted to him; another, wildly jealous. When he becomes important to a woman, drama and disruption often follow his entry into her life; as she now must follow his typical high and low swings.

The Dionysus man genuinely likes women, and from nursery school on he has probably had close female friends with whom he shares interests, confidences, and a depth of friendship that most men do not have with women.

RELATIONSHIPS WITH MEN

A Dionysus man is usually out of step with his fellows. He's not at home in the locker room or the board room because male relationships in these settings are so impersonal and goal related. He is too much an individual to be much of a team player, too little interested in competition, and too unconforming to manage to be "one of the guys."

Paradoxically, he may have closer male friendships than men who do fit in with their fellows. A number of male friends may be deeply important to him, in different ways. With a Hermes friend, he reaches conversational depths, and a Hephaestus finds that Dionysus really appreciates what he creates, that he touches his works of art with the same reverence that Hephaestus felt when he made them. Apollo is also drawn to Dionysus, who is his opposite.

Dionysus was a god who could weep over a friend, as a Dionysian man might also. When his friend Ampelos died, Dionysus wept over his grave and was consoled in part by the grapevine and by the wine that sprang up from his tears.

SEXUALITY

Expression of an innate, intense sexuality is an essential issue for Dionysus. A Dionysus man may be heterosexual, homosexual, or bisexual. Whether he is a wildly promiscuous rock musician or a celibate priest, sexuality is a forefront concern. Naturally sensual, his erotic nature is easily evoked. He may put as much of his considerable psychic energy into the sexual realm, as another man might put into his career. He can have ecstatic sexual experiences, sometimes further enhanced by music or intoxicants without being in a deep personal relationship. A sensitive partner may be aware that he is so much into making love, moving into an altered state of consciousness himself, that there is something impersonal about his lovemaking. At that moment, he may be having an archetypal Dionysian experience, not a personal communion.

He can be truly drawn repeatedly to a variety of women, or to repeated experience with the same woman if she, too, can love in the moment, as he does. Conquest is not a motivation; the experience itself is.

MARRIAGE

The traditional woman doesn't consider a Dionysus man "good husband material," which is an accurate appraisal. He can't be counted on to be a breadwinner with a lifetime nine-to-five job, or to make it to the summit of the business or professional world and thus to provide status, position, and security for her. Life with him will be unpredictable both economically and emotionally.

Problems arise when a woman falls in love with a Dionysus, and then on marrying him expects him to be somebody else—like the steady, predictable men she was not attracted to and now expects him to be. Marriage to him was probably her idea anyway, as he is likely to live in the moment and not think in terms of lifetime commitments. To expect marriage to make him monogamous is another mistake that may cause her pain.

And yet, again paradoxically and like the god, at some point in his life he may marry and honor the marriage, and love and cherish his wife, whom he knows empathically.

CHILDREN

A Dionysus man often is such a "big kid" himself that he is a hit with other people's children. However, his own children often have experiences that leave them feeling torn. He can be wonderfully exciting (when he's playful, he's imaginative and generous, and his happy moods are infectious), or terribly disappointing (when he's promised to do something special with them and doesn't remember, or has lost his previous enthusiasm for something that was to be a shared experience). To have a father who is a charming man who means what he says in the moment and can't be depended on to follow through can be shattering. His inconsistencies and lack of dependability are magnified if he becomes a divorced father—and there is a strong possibility that he will be.

The Dionysus man usually does not carry the traditional responsibilities of fatherhood very well:—the roles of breadwinner, disciplinarian, mediator between his family and the outer world, mentor, and role model of how to succeed in the world. Yet when his children were born he may have been deeply involved in his wife's labor and delivery, emotionally and physically present throughout. The birthing process may have been a shared mystical or ecstatic experience that bonds him to his children and his wife. Although a Dionysian man will never be temperamentally a traditional, distant, in-the-world Sky Father, it thus is possible for him to become an in-the-home, instinctively close to his children Earth Father.

MIDDLE YEARS

The Dionysus man at midlife can be in the middle of a major emotional crisis. If his excesses and lack of discipline have taken a toll, he may be facing alcohol or drug addiction, or work and relationship failures. Educational and professional deficiencies or an erratic work history now become glaringly evident. His marital situation is often no better. Many public Dionysus figures do not survive midlife; for example, death from drug overdoses claimed the lives of rock star Jim Morrison of The Doors, and actor John Belushi.

More commonly, the crisis of midlife goes on for years, with alcoholism often the most evident problem. Poet Dylan Thomas and actor Richard Burton had to struggle with alcoholism, with creative expression, and difficult relationships with women. These are the classic Dionysian midlife struggles. Thomas and Burton had all of them; a Dionysus man may also, or only one part.

Through heroic efforts to stay with meaningful work and to work through relationship issues of intimacy and commitment, a Dionysus man can, however, evolve into a man with depth and maturity who stays intense and integrates his ecstatic and creative moments into his life.

LATER YEARS

The Dionysus man's passage through midlife determines which of three patterns his later years will take.

One common pattern is the continuation of the midlife stuggle (with alcohol, work difficulties, or relationship problems) without resolution until death, which often comes prematurely.

A second pattern involves the combination of a Dionysus archetype and inherited wealth, which predisposes a man to stay the eternal youth inappropriately into old age. Whatever his sexual orientation, he usually has young companions as sexual partners, and having tried or done everything, life takes on a jaded quality.

A highly individual life of depth and meaning is the hard-won third possibility. Having integrated the Dionysian into a mature personality, the man is able to live fully in the moment, that moment being part of a tapestry, an emotionally rich life that has continuity and commitments. Ecstatic experiences provide him with a sense of a spiritual oneness that underlies reality, of being part of nature and part of humanity. This spiritual integration makes death the next experience to embrace fully when it comes.

PSYCHOLOGICAL DIFFICULTIES

When Dionysus determines the emotions and behavior of the man in whom the archetype lives, his potential for major psychological difficulties is greater than with any other archetype. How much damage results depends on the power of the archetype—how strong it is, relative to the weakness of the man's ego. Only a man with a strong and healthy ego can appropriately restrain the archetype's influence and choose how, when, with whom, and under what circumstances the Dionysus in him is lived out.

Moreover, a moralistic and puritanical society directs stronger negative messages at Dionysus than perhaps at any other archetype—another reason why Dionysus leads to psychological difficulties. Self-esteem problems can result, as well as adverse effects from repressing the archetype.

DISTORTIONS IN SELF-PERCEPTION: LOW SELF-ESTEEM AND INFLATION

Our cultural stereotype of what a boy or man should be like tells a young Dionysus that there is something wrong with him. He learns very early that he is too emotional, or too intense, or interested in things that only girls care about. His self-esteem naturally suffers.

On the other hand, the divine child aspect of the archetype gives him a sense of specialness and privilege that is unrealistic.

Often he fluctuates from one pole to the other, now feeling inadequate to the task at hand, next feeling that what he is about to embark on will make him instantly famous.

Lacking constancy of self-perception, and having so much of his positive self-esteem based on purely subjective feelings, may make it impossible for him to get a realistic sense of himself or his worth. The reaction of others to him is often equally inconsistent. People react negatively and positively to him, hardly ever just neutrally.

STAYING THE ETERNAL YOUTH

The god Dionysus was a youthful god. One famous description of him was as an elegant young man with long hair flowing over his shoulders, clad in a purple robe. In this myth, he was kidnaped by pirates who assumed he was a king's son, for whom ransom would be paid. The image is quintessentially that of a privileged eternal youth. And when this archetype goes hand-in-hand with wealth, what results is the sensuous playboy—the young Aly Khan, for example. Many men who become identified with Dionysus as the eternal youth actually bear some similarity to their rich and famous equivalents, in that they may live for the next party or the next intense affair. The possibility of staying an eternal youth is present whenever Dionysus is the dominant archetype.

THE STUGGLE WITH OPPOSITES

Men with Dionysian personalities struggle with paradox and opposites that exist side by side within. In them—as in the god—rapture and destruction, passion and coldness, immediacy and distance, may all coexist.

The playwright and screenwriter Sam Shepard—who is himself an example of a Dionysus man—described the task of holding these opposites:

> Somewhere there's a myth about the wolf and the sheep. . . . And the process of keeping alive is trying to have these two cohabit, trying to carry on a balance between these two parts, because one's always trying to devour the other. The one that wants to devour—the wolf—operates on impulse and is pretty insane. There's definitely a struggle going on, and it's answered in differ-

ent ways. Some people do it with drinking or drugs. The difficulty is trying to accept that this is the condition you're living with, the condition of these two parts banging up against each other, and the constant threat of being overthrown by one.[5]

PSYCHOSIS AS A POTENTIAL

Dionysus was known as the god who was mad and the god who drove his followers insane. He sent the mind reeling. When he suddenly appeared, his Maenads were transported into ecstasy and rapture, frenzied dancing and raging fury.

Something Dionysian can happen at rock concerts, especially when the star suddenly appears on stage, and the audience goes mad. There is the frenzy, the drugs, the dancing, and on faces in the audience, expressions of ecstasy and rapture. Occasionally, as at the Rolling Stones concert in Altamont, there is also violence and terror.

When Dionysus the god appeared to his followers, pandemonium broke out, followed by a numbed silence or sorrowful melancholy after he just as suddenly disappeared. This arc, from ecstatic heights and communion with the god to melancholy, describes a psychological process of intense inflation followed by a benumbed depression, or a period of hallucinations and delusional behavior followed by shocked horror and guilt.

Frederick Nietzsche, the German philosopher who wrote *Thus Spake Zarathustra* experienced eleven years of degenerating mental illness. Equating his madness and the dissolution of his psyche with the dismemberment of Dionysus, Nietzsche stressed the ecstatic, excessive, barbarian, titanic, even criminal aspects of Dionysus.[6]

SIDE EFFECTS OF THE GIFT OF THE VINE: SUBSTANCE ABUSE PROBLEMS

The worship of Dionysus involved drinking wine or other sacramental intoxicants in order to attain a state of communion with the god. His followers felt that they were taking the god within themselves and were god-possessed.

If he seeks ecstatic or altered states of consciousness through the use of drugs, a contemporary Dionysus is susceptible to substance abuse problems. He may risk his mental and physical health if he takes hallucinogenic or mood-altering drugs.

When I was an emergency room psychiatric resident at San Francisco General Hospital in the 1960s, people were often brought in under the influence of hallucinogenic drugs and stimulants they had bought on the streets. Drugs that they took to feel good brought them paranoia and terror, or put them in physical danger as they disregarded traffic or heights, or threatened the safety of others if they acted on delusions or misperceptions induced by the drugs they had taken. A decade or more later, hallucinogenic "designer" drugs that differ by a single molecule from prescribed drugs are being made by sophisticated, profit-minded chemists, to stay one step ahead of whatever is on the illegal list. The risk now is to young urban professionals. Drugs sold as promising a "god experience," have in some incidences led to death.

Contemporary users find that drugs taken to provide a temporary high may be followed by hangovers, despair, and addiction. When people sought communion with Dionysus, he induced ecstatic heights followed by melancholy and depression, or hallucinations followed by horror and guilt: it's no different today.

Communion with God can be a major unconscious motivation for drinking that leads to alcoholism. Bill W., cofounder of Alcoholics Anonymous, had an exchange of correspondence with Jung that illuminates this connection between alcoholism and spirituality. Bill W. wrote to tell him of the importance of a conversation that Jung had had in the 1930s with Rowland H. that had played a significant role in the founding of AA (Rowland H. was an alcoholic and former patient of Jung's, whom Jung in this conversation told that he could not help.)

"When he (Rowland H.) then asked you if there was any other hope, you told him that there might be, provided he could become the subject of a spiritual or religious experience."

(Taking Jung's words to heart, Rowland H. then sought and found the spiritual experience that did help him.)

Jung replied, "His craving for alcohol was the equivalent, on a low level, of the spiritual thirst of our being for wholeness, expressed in medieval language: the union with God."

"You see," Jung wrote, "'alcohol' in Latin is *spiritus,* and you use the same word for the highest religious experience as well as for the most depraving poison. The helpful formula therefore is: *spiritus contra spiritum*."

The phrase *spiritus contra spiritum* translates into the principle of using spiritual communion against the addiction of alcoholic spirits; substituting God (in whatever form that has meaning for that individual) for alcohol. When the use of alcohol or any other substance is motivated by Dionysus, a man or woman is seeking spiritual communion through these means; when this is the case, it's no wonder that a relationship with God helps bring about sobriety.

PSYCHOSOMATIC SYMPTOMS

Dionysus was thought to enter the body of his worshipers, much as alcohol courses through blood vessels, affecting the senses, influencing both body and mind. When Dionysus is a strong archetype, that man is embodied—that is, he reacts with his body, which is for him a sensory organ, and he feels emotions in his body. Being totally in his body when he dances or makes love is the positive expression of this embodiment. Having his body react psychosomatically is the negative aspect. He is susceptible to conversion symptoms—hysterical paralysis or blindness, for example. Anorexia is another expression of his susceptibility to mind-body illness.

He also can become fearful of having something wrong with his body, because he expresses emotions through his body and is highly aware of his body sensations. He will be disturbed by an ache or a pain that another man, who lives in his head, would not even be aware of.

PSYCHOLOGICAL DIFFICULTIES FOR OTHERS

If a Dionysus man is a significant man in a woman's life, it goes without saying that her life is not boring. How tumultuous, how joyful or how painful depends on him, on who she is, and on the structure of the relationship—is it an unusual friendship or a new affair? A living-together arrangement or a marriage? Equally important, what hopes does she hold for the relationship?

If there is a hopeful Hera (Goddess of Marriage, archetypal wife) in her, who expects a torrid affair to turn into an enduring, monogamous marriage, the relationship could be disastrous to her, exposing her to her own worst shadow aspects—her vindictiveness and jealousy.

However, Dionysus is most often a significant figure at a time of major transition. He may enter a woman's life and "call her away from hearth and home to revel," and in so doing, he may break up her home and marriage, and activate the passion and the anger that she has repressed all her life, first as the good girl and then as the good wife. The major casualties may be her children.

The period after a marriage has ended because the husband has left is another transition time when a Dionysus man often enters a woman's life. Here he is again an initiator, a sensual man who arouses her eroticism and emotionality. He may introduce her to intoxicating drugs, to pulsating music, or to ecstatic meditative practice. Or a Dionysus lover may enter the scene after the life has gone out of a marriage.

Recall that Dionysus the god transformed women into frenzied Maenads who shared his fate and could be torn apart and dismembered or cruelly persecuted; this is the darkest potentiality of becoming involved with a Dionysus man. Here women who are like Persephone in their susceptibility to be abducted into the underworld—as a metaphor for significant depression and loss of reality—are the most vulnerable. Also, because of their chameleonlike adaption to a powerful personality, they can become compliant followers of a Charles Manson, or like kidnaped and abused Patty Hearst, can come under the domination of a criminal Dionysus. Moreover, although Dionysus was a male god who called to women, the archetype can be lived through both men and women, and those who respond can be of either sex, or both can be of the same sex.

WAYS TO GROW

The psychological work that the Dionysus man (or woman) must do in order to grow is more complex than others because the archetype is more complex. An observing and accepting ego is needed. Other archetypes may have to be developed, not just as a means of becoming less one-sided but for survival. Two major tasks may have to be undertaken—a heroic encounter with the unconscious and a committed relationship—in order for him to have the ordinary life he eventually seeks, though it's not likely that he ever will be an ordinary person.

DEVELOPING AN OBSERVING AND ACCEPTING EGO

A person can contain or embrace this archetype without repressing it, going mad, doing violence, or being thrown out of ordinary company if he has a strong observing ego that accepts whatever thoughts and images that come to mind, whatever sensations are felt in the body, whatever passions surge up without judgment and shame, or having to act on them. If Dionysus is a powerful archetype in you, you may find simply knowing that this is the attitude to strive for to be helpful. Psychotherapy is the means to develop or strengthen the ego and work on self-acceptance, especially if rejection and judgment were childhood experiences.

DEVELOPING ALLIES: ZEUS, HERMES, AND APOLLO

In the mythology of Dionysus, several gods gave him crucial help. Zeus, Hermes, and Apollo, his allies, are archetypes that a Dionysus man needs to develop.

Zeus saved Dionysus's life twice, first by taking him from his dead mother's womb and sewing him into his thigh. Then, when Hera drove his foster parents mad, Zeus rescued him once again. A positive father archetype—personified as a caring and strong Zeus—can definitely help a Dionysus man accept being out of step with his fellows and can help him to live with irrational thoughts or intense feelings without acting on them or becoming self-rejecting. A Dionysus man can develop a positive father Zeus archetype in himself naturally if his actual father loves and accepts him. This development can also be fostered by a positive relationship with a father figure mentor or therapist.

Hermes was midwife at Dionysus's birth or the god who took Dionysus to his foster parents. As the Messenger God, Hermes easily traveled among the underworld, the earth, and the heights of Olympus. The ability to go from the depths to the heights without getting trapped emotionally is an ability that Dionysus men need to cultivate. A Dionysus man exists in the present, which is the only reality for him. Consequently, if he descends "into the pits" and is depressed, it feels unending and eternal to him. This despair can lead to thoughts of suicide as "the only way out." Hermes, however, knows that wherever he is, is only temporary.

Hermes was also the communicator god. By learning to put his feelings into words and sharing them with others, a Dionysus man develops this aspect of Hermes. Others often then can help him gain a wider perspective, which is helpful.

Rational Apollo is the third ally that a Dionysus man needs to develop. In his rituals, Dionysus shared Delphi with Apollo. Both gods were worshiped at Delphi—Dionysus in the three winter months, Apollo during the remainder of the year. These two gods are the traditional opposites. Apollo is the rational, linear thinker who valued clarity, who as Sun God could see everything from an objective distance. He is a personification of left-brain function. Dionysus is the irrational, emotional, embodied god who was subjective, in whom opposites and contradictions occurred side by side; he personifies right-brain function. Both need to be present in a man's psyche. A good education is the means through which a Dionysus man usually develops the Apollo archetype's ability to think rationally.

THE HERO'S TASK: THE JOURNEY TO THE UNDERWORLD

If he is to grow psychologically, the Dionysus man must leave behind his identification with the divine child and eternal adolescent, and become the hero. Psychologist Erich Neumann, in his classic desciption of the origin and growth of male consciousness, writes of the need for the androgynous son-lover to become the hero. To do this, Neumann says that he must deliberately expose himself to the unconscious and the nonego, which is the darkness, nothingless, the void, the bottomless pit, the underworld, the primordial womb of the Great Mother where the ego can dissolve into the unconscious and be devoured or overcome by irrational fears—the monsters and evils of the unconscious. The hero must endure the perils of the underworld and emerge with his ego intact and strengthened by the encounter.[8]

In his mythology, the last thing that Dionysus undertook before taking his place on Olympus was this hero's task. He was determined to rescue his mortal mother Semele, who had died and now was in Hades. One access to the underworld was through a bottomless pool in the marsh of Lerna. Dionysus dived in and in due time came to the dark house of Hades. There he secured his mother's freedom and led her up to the earth, and then to Olympus.

Psychologically, Dionysus separated his personal mother from the Great Mother, overcoming his fear of the unconscious and the masculine ego's fear of the devouring feminine. When a man can love and react to his mother (as well as any other woman) as a life-sized woman who has no terrible powers over him (who cannot emasculate him), he has accomplished an equivalent act. He has freed his personal mother from the Great Mother. His adolescent ego has become a heroic ego; he has grown up.

PERSONAL COMMITTED LOVE: FINDING ARIADNE

In his travels, Dionysus came across Ariadne on the island of Naxos. She had been abandoned there by Theseus, who had used her to help him kill the Minotaur and escape from Crete. Half-way home to Athens, Theseus sailed off while she was asleep on a lonely beach, where Dionysus found her. Dionysus loved her and honored her. For Dionysus's sake, Zeus made her an immortal, granting her eternal life and eternal youth.

Erotic relationships for a Dionysus man are likely to be intense and ecstatic: the sense of merging that he readily recreates leads both he and his partner to feel that they are extremely close, and yet some personal connection can be missing. The experience is impersonal or transpersonal (like Dionysus's many relationships with his Maenads) until he finds himself with compassion and empathy for a particular woman, as Dionysus the god may have felt on finding abandoned and betrayed Ariadne. Only when he forms a bond to a person whom he loves also when he is not making love does a Dionysus man move beyond being an archetypal lover into a personal relationship.

PART IV

Finding Our Myths: Re-membering Ourselves

When we know who the gods are, they can tell us more about who we are. In some of them, we can see reflections of ourselves, as they mirror the grandeur, meaning, and limitations of the archetypes we live out. Other gods tug at our memory, and we recall that we once did know them. In another, we might see the face of the god we rejected, the archetype we feared made us unacceptable.

After reading about the gods, which of them did you find has shaped your personality the most? Now you may know why it was easy for you to succeed in the world, and at what cost, or why success in the world has been so difficult to attain.

Travelers on the way to Athens—metaphorically those men (and women) whose goal is success, who seek to be at the center of power, commerce, or intellectual achievement—were caught by Procrustes, placed on his bed and either stretched to fit or cut down to size. "Procrustean" has come to mean arbitrary, often ruthless disregard of individual differences. Conformity is the contemporary procrustean bed; the stereotype of what a man is expected to be does violence to men's psyches. A man then becomes cut off from parts of himself that don't fit, or the part that does fit is stretched to occupy the space.

The world as we know it is a place where men are shaped by the patriarchy to be lonely heroes. Men are expected to leave their mothers and renounce any sameness with them. Fathers are distant and withholding of themselves. Men compete with other men, deny vulnerability, reject what is unaccepted, and repeatedly separate from less able companions, and go on.

Psychological dis-memberment results when men (and women) are cut off from archetypes that didn't fit the procrustean bed as well as from attachments to people that they are expected to let go of as they go on. Furthermore, because control of emotions is part of the male stereotype, a man also becomes cut off from his own feelings.

The next chapter "Finding Our Myths: Re-membering Ourselves" is about reconnecting with what we have been cut off from and finding the way home. The homecoming we seek has to do with being accepted and loved, welcomed as we truly are, embraced in our totality.

"The Missing God" is the last chapter of the book. He is the predicted son who would supplant Zeus and come to rule gods and men. This is the archetype that can become the ruling principle in a man's psyche, and if it did in enough men, would change the culture as well.

11.

Finding Our Myths: Re-membering Ourselves

For men, life is a series of separations and disidentifications, beginning with mother, whom they must leave and whom they must not be like. Expected to be little men, who do not cry, they go to kindergarten and from there, year after year, have two cultures to cope with. Inside the classroom, the world—especially in the beginning—is a feminine-ruled one. The teacher is a woman who rewards cooperation and neatness, order and schoolwork.

In the schoolyard, the bigger boys are the bosses and being accepted by a male peer group is essential, because an isolated boy can be picked on or scapegoated. Conformity to the group norm is essential for survival in the schoolyard, and the dynamics of identification with the aggressor are played out there. A boy must straddle the two worlds of school and schoolyard, and he may fail at one or both. The bright boy athlete is often most able to play freely in both worlds; his athletic prowess is a source of respect that makes it possible.

I hear of golden periods in boyhood and adolescence from a few men—times when they could be unselfconsciously themselves with other boys. My impression is that these boys were lucky, that it wasn't the norm. They were preadolescent or adolescent buddies who spent every spare moment together, and they had lots of spare moments—as children of middle-class parents don't seem to have any more. Or they were boys who became close in boarding schools.

Real love for one another got generated only in these golden periods. Then came the time of separation, as repeatedly happens to men. At every step on the traditional path men are supposed to follow, there is some variation of separating sheep from goats, or boys from men, or achievers from nonachievers. Men who are successful in the world must undergo a whole series of separations from peers who did not keep up.

As the patriarchal world requires separation after separation of men, each cutting away cuts two ways: the boy who separates from his mother separates from her emotionally and cuts himself off from the inner part of himself that was close to her. The boy who goes to school and finds he cannot show his innocence or ignorance, because it makes him an object of ridicule, adapts by imitating the acceptable attitude. Thus he cuts himself off from the innocent boy in himself. The boy who had a best friend who couldn't keep up with him, not only cut off his friendship, but also cut off the part of himself that mourned his friend. The boy who could cry when he was sad and learned not to, stopped his tears by walling himself off from his emotions. And there is a "men from the boys" cut-off time, when something that is still tender in a young man is sacrificed so that he may join the ranks of men.

In a patriarchal Zeus world, where economic rewards determine what has value, most successful men work with mental skills, in offices. Some of them are in their element, and thrive on this environment. A great many do not. Some are men who would love to till the soil, or make things with their hands, or make music, or teach young children, or do any number of things, and do not; they cut themselves off from this part of themselves to go to work in an office.

The losses add up, until somewhere around midlife depression sets in, and with it come feelings of sorrow, loneliness, a sense of meaninglessness.

RE-MEMBERING

There is an alternative—which often doesn't present itself until mid-life—on which men I see in my practice embark on out of necessity when life becomes painful and empty, or arid and flat. They seek to find what is true for them, to uncover their feelings and find meaning in their lives. They may be men who have made a place for themselves in a competitive world, and who are in control of much of their lives. Yet depression, anxiety, ulcers, hypertension, a heart attack, bad dreams, or a major relationship crisis has signaled that something is terribly wrong, sending them on a journey of self-discovery to find what happened to them in the past and what is going on in their depths now. For each man, the process is a gradual descent to find buried feelings, to discover his inner world, where he can pick up the threads of his personal story. This story always begins in childhood: who was he then—what gave him joy? What delighted him? What could he be absorbed in doing? Who loved him? And, in contrast—what shamed him? What was not acceptable to others about him or his family? Who did he try to be? Whose love and approval did he try to get? How was he treated, and by whom?

He finds that "whomever" he buried and split off from his conscious awareness and left in the past—the child he was at various ages, his parents as larger-than-life figures, a caretaker, a pet, siblings as they were then, people he once loved or feared—still are alive inside. And "whatever" was buried also still exists in his inner world—innocence, betrayal, fear, joy, guilt, shame, love, and archetypes that he denied were a part of him. There are adolescent and adult dis-memberments also: major loves and friendships that he cut himself off from, a child he might have fathered, a homosexual friend he rejected, an Asian "wife" left behind in Korea, Japan, or Vietnam, a woman who was love of his life whom he could not marry—the people and corresponding parts of himself that didn't "fit" and were "dismembered."

Whatever is dis-membered and buried through repression is "buried alive": when it's uncovered, it exists as it was. This truth is especially dramatic when, as is common, what got buried was unexpressed grief. Once tapped, it's as if the loss were yesterday, not decades ago or even last year. Smoldering rage is much more accessible; like hot coals covered by a layer of earth in a firepit, anger lies below the surface in many, perhaps even most men, though it is as deeply repressed as is grief in some of them.

And even more important than uncovering feelings is resurrecting (or re-membering) "who" got "buried alive": the sacrificed child, who was put away when he was not acceptable or not wanted or was abused and ashamed; the inspired adolescent, who was ridiculed and then seen no more; whoever was seemingly inappropriate; the denied archetypes that now could revitalize his life.

Discovering what happened and why carries into the present. Each of us has a personal story, with a cast of characters and a role we were cast in by our family, a story that we continue to unconsciously live, recruiting others to play the familiar roles, until we become aware of the underlying plots and subplots.

Who you tried to be and how you were seen by others may be very different from your own archetypes and thus your own myth.

FINDING YOUR MYTH

Through knowing the gods as archetypes, you can see yourself and others more clearly. You can identify whom you most naturally resemble, see which one you may have tried to be, and which of them you have not accepted. When knowledge of the mythic dimension comes into your possession, it can help you find your bearings and a path that is true for you; one that reflects who you authentically are, which makes life meaningful.

If you had "Aha!" reactions as you read this book, your intellect and feelings came together as personally known intuitive truth. Your heart or your body affirmed what your head was learning. However, if knowledge of the gods has so far only been intellectually grasped and myths are only old stories, then you still don't really *know* and are missing the heart of the message of this book. For knowledge of the gods is only a means to empower authenticity, its value lies in making it possible to say, "This matters to me!" and to act accordingly.

Paradoxically, it is still necessary to find your myth, even if you were told them all, and related to none of them personally. For you don't need to know what your myth is, you only have to live it.

How?

In the following dialogue, mythologist Joseph Campbell tells us:

"How is a person to go about finding his or her myth?" a young man in a lecture audience once asked Campbell, who

286

responded with a question of his own: "Where is your deepest sense of harmony and bliss?"

"I don't know—I'm not sure," he answered.

"Find it," Campbell sang back—"and then follow it."[1]

FINDING HARMONY AND BLISS

Harmony is being on the right path, being one with it—making a living doing work that is absorbing and consistent with your personal values, doing what you have a gift for. Harmony is being with a partner or companions or alone, with animals or with nature, in a particular city or country or place, and having a sense of "ringing true" there. Harmony is experiencing deep grief that corresponds to deep loss. Harmony is uninhibited, unselfconscious spontaneity, the immediacy of laughter, the welling up of tears. Harmony happens when behavior and belief come together, when inner archetypal life and outer life are expressions of each another, and we are being true to who we are. And only we can say and know: "I feel at home here," "I am totally absorbed doing this." "It gives me joy." "I love you." "This is bliss."

Bliss and joy come in moments of living our highest truth—moments when what we do is consistent with our archetypal depths. It's when we are most authentic and trusting, and feel that whatever we are doing, which can be quite ordinary, is nonetheless sacred. This is when we sense that we are part of something divine that is in us and is everywhere.

THE COURAGE TO ACT

To know what really is important to you, to have a real sense of who you are and what would be deeply satisfying and archetypally true, is not enough. You must also have the courage to act. As noted earlier, our word "courage" comes from the French word *coeur*, "heart": courage is a willingness to act from the heart, to let your heart lead the way, not knowing what will be required of you next, and if you can do it.

There are crucial forks and stepping-off places in every road. What should you do when compassion for an outsider conflicts with belonging to a group, for example? For men, group conformity is a powerful force; and the cost of going against the group is to risk being outside of it, possibly to have the hostility of the group then turned on you, be shunned, or be linked with whomever the group devalues.

With this as the possible penalty, do you go along with the group when the group goes against a person or a principle that matters to you? There is a cost to pay either way. Many a man feels guilty to this day for something he did with a group he was in. He may keep it as a dirty secret, may repress it from his mind, may become phobic or paranoid, or the experience may give him courage to act differently next time. As one man said to me, "I didn't lift a finger and just watched what happened. I will never forget and I will never let it happen again."

When a man decides to act on his principles and from his heart, and goes against the group, he takes a risk. It is likewise a risk for him to leave work that pays well to seek work he loves—with no guarantees. Or set out to manifest a dream. Or, for love, abdicates a secure place in the world. In these situations, he takes a fork in the road, leaves the broad road traveled by others, to live his own personal myth. By acting from his heart, and doing what is true for him, he will probably travel at least at the beginning without outer companions, but he very likely will not feel alone—for ego and archetypes are connected; the "gods" are with him.

When a man (or woman) follows the bliss—and acts from his heart and his authentic being, that commitment seems in turn to energize the world. I have a card tacked up on a bookcase, a quote from Goethe that says what I have experienced myself, and over and over, seen to be true for others. It says,

> Until one is committed, there is hesitancy, the chance to draw back, always ineffectiveness, concerning all acts of initiative (and creation). The moment one definitely commits oneself, then Providence moves too. A whole stream of events issues from the decision. Whatever you can do or dream you can, begin it. Boldness has genius, power and magic in it.

THE GEOGRAPHY OF THE JOURNEY

In each of the separate chapters about the gods, the sections on psychological difficulties and ways to grow provide specific information about the difficult psychological terrain associated with a particular god or archetype. Psychological difficulties are the shadow areas of the particular archetype. If we are taken over by the dark side of an archetype, it will possess us until we differentiate from it and struggle free from its hold.

Others may help us. We may be unconscious of the negative effects of something we do and even resist knowing this until a series of confrontations brings this to light. Or we may be overly critical or fascinated by another person's actions or attitude that turn out to belong to an archetype that we need to acknowledge as part of ourselves.

In the shadow (as Jungians define it) lies everything that is yet unborn or not yet conscious within us, which includes the positive potential of archetypes that have not yet seen the light of day, as well as whatever our conscious attitude deems unacceptable and keeps hidden there (which are the same as the contents of the psychoanalytic id).

THE MISSING FEMININE PRESENCE

Powerful goddesses are notably absent from patriarchal mythology or theology, just as mothers and wives are either powerless or unimportant in the stories of the Greek gods. In Greek mythology, the father god is supreme, and the struggle of fathers and sons the important conflict. Though not the subject of this book, real mothers are major presences in the lives of real mortal men, and women have enormous significance in their lives. Even more unseen and unacknowledged is the influence of a man's anima, which Jung described as the largely unconscious feminine side of a man, which affects his moods, emotional bonds, and how he perceives women. Psychologically perceptive men who read *Goddesses in Everywoman* saw the goddesses in themselves: they found that a feminine archetype corresponded to the feminine part of themselves, or that the image of a particular goddess is "who" they sought in women. The goddesses and their influence are largely in the shadow in individual men's psyches, and what they represent as been minimized or devalued in the culture, as in mythology.

289

A GUIDE ON THE JOURNEY: HERMES

In ancient Greece, travelers prayed to be accompanied by the Messenger God, Hermes. Hermes gifts of communication, quick thinking, inventiveness, friendliness, and even a little larceny all help travelers. Contemporary men (and women), whose occupations literally take them on the road, may know only this part of the archetype. But for those who also see life as a spiritual journey, Hermes is known as the Guide of Souls.

This Hermes, the Guide of Souls, speaks through Joseph Campbell, when he advises us to "follow the bliss." This Hermes is Yoda in *Star Wars,* the wise, gentle, ancient being who helped Luke Skywalker master his own fears and not be taken in by illusions. This Hermes is Jung writing about the archetypes of the collective unconscious, bringing this whole inner world into intellectual awareness. This Hermes bridges worlds with his understanding, and brings word to us of the realm of the soul. He knows that the soul exists after death. He travels between the underworld and the highest places in the sky world, and knows the terrain in between. This Hermes can discern the purity of an experience, just as the substance mercury will only bond with precious metals. He is a guide on the path to individuation who helps us know what is personally authentic, and supports our potential for growth and wholeness. When we listen to this Hermes, we recognize the truth of what he says.

Since Hermes, the Guide of Souls, is an archetype, it is part of each of us, potentially available to everyone, especially when we contemplate where we are on our journey, and go inward to get our bearings. Hermes is called by a variety of names. People with a spiritual outlook sometimes call Hermes the "inner guide" or "inner voice." In the psychiatric literature about multiple personalities, Hermes is another name for what Ralph Allison, a psychiatrist who has done extensive pioneering work with such people, calls "the inner self helper."

The multiple personality has been popularized in *The Three Faces of Eve* by C. H. Thigpen and *Sybil* by Flora Schreiber, so that many people may know that the multiple personality can have many separate personalities of both sexes and all ages living within one body. These personalities are cut off from one another and usually have limited or no knowledge of one another, which is not surprising, since each developed as a means to forget and get away from intolerable abuse and pain. In contrast, the personality Allison describes as "the inner self helper" knew all the personalities, and could provide information about each one and what had happened in the patient's life. He found that this inner self helper was androgynous, felt only love and goodwill, and described itself as feeling close to God. With the help of the inner self helper in psychotherapy, the many fragmentary personalities become aware of the others, after which they can voluntarily integrate into one personality.

To a lesser extent, because the damage done is less (but on a continuum that links the multiple personality with the reasonably well-adjusted person), a very similar task needs to be done whenever the individuation journey begins, usually somewhere in midlife. The task is not to knit together separate personalities, but to reconnect with cut-off parts of ourselves. Psychological "dis-memberment" takes place in the first half of life of most men, who do to themselves what Procrustes did to men on their way to Athens—cut off whatever didn't fit. To heal and make whole takes "re-membering." To do this, we must go downward or inward to find the pieces and bring them back to light. This is the task of Hermes.

It was Hermes who brought Persephone out of the underworld, it was he who rescued the infant Dionysus, who was the dismembered god, and it is this archetype in us that can bring the repressed feminine or the divine child in each of us into consciousness. Thus his task is not only to find what was personally repressed, but also to resurrect archetypes that have been culturally buried.

As deities, Hermes and Hestia, Goddess of the Hearth, were paired together as part of the structure of the home; a *herm* or stone pillar representing Hermes stood at the doorway of each house; within and at the center of the household was Hestia's hearth. These two deities, one as guardian and guide, the other as the source of warmth and illumination, symbolize aspects of the archetype of the Self.

HESTIA—THE SACRED FIRE IN THE TEMPLES OF THE GODS

In ancient times, the traveler might seek to visit the temple of a particular god or goddess to invoke help or pay respects to a deity when the road taken took him by a temple. On our life journey, we are like these travelers, who came across the temples of different gods on different stretches of the road. The viscissitudes of life constellate situations that are archetypal, so that on one part of the journey, we encounter a particular god or archetype; at another place, we visit the temple of another god.

If we were to go inside the temple of a god, we would also find an unseen goddess was there. This was Hestia, the eldest Olympian, who was present in the temples of all the other deities. Hestia was Goddess of the Hearth and Temple. She was the fire at the center of a round hearth—an image that is a three-dimensional mandala, symbol of the archetype of the Self, which Jung considered the center of the personality, the archetype of meaning and wholeness.

Hestia's presence made house and temple sacred places. A new bride took the fire from her family hearth to her new house, and only then was it sanctified. The fire colonists brought to new temples from the home temple made the new building sacred. Hestia's fire was thus both the center and the connecting link.

Hestia was an anonymous goddess in that she had no persona, no characteristic outer appearance. Thus there were no paintings or statues of her. She was a virgin goddess, which meant that she had a "one unto herself" quality; she did not need anyone else to feel whole and intact.

As a goddess she is an archetype in women. But she clearly is a presence in the psyches of many men as well, men who need physical order, free of clutter and noise, in order to feel centered in themselves. Men who need and enjoy solitude, finding it gives energy to other aspects of themselves, men who have a sense of wholeness and intactness.

Hestia was the fire at the center of a round hearth in the temple of each deity, an image that corresponds to the sacred dimension of each archetype. When what you do gives you a sense of meaning that feels deeply connected to who you really are, an archetype is active in you that specifically relates both to the activity and at the same time to the Self. A man (or woman) who is totally absorbed creating something in his studio or workshop, for example, is in a psychological space that metaphorically corresponds to being in the temple of Hephaestus. When an ecstatic quality enters lovemaking and there is a sense of communion, love is being made in the temple of Dionysus. When an athlete on a playing field enters a timeless moment and feels as if he has all the time in the world to make a pass, even as opposing players are charging towards him, he is a centered Ares, who in the midst of action is simultaneously in contact with his own inner still point—symbolized by the fire at the center of the hearth in Ares temple.

When mortals met the gods and goddesses outside of the temple, they no longer were in the precinct of Hestia's hearth. Then the encounter with the god, as that with the archetype, might well be beneficial but it could also be risky, with negative or destructive possibilities. Gods often took people by surprise and overpowered them. They forced their will on mortals, seduced, abducted, or punished them. Correspondingly, an archetype can seduce or overpower a man (or woman); when this happens psychologically, that person now identifies with one god who takes him over. The businessman who has been taken over by the Zeus archetype, for example, throws himself totally into acquiring position and power; he has no personal life, and no one seems to matter to him. Identification with one god's positive or negative attributes inflates the importance of this one archetype; to identify with a god also makes you feel important. This personal inflation is what makes the identification with a god seductive.

In contrast, when you feel gratitude for the experiences of harmony and bliss that come when you do work you love, or are with people special to you, or enjoy solitude, you are aware that there is depth and meaning in your life. That consciouness and thankfulness parallels visits mortals made to the temples of their gods.

A mortal entered a temple by choice, conscious of what he was doing. Within the temple, he encountered an image, usually a statue of the god. He felt the presence or energy of that particular deity. Although he focused on the deity whose temple it was, Hestia was also present, in the fire and in the clean-swept temple. This is a metaphor for a man (or woman) who lives authentically because he is in conscious relationship to one or more activated archetypes, through which he feels centered and that affords a clarity and certainty that there is a sacred dimension in his life.

HOMECOMING

On a journey, a traveler might enter the temples of many gods or goddesses, or he might pass them all by, or he might stop at the temples of only one particular deity. He counted himself fortunate, as indeed he was, if Hermes accompanied him as guardian and guide. However far his journey took him, each traveler also looked forward to an eventual homecoming.

Hermes could accompany the traveler as far as the door, where the herm or stone pillar stood. Then the traveler crossed the threshold and was home. Home was made sacred by Hestia's presence in the fire at the center of the round hearth. The homefire welcomed the returning family member or the new-born one.

In ancient Greece, a newborn was ritually made a member of the family when he was five days old. In this rite, the child was carried around the hearth by his father and introduced to Hestia and to his family. This ritual of acknowledgment and welcome—of homecoming—consciously recognized new life as part of the whole.

It's possible to come home.

"Home" is a psychological destination where we connect with a spiritual center, just as in ancient Greece, home was a sacred place of homecoming because Hestia was there. As a symbol of the Self, or the center of the personality, we experience our own "Hestia" as an inner still point associated with a sense of wholeness. We find Hestia whenever we enter a sanctuary and find a welcoming hearth. It may literally be home, or a place of solitude and peace, or in the arms of another person, or at play, or at work, or in a place of worship, or in nature. Wherever and whenever we find ourselves "at home," we also find harmony and bliss, and we are living our personal myth.

12.

The Missing God

There is a missing god among the Olympians—the son of Metis and Zeus, whose birth was foreseen, and who was to supplant his father Zeus and rule with an all-loving heart. For him to be born, Metis—feminine wisdom—would have to emerge once more into western culture and into our consciousness. A son of Metis and Zeus would have had an exceptional pair of parents. When the Great Goddess in her several aspects was the Mother God, fatherhood was not important, possibly not even recognized. When the Sky Father gods established patriarchal supremacy, the pendulum swung the other way: goddess and women were subjugated, which has been the historical and theological condition for several thousand years now. Male gods have had dominion, and none of them either in Greek mythology of Judeo-Christianity has had both a strong and wise mother and a powerful and loving father. Few humans have, either.

ZEUS: FATHER ARCHETYPE IN TRANSITION

In his mythology as a Sky Father, Zeus changed. He began as a threatened father, who swallowed Metis to abort a son he feared would defeat him and take over (as his father Cronus had feared and hence consumed his children, while Cronus's father Uranus, the first father, had buried his). Zeus then became a father of many children—the Olympians, and the lesser deities and demigods. He was a distant father who approved of some of his many children, rejected others, and was often protective of them from afar. He was thus unlike his father and his grandfather before him: they had no positive paternal feelings and did not want children. But with his son Dionysus, the youngest Olympian and the child whom he rescued and then nurtured himself, Zeus had made yet another change.

The mythology of the sky gods (Uranus, Cronus, and Zeus) reflect changes in the father archetype that have biblical parallels—the God of the Old Testament was a jealous and vengeful god who evolved into the loving and forgiving God of the New Testament. Dionysus was the only Olympian with a mortal mother—like Jesus. Both were persecuted, sacrificed, and reborn or resurrected. Images of Dionysus as a divine child are sometimes mistaken for the infant Jesus: the child held by the Black Madonna of Montserrat, for example, holds what looks like a pine cone or upside-down pineapple—the thyrsus, a symbol of Dionysus.

The father archetype is changing, and as more men shift in this direction a new father archetype has come into the culture. As each new generation of men become fathers, they join others who in the last third of the twentieth century have been present during their women's labor and delivery. These men usually bond with their infant children and are often involved fathers, not emotionally distant or unavailable Sky Fathers. They mirror the evolution of Zeus from a distant sky god to one who created a womb space for his son in his own thigh. When he did this, Sky Father Zeus took on an earthy aspect, as contemporary men also do. And some men are becoming Earth Fathers altogether.

In *Earth Father/Sky Father,* Arthur and Libby Colman describe the Earth Father as a man who interacts with his family on a day-to-day basis. For an Earth Father, his family is his primary focus. Even when he is away from home, his consciousness is with his children. At home, his activities will be nurturant, focused on the intimate parenting behaviors that sustain relationships within the family. The Colmans emphasize the value of this kind and quality of fathering, and the difficulty doing this in a patriarchy:

> Of all the images of parenting, that of earth father is farthest removed from the values and ambitions instilled in growing boys in America. It may be the hardest image for a man to feel truly enriched by, and yet it represents a most fundamental level of parenting. Rather than being a hero, a disciplinarian, a bridge to the outside world, or a force to be overcome, the earth father

takes on the job of providing his children with the basic trust and inner security with which to grow up and out of the family towards independence and a unique identity.[1]

In my practice, I've heard professional men whose position in the world placed them like Zeus, on summits, wish that they could stay home with the children. I hear of the pleasure they take giving their children their baths or being the one who reads the bedtime story. These fathers do not resent their little boys, but love them fiercely. Some would not even leave an unhappy marriage, because it would mean losing a daily contact with their children.

Thus in contemporary American men, the archetype of the father is changing. Although the patriarchal Sky Father still dominates, one at a time individual men are changing. Possibly reflecting a similar transition, western political and religious leaders no longer have the authority they once had. They aren't considered infallible anymore, they don't find it as easy as it once was to order young men to lay down their lives fighting wars. They are less personally like Zeus.

METIS: THE EMERGING WISE MOTHER ARCHETYPE

Very little information is given about Metis in Greek mythology. This silence might be expected: she was tricked into becoming small and then swallowed, so whoever she once was would be minimized if known at all. We hear only that she had helped Zeus free his brothers and sisters, who had been swallowed by Cronus. It was she who knew how and provided the emetic. Metis was a goddess of wisdom, a divinity worshiped long before Zeus and the Olympians. We also know that she was his first consort and it had been predicted that she would have two children, a daughter with courage and clarity equal to any man, and a son, "a boy of all-conquering heart, who would become king of gods and men."[2] Thus when Metis became pregnant, Zeus feared that the child she was carrying was the predicted son who would supplant him. This was why he tricked her into becoming small and then swallowed her.

As it turned out, the child she was carrying was not the son, but the daughter, Athena, who emerged out of Zeus's head, as a full-grown woman wearing golden armor. Athena had no memory of her mother, and considered Zeus her sole parent.

Metis, as divine feminine wisdom, was indeed swallowed by the patriarchy, and disappeared from the Western world. The myth reflects what happened historically (probably between 4500 B.C. and 2400 B.C.): successive waves of Indo-European invaders, with their warrior gods and father-based theologies, subjugated the people of old Europe, who for 25,000 years had followed mother-based religions and developed a peaceful, culturally advanced civilization that was unstratified, agricultural, and egalitarian. Because their cities were unfortified and exposed and because they lacked military skills, they were conquered by the horse-riding, sky god-worshiping invaders who imposed their patriarchal culture and religion on the defeated people.

The Goddess (known by many different names) became the subservient consort of the invader gods, and her attributes and powers were absorbed (swallowed) or came under the domination of a male deity. Even the power of giving birth or creating life, which had been the natural realm of women and the Goddess, became co-opted, and sky gods now created life through their words and will, or gave birth through the head.

Women forgot her, thus resembling Athena, who was born as a fully grown woman out of Zeus's head, with no recollection of her mother Metis. Like Athena, most women are daughters of the patriarchy, who have recognized the divinity only of God the Father. Women have not (until recently) remembered a time "when God was a woman." Lost to memory was the existence of God the Mother, the Goddess, the feminine face of God. In the last decade, "Metis" is re-emerging and being remembered. In a contemporary women's journal, *Women of Power*, this renaissance is described:

> The ancient spiritual voice of woman now speaks its long-hidden wisdom and becomes an active force for the conscious evolution of our world. . . . This emerging voice speaks of the recognition of the interconnectedness of all life; the awareness that everything has consciousness and is sacred; the re-membering of our selves as sacred beings, and the loving of our psyches, bodies, and emo-

tions; the empowerment of women and all oppressed peoples; the creation of world peace, social justice, and environmental harmony; the activation of spiritual and psychic powers; the honoring of woman's divinity; and reverence for the earth, and the celebration of her seasons and cycles, and those of our lives.[3]

Women's spirituality is re-emerging into our culture as a dimension of the women's movement, and the renewal coincides synchronistically with significant new archeological discoveries showing evidence of the historical matriarchal period. This long, peaceful, goddess-worshiping period of history is described in *The Goddesses and Gods of Old Europe,* by Marija Gimbutas; in *When God Was a Woman,* by Merlin Stone; and in *The Chalice and the Blade* by Riane Eisler. The Nag Hammadi scrolls, known more widely as the Gnostic Gospels—about which Elaine Pagels has written a book by this title—reveal that Sophia or a feminine aspect of God was known and honored by the Gnostic Christians. Eastern Orthodox Christians worshiped Sophia. Her greatest shrine, the Hagia Sophia (the church of the Holy Sophia, or Holy Female Wisdom) was built in Constantinople (now Istanbul). Roman Christians later claimed that it was dedicated to a minor virgin martyr. In Jewish mysticism, Sophia's name was Shekina. Metis, Sophia, and Shekina are different names for the same forgotten feminine wisdom that was once deified.

For many centuries, feminine wisdom, by any name, has been unseen and been forgotten; if seen, it was not defined as wisdom. For example, when it came to making ethical choices, women used to be defined as being less ethical than men. Carol Gilligan, in her book *In a Different Voice,* suggested that most women might perceive an ethical situation differently from most men, valuing the person and relationships over abstract principle, and that this choice did not reflect inferior ethics, but different values. When affiliation values are considered equal to principle, then compassion and justice can exist together, and both are completed by the other. Carol Gilligan here voiced a Metis position, with the courage and mental clarity to confront and do academic battle—a contemporary Athena who has remembered Metis.

We see women speaking up about their perceptions and values all the time now, in their personal lives as in the academic world or workplace. And the first time ever, perhaps, it's possible for women as a group—for there always are exceptional individuals—to become strong and wise mothers, who do not have their minds or will swallowed up by their husbands, do not shrink from voicing their values, and if necessary, can intervene and protect their sons and daughters.

THE SON OF METIS AS A NEW ARCHETYPE

Although the archetype of the son with a loving heart has been present as Jesus in the West, and as Krishna in the East, their presence in the culture did not change the basic power structure of the patriarchy. Zeus on the mountain top with his thunderbolt has continued to be the ruling principle in the culture, and will remain so as long as we look to superior force or weapon superiority for our security, and consider isolation from others both possible and desirable.

For a long time, Zeus's position has seemed logically unassailable. But now we have seen how radioactive particles from a nuclear accident at Chernobyl, near Leningrad, contaminated milk in the Netherlands, and how the destruction of rain forests in Brazil can change the atmosphere of Earth, and how a nuclear war leads to a nuclear winter for the planet. We become increasingly aware of our interdependence, of how we share this planet and its fate together. Zeus is still the ruling power principle, but what will happen to Zeus as our consciousness grows that his thunderbolt cannot be used without destroying life on Earth?

Global consciousness, environmental concerns, ecology, women's spirituality, and nuclear disarmament are expressions of the re-emergence of Metis as a metaphor for the wisdom that we are all related to one another and to the mother archetype. This is a time of cultural transition, a time of re-membering Metis, as feminine wisdom, as Mother Nature, as the sacredness of Earth, or the divinity of God the Mother returns to the culture, at the same time that the father archetype as seen in contemporary men is changing.

NEW ARCHETYPES AND MORPHIC FIELDS

In *A New Science of Life: The Hypothesis of Formative Causation* (1981), Rupert Sheldrake, a theoretical biologist, proposed a radical new theory of how living things learn and assume new forms. His theory provides an explanation of how new arche-types can come into being—and thus how human nature could change.

Sheldrake's hypothesis is this: when a behavior is repeated often enough, it forms a "morphogenetic (or form-shaping) field." This field (which Sheldrake now calls "morphic") has a kind of cumulative memory based on what has happened to the species in the past. All members of the species (not just living organisms, but also protein molecules, crystals, and even atoms) are tuned into their particular morphic field, which ranges across space and time through a process called "morphic resonance."

In the realm of crystals, for example, the theory says that the form or structure the crystal takes depends on its character-istic field. Moreover, a new compound would be hard to crystal-lize the first time, but after that first time it should get easier and easier to crystallize because of the influence of the morphic field (or "memory") of each previous crystallization. This fact is very well known among chemists, notes Sheldrake.

Applied to us, Sheldrake's theory explains how fundamental (or archetypal) changes in human beings might also come about. At first a change in attitude or behavior is difficult, but as more and more individuals change, it becomes progressively easier for other people to do so, and not just through direct influence. According to Sheldrake, people tune into the new pattern within the morphic field through morphic resonance and are affected by it, explaining how change becomes progressively easier. At some point, the number of individuals needed to tip the scales is reached; there is a new archetype in the collective unconscious.

Sheldrake himself equated the two ideas:

> "The approach I am putting forward is very similar to Jung's idea of the collective unconscious. The main difference is that Jung's idea was applied primarily to human experience and human col-lective memory. What I am suggesting is that a very similar prin-ciple operates throughout the entire universe, not just in human beings."[4]

THE HUNDREDTH MONKEY: A CONTEMPORARY MYTH

The Hundredth Monkey is the name of a new myth. It's a story that has arisen, been repeated, and written about only in the last two decades. It is of very recent origin and yet, like Greek myths that tell of the Trojan war, it's not clear where fact ends and metaphor begins. The story was based on scientific observations of monkey colonies in Japan. The most widely read version was written by Ken Keyes, Jr., which I condense and paraphrase as follows:

Off the shore of Japan, scientists had been studying monkey colonies on many separate islands for over thirty years. In order to keep track of the monkeys, they would drop sweet potatoes on the beach for them to eat. The monkeys would come out of the trees to get the sweet potatoes, and would be in plain sight to be observed. One day an 18-month-old female monkey named Imo started to wash her sweet potato in the sea before eating it. We can imagine that it tasted better without the grit and sand; maybe it even was slightly salty. Imo showed her playmates and her mother how to do it, and her friends showed their mothers, and gradually more and more monkeys began to wash their sweet potatoes instead of eating them grit and all. At first, only the adults who imitated their children learned, and gradually others did also. One day, the observers saw that all the monkeys on that particular island were washing their sweet potatoes.

Although this was significant, what was even more fascinating to note was that when this shift happened, the behavior of monkeys on all the other islands changed as well; they now all washed their sweet potatoes—despite the fact that monkey colonies on the different islands had no direct contact with each other.

Here was validation for the morphogenic field theory: it could account for what had happened. The "hundredth monkey" was the hypothesized anonymous monkey that tipped the scales for the culture: the one whose change in behavior signaled the critical number of changed monkeys, after which all the monkeys on all the islands washed their sweet potatoes.

The Hundredth Monkey is a New Age allegory that gives hope to people who have been working on changing themselves and saving the planet, and wondering if their individual efforts will make any difference at all. As a myth, the Hundredth Monkey is a statement that affirms a commitment to work on something, like ridding Earth of nuclear weapons—even if the effect is invisible for a long time. If there is to be a hundredth monkey, there has to be a human equivalent of Imo and her friends; someone has to be the twenty-seventh and the eighty-first and the ninety-ninth monkey, before a new archetype can come into being.

Sheldrake's hypothesis provides us with an understanding of how change in a species might come about through the actions of individuals who, one at a time, do something new. If the son of Metis is to supplant Zeus in the culture, that change may come about only after a critical number of individual men (and women) trust love more than power and base their actions on this principle. As more and more people do so, according to Sheldrake's hypothesis, it will become easier and easier, until one fine day, someone will be the anonymous hundredth monkey.

Most men and women, however, feel neither the need nor the faith to tackle changing the world. Those who do try are encouraged by the Hundredth Monkey, because it is a myth that describes what they are drawn to do anyway. Whenever we recognize ourselves in a myth, it is empowering. A myth that evokes an "Aha!" helps us stay true to what moves us deeply, to be our authentic selves.

Besides speaking to those who are inwardly motivated to make a difference in the outer world, the Hundredth Monkey is also a metaphor for what goes on in an individual psyche. In the inner world, doing is becoming: if we repeat a behavior motivated by an attitude or a principle enough times, eventually we become what we do.

SON OF METIS AS A PERSONAL ARCHETYPE

In the *Star Wars* movies, Luke Skywalker relies on what his heart knows or hopes for—that there is a loving father in Darth Vader. He knows that he, the son, must not be tempted by hopelessness and fear to give up on the possibility and so become one of them, as the Emperor had assured Darth Vader he would. In his life-and-death struggle with Darth Vader, Luke kept faith with the intuition that a loving father could exist within this dark figure, and by acting on that belief, drew him out. As contemporary mythic figures, the Emperor and Darth Vader are updated versions of Uranus and Cronus, hostile fathers who resent or fear their sons. Luke is the son with the loving heart who defeats the negative father in order to liberate the loving one.

Stephen Spielberg's extraordinarily successful movie *E. T.* is another contemporary myth about a boy who trusts his own heart. Once again, men in power are in charge of the situation, this time clothed as rational scientists. *E.T.*, the innocent extra-terrestrial, is taken captive as a specimen, and when it seems that he has died from isolation—as infants who are not loved and touched have done—the boy's love brings him back to life.

Likewise, a boyish hero, Frodo, is the main protagonist of J. R. R. Tolkien's trilogy, *The Fellowship of the Ring*. Frodo is a hobbit; hobbits are about the size of preadolescent boys, with furry feet and endearing qualities such as loyalty and trust and vulnerability. The task that Frodo and his friends take on—and successfully accomplish—is formidable: to destroy the Ring of Power, and not be seduced into using it instead.

In these films and books, the protagonists come to a moment of inner truth or faith, on which the outcome of the story depends. Individual men and women in a patriarchy make the very same choices: will we identify with the aggressor that Darth Vader symbolized? Will we trust each other as part of the fellowship or be seduced by the power of the Ring? Will we trust our hearts and believe, or will we accept that something or someone is hopeless because experts say so? Will we look out only for ourselves, or will we keep faith with our companions?

In contemporary myths, as in Greek mythology, Metis—feminine wisdom—is absent but "her" values, which emphasize affiliation with others and connection to the earth and all life are emerging. And as men (and women) reconnect with feminine wisdom, as many women are now doing, we reconnect with a missing parent, and find the missing god in ourselves.

It's been my impression that we all come into the world as children who want love, and if we can't get love, we settle for power. When we remember Metis, we remember that love is what we really wanted all along.

On a personal level, once power becomes the ruling arche-type in a man's (or woman's) psyche, that person's choices are made in order to achieve position, keep power, look good, and be in control. Power choices are not made for love—for the love (or bliss) of it, for the love (or joy) of doing it, out of love for someone or something, or for the love (or good) that is generated. When we become conscious that our choices have to do with deciding which principle we will base them on, we can decide to go for what we love—for what has meaning or is true for us personally.

Life continually presents us with moments of decision. When we consciously make a choice that is based on love and wisdom, knowingly rejecting an alternative that would enhance our power, the first courageous decision is often the hardest. Each next time, it may become easier, until what once would have been the difficult choice becomes the natural one. Then, love becomes the ruling principle in our psyche.

The last paragraph was to be the end of the book, but before the manuscript went to the typesetter, I found myself thinking about endings, and some lines from T. S. Eliot's *Four Quartets* came to mind that I have found comforting, know are true, and take heart from. You might also.

> "What we call the beginning is often the end
> And to make an end is to make a beginning.
> The end is where we start from."[5]

Love to you.

Appendix: Who's Who in Greek Mythology

Aphrodite (af ro dī′ tē), Goddess of Love and Beauty, known as Venus to the Romans. The unfaithful wife of Hephaestus, lame God of the Forge, she had many affairs with gods and mortals, most notably with Ares the God of War.

Apollo (a pol′ ō), also called Apollo by the Romans, the handsome God of the Sun; lawgiver, archer, and patron of fine arts; a son of Zeus and Leto; twin brother of Artemis. Sometimes also referred to as Helios.

Ares (á rēs) or Mars as he was called by the Romans, was the God of War, and archetypal warrior, lover, and dancer. He was the son of Zeus and Hera, who was despised by his father for his battle lust. He was the lover of Aphrodite, with whom he fathered a daughter, Harmonia, and two sons—Fear (Deimos) and Panic (Phobus) who joined him on the battlefield.

Artemis (ar′ te mis), whom the Romans called Diana, was Goddess of the Hunt and Moon. She was the daughter of Zeus and Leto, and twin sister of Apollo, God of the Sun.

Athena (a thē′ na), known as Minerva to the Romans, Goddess of Wisdom and Handicrafts, patron of her namesake city Athens, and protector of numerous heroes. Usually portrayed wearing armor, and known as the best strategist in battle. She acknowledged only one parent, Zeus, but was also the daughter of wise Metis, the first consort of Zeus, whom he swallowed.

Cronus (krō′ nus), or Saturn (Roman). A Titan and the youngest son of Gaia and Uranus, who emasculated his father and became the chief god. Husband of Rhea and the father of six of the Olympians (Hestia, Demeter, Hera, Hades, Poseidon, Zeus) who swallowed the first five when they were born. He in turn was overpowered by his youngest son, Zeus.

Demeter (de mē' ter), known as Ceres to the Romans. Demeter was Goddess of Grain, and the mother of Persephone, whom Hades abducted into the underworld.

Dionysus (dī o nī' sus), known as Bacchus to the Romans, God of Wine and Ecstasy. He was the son of Zeus and Semele, and Zeus incubated him in his thigh. His archetypal roles are as ecstatic lover, wanderer, and mystic.

Gaia (gī' a), the Goddess Earth. Mother and wife of Uranus (sky), mother of the Titans and grandmother of the first generation of Olympians.

Hades (hā' dēz) or Pluto (Roman), ruler of the underworld, a son of Rhea and Cronus, abductor-husband of Persephone. Brother of Zeus and Poseidon, and one of the three aspects of the father archetype. He ruled over the realm of souls, and the collective unconscious.

Hephaestus (he fes' tus), known as Vulcan by the Romans, lame God of the Forge, the only Olympian god who worked. He was the cuckolded husband of Aphrodite, the rejected son of Hera, who was his sole parent, and he was also rejected by Zeus, his nominal father. Archetypal roles as the craftsman, artisan, cripple, loner.

Hera (her' a), also known as Juno to the Romans, was Goddess of Marriage. Married to Zeus, who was a philanderer, she was portrayed as a vindictive and jealous wife.

Hermes (hur' mēz), better known by his Roman name Mercury. The messenger of the gods, the patron god of trade, communication, travelers, and thieves. He conducted souls to Hades, rescued Dionysus, and brought Persephone back from the underworld. He had an affair with Aphrodite, with whom he fathered Hermaphroditus.

Hestia (hes' ti a), also known as the Roman goddess Vesta. The Goddess of the Hearth and Temple, least known of the Olympians. Her fire made home and temple sacred. Personifies the archetype of the self.

Persephone (per sef′ ō nē), also referred to by the Greeks as the Kore (kō′ rē) or the maiden, and called Proserpina by the Romans. The abducted daughter of Demeter, Persephone became queen of the underworld.

Poseidon (pō sī′ don), God of the Sea, and Earth-shaker, an Olympian more commonly known by his Roman name, Neptune. He vied with Athena for Athens and lost. Brother of Zeus and Hades, one of the three aspects of the father archetype.

Rhea (rē′ a), daughter of Gaia and Uranus, sister and wife of Cronus. Mother of Hestia, Demeter, Hera, Hades, Poseidon, and Zeus.

Uranus (ū rā′ nus), the first sky god, Gaia's son and her husband. Father of the Titans, he was emasculated and overthrown by his youngest son, Cronus.

Zeus (zūs), called Jupiter or Jove by the Romans; chief god of the Olympians, God of Lightning and Thunder, youngest son of Rhea and Cronus. He overthrew the Titans and established the supremacy of the Olympians as rulers of the universe. Philandering husband of Hera, he had many wives prior to her, many affairs, and numerous offspring from these liaisons—some were the second-generation Olympians, others were the heroes of Greek mythology.

GOD ARCHETYPE CHART

God	Category	Archetypal Roles	Significant Others
Zeus (Jupiter, Jove) God of Sky and Lightning Realm of Will and Power	Patriarchal god	King, Sky Father Executive, alliance maker Philanderer	Wife (Hera) Children (Olympian sons and daughters
Poseidon (Neptune) God of Sea, Earth-Shaker Realm of Emotion and Instinct	Patriarchal god	King, Earth Father Instinctive, emotional man, Implacable enemy	Wife (Amphitrite) Enemies (Odysseus)
Hades (Pluto) God of the Underworld Realm of Souls and the Unconscious	Patriarchal god	King Recluse	Wife (Persephone) Images (or shades)
Apollo God of Sun	Favored son	Successful goal setter Sibling	No major important others Siblings (Artemis, Hermes)
Hermes (Mercury) Messenger God	Favored son	Communicator, guide Trickster	Transiently important others Friends
Ares (Mars) God of War	Rejected son	Warrior, dancer, lover Embodied man	Lover (Aphrodite) Children
Hephaestus (Vulcan) God of the Forge	Rejected son	Craftsman Creative man	Wife (Aphrodite)
Dionysus (Bacchus) God of Ecstasy and Wine	Nurtured son	Mystic, wanderer Ecstatic lover	Women Wife (Ariadne)

GOD CHART (CONTINUED)

God	Jungian Psychological Type/Sense of Time	Psychological Difficulties	Strengths
Zeus	Usually extraverted Definitely thinking Both intuition and sensation Present and future	Ruthlessness Emotional immaturity Inflation	Ability to use power Decisiveness Generativity
Poseidon	Either extraverted or introverted Definitely feeling Past and present	Destructive emotionality Emotional instability Low self-esteem	Loyalty Access to feelings
Hades	Definitely introverted Definitely sensation Timeless	Social invisibility Depression, distortion of reality Low self-esteem	Rich inner world of images Detachment
Apollo	Usually extraverted Usually thinking Usually intuition Future	Emotional distance Arrogance Venom	Ability to set goals and reach them Appreciation of clarity and form
Hermes	Usually extraverted Definitely intuitive Usually thinking Aware of past, present, future	Impulsiveness Sociopathy Eternal adolescent	Capacity to understand meaning Communicator of ideas Friendliness

Ares	Definitely extraverted Definitely feeling Definitely sensation Immediate present	Emotional reactivity Scapegoat and abuser Low self-esteem	Integration of emotions and body Emotional expressiveness
Hephaestus	Definitely introverted Definitely feeling Definitely sensation Present	Social inappropriateness Buffoon Low self-esteem	Creativity Capacity to see and make beauty Skill with hands
Dionysus	Either extraverted or introverted Definitely sensation Immediate present/timelessness	Distortions in self-perception Substance abuse Poor self-esteem	Appreciation of Sensory Experience Love of Nature Passionate Intensity

Chapter Sources and Notes

The primary sources for each chapter are listed first, followed by footnoted references for direct quotes.

All references to Jung's *Collected Works* (abbreviated CW) are taken from *Collected Works of C. G. Jung*, edited by Sir Herbert Read, Michael Fordham, and Gerhard Adler; translated by R. F. C. Hull; Executive Editor, William McGuire; Bollingen Series 20 (Princeton, N.J.: Princeton University Press, various publication dates).

Frontispiece quote from Joseph Campbell, quoted by Keith Thompson, in "Myth as Soul of the World," *Noetics Sciences Review* (Winter 1986) p. 24.

PREFACE

NOTES

1. Daniel Levinson, *The Seasons of a Man's Life* (New York: Ballantine, 1978), p. 109.
2. Michael E. McGill, *The McGill Report on Male Intimacy* (New York: Harper & Row, 1986), p. 157.
3. Jean Baker Miller, *Toward a New Psychology of Women* (Boston: Beacon Press, 1976), pp. 3–12.

CHAPTER 1: THERE ARE GODS IN EVERYMAN

SOURCES

Bolen, Jean Shinoda. "Which Goddess Gets the Golden Apple?" In *Goddesses in Everywoman*. San Francisco: Harper & Row, 1984, pp. 263–277.

Jung, C. G. "Archetypes of the Collective Unconscious" (1954). In *CW*, vol. 9, part 1 (1968), pp. 3–41.

Jung, C. G. "The Concept of the Collective Unconscious." In *CW*, vol. 9, part 1, pp. 42–53.

Levinson, Daniel. *The Seasons of a Man's Life*. New York: Ballantine Books, 1978.

McGill, Michael E. *The McGill Report on Male Intimacy.* New York: Harper & Row, Perennial Library, 1986.

Miller, Jean Baker. "Domination-Subordination." In *Toward a New Psychology of Women.* Boston: Beacon Press, 1976, pp. 3–12.

NOTES

1. William Broyles, Jr., "Pushing the Mid-life Envelope," *Esquire,* June 1987.
2. Rollo May, *The Courage to Create* (New York: Bantam Books, 1975), p. 45.

CHAPTER 2: FATHERS AND SONS

SOURCES

Colman, Arthur, and Colman, Libby. *Earth Father, Sky Father: The Changing Concept of Fathering.* Englewood Cliffs, NJ: Prentice-Hall, 1981.

Davis, John H. *The Kennedys: Dynasty and Disaster 1848–1984.* New York: McGraw-Hill, 1984.

Dinnerstein, Dorothy. *The Mermaid and the Minotaur: Sexual Arrangements and Human Malaise.* New York: Harper Colophon Books, 1977.

Hesiod. *Theogony.* Translated and introduced by Norman O. Brown. Indianapolis: Bobbs-Merrill, 1953, 1982.

The Holy Bible, Revised Standard Version (RSV). New York: Nelson, 1953.

Jung, C. G. *Memories, Dreams, Reflections.* Recorded and edited by Aniela Jaffe, translated from the German by Richard and Clara Winston. New York: Pantheon, 1961.

Lucas, George. *Star Wars* (motion picture).

Lucas, George. *Return of the Jedi* (motion picture).

Masson, Jeffrey Moussaieff. *The Assault on Truth: Freud's Suppression of the Seduction Theory.* New York: Farrar, Straus & Giroux, 1984.

Mayerson, Philip. *Classical Mythology in Literature, Art, and Music.* New York: Wiley, 1971.

Miller, Alice. *For Your Own Good: Hidden Cruelty in Child-Rearing and the Roots of Violence.* Translated by Hildegarde and Hunter Hannum. New York: Farrar, Straus & Giroux, 1983.

Miller, Alice. *Thou Shalt Not Be Aware: Society's Betrayal of the Child.* Translated by Hildegarde and Hunter Hannum. New York: New American Library, 1986.

Samuels, Andrew, ed. *The Father: Contemporary Jungian Perspectives,* Edited and introduced by Andrew Samuels. New York: New York University Press, 1985.

NOTES

1. Hesiod, *Theogony,* trans. and intro. Norman O. Brown (Indianapolis: Bobbs-Merrill, 1953), p. 57.
2. Hesiod, p. 58.

3. C. G. Jung, "Sigmund Freud," in *Memories, Dreams, and Reflections*, ed. Aniela Jaffe, trans. Richard and Clara Winston (New York: Pantheon, 1961), pp. 159–162.
4. Alice Miller, *Thou Shalt Not Be Aware: Society's Betrayal of the Child*, trans. Hildegarde and Hunter Hannum (New York: New American Library, 1986), p. 145.
5. Miller, p. 145.
6. Bruce Ogilvie, "Interview," *Omni* (September 1987), p. 82.
7. Gen. 22:7–8. *The Holy Bible*, RSV (New York: Nelson, 1953), p. 20.
8. Gen. 22:12.
9. Gen. 22:16–17.
10. George Lucas. *Return of the Jedi* (motion picture).

CHAPTER 3: ZEUS

SOURCES

Bolen, Jean Shinoda. "Hera: Goddess of Marriage, Commitment Maker and Wife." In *Goddesses in Everywoman*. San Francisco: Harper & Row, 1984.

Colman, Arthur, and Colman, Libby. *Earth Father, Sky Father: The Changing Concept of Fathering*. New York: Prentice-Hall, 1981.

Graves, Robert. *The Greek Myths*. Vol. 1. New York: Penguin Books, 1955, 1960.

Guthrie, W. K. C. *The Greeks and Their Gods*. Boston: Beacon Press, 1950.

Hamilton, Edith. *Mythology*. Boston: Little, Brown, 1942.

Hesiod. *Theogony*. Translated and introduced by Norman O. Brown. Indianapolis: Bobbs-Merrill, 1953, 1982.

Iaccocca, Lee, with William Novak. *Iacocca: An Autobiography*. New York: Bantam Books, 1984.

Kerenyi, C. *Zeus and Hera: Archetypal Image of Father, Husband, and Wife*. Translated from the German by Christopher Holme.

Bollingen Series LXV, Vol. 5: *Archetypal Images in Greek Religion*. Princeton, NJ: Princeton University Press, 1975.

Kerenyi, C. "Stories of the Titans," "Zeus and his Spouses." *The Gods of the Greeks*. Translated from the German by Norman Cameron. England: Thames and Hudson, 1951, 1979.

Mayerson, Philip. "Battles of the Titans and the Rise of Zeus," "The Gods of Mount Olympus, Zeus." In *Classical Mythology in Literature, Art, and Music*. New York: Wiley, 1979.

Stassinopoulos, Arianna, and Roloff Beny, "Zeus." In *The Gods of Greece*. New York: Abrams, 1983, pp. 115–131.

Stein, Murray. "Hera: Bound and Unbound." *Spring* (1977) pp. 105–119.

NOTES

Epigraph: Edith Hamilton, *Mythology* (Boston: Little, Brown, 1942), p. 25.
Epigraph: Arianna Stassinopoulos and Roloff Beny. *The Gods of Greece* (New York: Abrams, 1983), p. 131.

1. Lee Iacocca with William Novak, *Iacocca: An Autobiography* (New York: Bantam Books, 1984), pp. 55–56.

CHAPTER 4: POSEIDON

SOURCES

Colman, Arthur, and Colman, Libby. *Earth Father/Sky Father*. Englewood Cliffs, NJ: Prentice-Hall, 1981.

Grant, Michael, and Hazel, John. *Gods and Mortals in Classical Mythology: A Dictionary*. New York: Dorset Press, 1979.

Graves, Robert. *The Greek Myths*. Vol. 1, "16. Poseidon's Nature and Deeds." Middlesex, England: Penguin Books, 1955.

Grimm Brothers. "Iron Hans." In *Sixty Fairy Tales of the Brothers Grimm*. Illustrated by Arthur Rackham, Translated by Mrs. Edgar Lucas. New York: Weathervane Books (Crown Publishers), 1979, pp. 319–325.

Mayerson, Philip. "Poseidon (Neptune)." In *Classical Mythology in Literature, Art, and Music*. New York: Wiley, 1971, pp. 94–105.

Shaffer, Peter. *Equus*. New York: Avon Books, 1975.

Stassinopoulos, Arianna, and Roloff Beny. "Poseidon." In *Gods of the Greeks*. New York: Abrams, 1983, pp. 42–51.

Walker, Barbara G. "Trident." *The Women's Encyclopedia of Myths and Secrets*. San Francisco: Harper & Row, 1983.

NOTES

Epigraph: Arianna Stassinopoulos and Roloff Beny. *Gods of the Greeks* (New York: Abrams, 1983), p. 42.

Epigraph: Homer, "Hymn to Poseidon," in *The Homeric Hymns*, trans. Charles Boer (Irving, TX: Spring Publications, 1979), p. 86.

1. Dylan Thomas, "Do Not Go Gentle into That Good Night," in *Deaths and Entrances*, 1946.

CHAPTER 2: HADES

SOURCES

Grant, Michael, and Hazel, John. *Gods and Mortals in Classical Mythology: A Dictionary*. New York: Dorset Press, 1979.

Graves, Robert. "The Gods of the Underworld," in *The Greek Myths*, Vol. 1 (Middlesex, England: Penguin Books, 1955), pp. 120–125.

Kerenyi, C. *Eleusis: Archetypal Image of Mother and Daughter*. Translated from the German by Ralph Manheim. New York: Schocken Books, 1977.

Mayerson, Philip. "The House of Hades: Gods of the Underworld," in *Classical Mythology in Literature, Art, and Music*. New York: Wiley, 1971, pp. 227–247.

Otto, Walter F. *Dionysus: Myth and Cult*. Translated and introduced by Robert B. Palmer. Bloomington: Indiana University Press, 1965.

Stassinopoulos, Arianna, and Roloff, Beny. "Hades." In *Gods of the Greeks*. New York: Abrams, 1983, pp. 187–189.

Walker, Barbara G. "Hel" and "Hell." In *The Woman's Encyclopedia of Myths and Secrets*. San Francisco: Harper & Row, 1983, pp. 380–390.

NOTES

Epigraph: Philip Mayerson, in *Classical Mythology in Literature, Art, and Music*. (New York: Wiley, 1971), p. 229.

Epigraph: Arianna Stassinpoulos and Roloff Beny, in *Gods of the Greeks* (New York: Abrams, 1983), p. 187.

1. Walter F. Otto, *Dionysus: Myth and Cult*, trans. and intro. Robert B. Palmer (Bloomington: Indiana University Press, 1965), p. 116.

CHAPTER 6: APOLLO

SOURCES

Fontenrose, Joseph. *Python: A Study of Delphic Myth and Its Origins*. Berkeley: University of California Press, 1980.

Grant, Michael, and Hazel, John. *Gods and Mortals in Classical Mythology: A Dictionary*. New York: Dorset Press, 1979.

Guthrie, W. K. C. *The Greeks and Their Gods*. Boston: Beacon Press, 1955.

Homer. "The Hymn to Pythian Apollo" and "The Hymn to Delian Apollo." In *The Homeric Hymns*. Translated by Charles Boer. Irving, TX: Spring Publications, 1979.

Kerenyi, Karl. *Apollo: The Wind, the Spirit, and the God*. Translated from the German by Jon Solomon. Dallas: Spring Publications, 1983.

Mayerson, Philip. *Classical Mythology in Literature, Art, and Music*. New York: Wiley, 1971.

Otto, Walter F. *The Homeric Gods: The Spiritual Significance of Greek Religion*. Translated by Moses Hadas. Great Britain: Thames & Hudson, 1979.

NOTES

Epigraph: W. K. C. Guthrie, *The Greeks and Their Gods* (Boston: Beacon Press, 1980), pp. 73, 183.

Epigraph: Walter F. Otto, *The Homeric Gods: The Spiritual Significance of Greek Religion*, Trans. Moses Hadas (Great Britain: Thames & Hudson, 1979), p. 78.

1. W. K. C. Guthrie, *The Greeks and Their Gods* (Boston: Beacon Press, 1980), p. 184.

2. Walter F. Otto, *The Homeric Gods: The Spiritual Significance of Greek Religion*, Trans. Moses Hadas (Great Britain: Thames & Hudson, 1979), p. 76.

3. Otto, p. 64.

4. Homer, "The Hymn to Delian Apollo," in *The Homeric Hymns*, trans. Charles Boer (Irving, TX: Spring Publications, 1979), p. 157.

5. Homer, p. 157.

6. Homer, p. 157.
7. Karl Kerenyi, *Apollo: The Wind, the Spirit, and the God,* trans. Jon Solomon (Dallas: Spring Publications, 1983), p. 41.
8. "A Pair for the Court," *Newsweek,* June 30, 1986.

CHAPTER 7: HERMES

SOURCES

Brown, Norman O. *Hermes the Thief: Evolution of a Myth.* New York: Vintage Books, Random House, 1969.
Grant, Michael, and Hazel, John. *Gods and Mortals in Classical Mythology: A Dictionary.* New York: Dorset Press, 1979.
Guthrie, W. K. C. "The Divine Family: Section 5; Hermes." In *The Greeks and Their Gods.* Boston: Beacon Press, 1955.
Hillman, James. "Notes on Opportunism." In James Hillman, ed., *Puer Papers.* Irving, TX: Spring Publications, 1979.
Hirshey, Gerri. "Sting Feels the Burn." *Rolling Stone,* September 1985, p. 32.
Homer. "The Hymn to Hermes." In *The Homeric Hymns,* translated by Charles Boer. 2nd ed., rev. Irving, TX: Spring Publications, 1979.
Jung, C. G. "Psychology and Alchemy," *CW,* vol. 12 (1968).
Jung, C. G. "On the Mythology of the Trickster Figure," *CW,* Vol. 9, part 2, (1968) pp. 225–272.
Kerenyi, C. "Maia, Hermes, Pan and the Nymphs." In *The Gods of the Greeks.* Great Britain: Thames & Hudson, 1979.
Kerenyi, Karl. *Hermes: Guide of Souls.* Zurich: Spring Publications, 1976.
Lopez-Pedraza, Rafael. *Hermes and His Children.* Zurich: Spring Publications, 1977.
Mayerson, Philip. "Hermes." In *Classical Mythology in Literature, Art, and Music.* New York: Wiley, 1971.
Needleman, Jacob. *The Way of the Physician.* San Francisco: Harper & Row, 1985.
Otto, Walter F. "Hermes." *The Homeric Gods: The Spiritual Significance of Greek Religion.* Trans. Moses Hadas. Great Britain: Thames & Hudson, 1979.
Peisch, Jeffrey. "Sting." *Record,* September 1985.
Smith, Betty. "The Wayfarer God." C. G. Jung Institute of Los Angeles, Lecture Series, 1981. 4 tapes.
Stassinopoulos, Arianna, and Roloff Beny. "Hermes." *The Gods of Greece.* New York: Abrams, 1983.
Stein, Murray. "World of Hermes, God of Significant Passage: Reflections on the Mid-Life Transition." C. G. Jung Institute of San Francisco, Public Events Lecture Series, February 28, 1981–March 1, 1981.
Von Franz, Marie Louise. *Puer Eternus.* Zurich: Spring Publications, 1970.
Walker, Barbara G. "Alchemy" and "Hermes." In *The Women's Encyclopedia of Myths and Secrets.* San Francisco: Harper & Row, 1983.

NOTES

Epigraph: Arianna Stassinopoulos and Beny Roloff, *The Gods of Greece* (New York: Abrams, 1983), p. 190.

Epigraph: Walter F. Otto, *The Homeric Gods: The Spiritual Significance of Greek Religion,* Trans. Moses Hadas (Great Britain: Thames & Hudson, 1979), p. 124.

1. C. G. Jung, "Psychology and Alchemy," *CW,* vol. 12, pp. 293–294.

2. Murray Stein. "The World of Hermes, God of Significant Passage: Reflections on the Mid-Life Transition," lecture at C.G. Jung Institute, San Francisco, February 28, 1981, to March 1, 1981. Tape.

3. Homer, "Hymn to Hermes," *The Homeric Hymns,* Trans. Charles Boer (Irving, TX: Spring Publications, 1979), p. 29.

4. "Hymn to Hermes," p. 45.

5. Adelaide M. Johnson, "Sanctions for Superego Lacunae of Adolescence," in *Searchlight on Delinquency: New Psychoanalytic Studies,* edited by K. R. Eissler (New York: International Universities Press, 1949), pp. 225–245.

6. Gerri Hirshey, "Sting Feels the Burn," *Rolling Stone,* September 1985, p. 32.

7. Jeffrey Peisch, "Sting," *Record,* September 1985, p. 31.

8. Rafael Lopez-Pedraza, *Hermes and His Children* (Zurich: Spring Publications, 1957).

CHAPTER 8: ARES

SOURCES

Grant, Michael, and Hazel, John. *Gods and Mortals in Classical Mythology.* New York: Dorset Press, 1979.

Hall, James. *Dictionary of Subjects and Symbols in Art.* New York: Harper & Row, 1974.

Hamilton, Edith. *Mythology.* Boston: Little, Brown, 1942.

Homer. "Hymn to Ares." *The Homeric Hymns.* Charles Boer Translation, 2nd ed., rev. Irving, TX: Spring Publications, 1979.

Kerenyi, C. *The Gods of the Greeks.* Translated by Norman Cameron. Great Britain: Thames & Hudson, 1979. (Originally published 1951.)

Meyerson, Philip. "Ares (Mars)." *Classical Mythology in Literature, Art, and Music.* New York: Wiley, 1971.

Miller, Alice. *For Your Own Good: Hidden Cruelty in Child-Rearing and the Roots of Violence.* Translated by Hildegarde and Hunter Hannum. New York: Farrar, Strauss and Giroux, 1983.

Miller, Alice. *Thou Shalt Not Be Aware: Society's Betrayal of the Child.* Translated by Hildegarde and Hunter Hannum. New York: New American Library, 1984.

Otto, Walter F. *The Homeric Gods: The Spiritual Significance of Greek Religion.* Translated by Moses Hadas. Great Britain: Thames & Hudson, 1979.

Perera, Sylvia Brinton. *The Scapegoat Complex.* Toronto: Inner City Books, 1986.

Stassinopoulos, Arianna, and Roloff Beny. "Ares." *The Gods of Greece*. New York: Abrams, 1983.

Tripp, Edward. *The Meridian Handbook of Classical Mythology*. Originally published as *Crowell's Handbook of Classical Mythology*. New York: New American Library, 1970.

NOTES

Epigraph: Arianna Stassinopoulos and Roloff Beny, *The Gods of Greece* (New York: Abrams, 1983), p. 170.

Epigraph: Philip Mayerson, *Classical Mythology in Literature, Art, and Music* (New York: Wiley, 1971), p. 181.

1. Walter F. Otto, *The Homeric Gods:* trans. Moses Hadas (Great Britain: Thames & Hudson, 1979), p. 47.

2. Homer, "Hymn to Ares," *The Homeric Hymns*, trans. Charles Boer (Irving, TX: Spring Publications, 1979), p. 60.

3. Associated Press, "Sean Penn Sentenced—60 Days in Jail," *San Francisco Chronicle*, June 24, 1987.

4. Homer, *The Iliad of Homer*, trans. and intro. Richmond Lattimore (Chicago: University of Chicago Press, 1951), Book 1, Lines 206–211, p. 64.

CHAPTER 9: HEPHAESTUS

SOURCES

Bolen, Jean Shinoda. "Aphrodite and Hephaestus." *Goddesses in Everywoman*. New York: Harper & Row, 1984, pp. 247–248.

Corliss, Richard. "Andrew Wyeth's Stunning Secret." *Time*, August 18, 1986.

Hillman, James. "Puer Wounds and Ulysses' Scar." In James Hillman, ed., *Puer Papers*. Irving, TX: Spring Publications, 1979.

Jung, C. G. "Confrontation with the Unconscious." In *Memories, Dreams, Reflections*. Recorded and edited by Aniela Jaffe; translated by Richard and Clara Winston. New York: Pantheon Books, 1961.

Kerenyi, C. "IV. 3. Aphrodite, Ares and Hephaistos," "VII. 3. Athene and Hephaistos," "IX. Hera, Ares and Hephaistos." *The Gods of the Greeks*. Great Britain: Thames & Hudson, 1979.

Mayerson, Philip. "Hephaestus." *Classical Mythology in Literature, Art, and Music*. New York: Wiley, 1971.

Slater, Philip. "Self-Emasculation: Hephaistos." *The Glory of Hera*. Boston: Beacon Press, 1968.

Stassinopoulos, Arianna, and Roloff Beny. "Hephaistos." In *The Gods of Greece*. New York: Abrams, 1983.

Stein, Murray. "Hephaistos: A Pattern of Introversion." *Spring 1973*. New York: Spring Publications, 1973.

Stein, Murray. "Hera: Bound and Unbound." *Spring 1977*. Zurich: Spring Publications, 1977.

Stein, Murray. "Hephaistos: A Pattern of Introversion" and "Postscript on Hephaistos." In James Hillman, ed., *Facing the Gods*. Irving, TX: Spring Publications, 1980.

NOTES

Epigraph: Arianna Stassinopoulos and Roloff Beny, *The Gods of Greece* (New York: Abrams, 1983), p. 175.

Epigraph: Murray Stein, "Hephaistos: A Pattern of Introversion," *Spring 1980* (Irving, TX: Spring Publications, 1980), p. 35.

1. James Hillman, "Puer Wounds and Ulysses Scar," in James Hillman, ed., *Puer Papers* (Irving, Texas: Spring Publications, 1979), pp. 101–102.

2. Walter F. Otto, *The Homeric Gods: The Spiritual Significance of the Greek Religion*, trans. Moses Hadas (Great Britain: Thames & Hudson, 1979), p. 130.

3. C. G. Jung, *Memories, Dreams, Reflections*, ed. Aniela Jaffe; trans. Richard and Clara Winston (New York: Pantheon Books, 1961), pp. 173–175.

4. Richard Corliss, "Andrew Wyeth's Stunning Secret," *Time*, August 18, 1986.

5. Corliss.

6. Philip Slater, "Self-Emasculation: Hephaistos," in *The Glory of Hera* (Boston: Beacon Press, 1968), p. 193.

CHAPTER 10: DIONYSUS

SOURCES

Colman, Arthur, and Colman, Libby. *Love and Ecstasy.* New York: Seabury Press, 1975.

Freedman, Samuel G. "Why Artists Pay the Wages of Creativity." *San Francisco Chronicle*, Datebook, December 1, 1985, pp. 27–29.

Keen, Sam. *The Passionate Life: Stages of Loving.* San Francisco: Harper & Row, 1983.

Kerenyi, C. "Dionysos and His Female Companions." *The Gods of the Greeks.* Translated by Norman Cameron. (Great Britain: Thames & Hudson, 1979. (Originally published 1951.)

Hillman, James. "Puer Wounds and Ulysses' Scar." In James Hillman, ed., *Puer Papers*. Irving, TX: Spring Publications, 1979. pp. 116–118.

Hillman, James, "Dionysus in Jung's Writings." *Spring 1972.* New York: Spring Publications, 1972.

Hillman, James, "Dionysos." In Hillman, James, ed., *Facing the Gods*. Irving, TX: Spring Publications, 1980.

Lukoff, David, and Everest, Howard C. "The Diagnosis of Mystical Experiences with Psychotic Features." *Journal of Transpersonal Psychology* 17 (1985): 2.

Mayerson, Philip. *Classical Mythology in Literature, Art, and Music.* New York: Wiley, 1983.

Moore, Tom. "Artemis and the Puer." In James Hillman, ed., *Puer Papers*. Irving, TX: Spring Publications, 1979.

Neumann, Erich. *The Origins and History of Consciousness.* Foreword by C. G. Jung; translated from the German by R. F. C. Hull. Bollingen Series XLII. Princeton, NJ: Princeton University Press, 1970.

Otto, Walter F. *Dionysus: Myth and Cult.* Translated and introduced by Robert
B. Palmer. Bloomington: Indiana University Press, 1965.

NOTES

Epigraph: Tom Moore, "Artemis and the Puer," in James Hillman, ed., *Puer
Papers* (Irving, TX: Spring Publications, 1979), p. 176.
Epigraph: Walter F. Otto, *Dionysus: Myth and Cult,* trans. and intro. Robert B.
Palmer (Bloomington: Indiana University Press, 1965), p. 49.
1. W. F. Otto, *Dionysus: Myth and Cult,* trans. and intro. Robert B. Palmer
(Bloomington: Indiana University Press, 1965), p. 65.
2. Philip Mayerson, *Classical Mythology in Literature, Music, and Art* (New York:
Wiley, 1983), p. 249.
3. Otto, p. 176.
4. Otto, p. 121.
5. Samuel G. Freedman, "Why Artists Pay the Wages of Creativity," *San Francisco Chronicle,* Datebook, December 1, 1985.
6. James Hillman, "Dionysus in Jung's Writings," *Spring 1972* (New York:
Spring Publications, 1972), p. 199.
7. "The Bill W.—Carl Jung Letters," *Revision* 10 (1987): 21. Originally published in the *Grapevine,* January 1963.
8. Erich Neumann, *The Origins and History of Consciousness* (Princeton, N.J.:
Princeton University Press, 1970), pp. 152–169.

CHAPTER 11: FINDING OUR MYTHS

SOURCES

Allison, Ralph B. "A New Treatment Approach for Multiple Personalities."
American Journal of Clinical Hypnosis 17 (1974): 15–32.
Allison, Ralph B. *Minds in Many Pieces.* New York: Rawson Wade, 1980.
Bolen, Jean Shinoda. "Hestia." In *Goddesses in Everywoman.* San Francisco: Har-
per & Row, 1984, pp. 107–138.
Damgaard, Jacqueline A. "The Inner Self Helper: Transcendent Life Within
Life?" *Noetic Sciences Review* (Winter 1987), pp. 24–28.
Jung, C. G. "Concerning Mandala Symbolism." CW, vol. 9, Part I, pp. 335–
384.

NOTES

1. Keith Thompson, "Myths as Souls of the World" (Book Review: *Inner
Reaches of Outer Space,* by Joseph Campbell), *Noetic Sciences Review* (Winter
1986), p. 24.

CHAPTER 12: THE MISSING GOD

SOURCES

Colman, Arthur, and Colman, Libby. *Earth Father/Sky Father: The Changing
Concept of Fathering.* Englewood Cliffs, N.J.: Prentice-Hall, 1981.

Eisler, Riane. *The Chalice and the Blade*. San Francisco: Harper & Row, 1987.

Gilligan, Carol. *In a Different Voice: Psychological Theory and Women's Development*. Cambridge, MA: Harvard University Press, 1982.

Gimbutas, Marija. *The Goddesses and Gods of Old Europe: Myths and Cult Images*. Berkeley: University of California Press, 1982.

Godavitarne, Pia M., ed. "Statement of Philosophy." *Woman of Power*, no. 8 (Winter 1988), p. 1.

Keyes, Jr., Ken. *The Hundredth Monkey*. Coos Bay, OR: Vision Books, 1982.

The Nag Hammadi Library. Translated by members of the Coptic Gnostic Library Project of the Institute for Antiquity and Christianity; James M. Robinson, editor. San Francisco: Harper & Row, 1978.

Pagels, Elaine. *The Gnostic Gospels*. New York: Random House, 1979.

Sheldrake, Rupert. *A New Science of Life: The Hypothesis of Formative Causation*. Los Angeles: Tarcher, 1981.

Sheldrake, Rupert. "Mind, Memory & Archetype: Morphic Resonance and the Collective Unconscious." *Psychological Perspectives* 18 (1987): 1.

Sheldrake, Rupert. "Society, Spirit & Ritual: Morphic Resonance and the Collective Unconscious." *Psychological Perspectives* 18 (1987): 2.

Stone, Merlin. *When God Was a Woman*. New York: Harcourt Brace Jovanovich, 1976.

NOTES

1. Arthur Colman and Libby Colman, *Earth Father/Sky Father* (Englewood Cliffs, NJ: Prentice-Hall, 1981), p. 31.
2. Hesiod, *Theogony*, trans. Richard Lattimore (Ann Arbor: University of Michigan Press, 1959), p. 177.
3. Pia M. Godavitarne, ed., "Statement of Philosophy," *Woman of Power*, no. 8 (Winter 1988), p. 1.
4. Rupert Sheldrake, "Mind, Memory and Archetype: Morphic Resonance and the Collective Unconscious," *Psychological Perspectives* 18 (1987): 25.
5. Eliot, T.S. *Four Quartets*. "Little Gidding" (lines 214–216). New York: Harcourt Brace Jovanovich, 1943.

Bibliography

This bibliography is divided into four sections: (1) Mythology; (2) Archetypal Psychology (Jungian Analytical Psychology); (3) Psychology of Men (other than Jungian); and (4) General Psychology, Theology, Religion (relevant to this book).

1. MYTHOLOGY

Brown, Norman O. *Hermes the Thief: Evolution of a Myth.* New York: Vintage Books, Random House, 1969.

Bullfinch's Mythology. Middlesex, England: Hamlyn, 1964.

Bullfinch's Mythology: The Greek and Roman Fables Illustrated. Compiled by Bryan Holme, with an Introduction by Joseph Campbell. New York: Viking Press, 1979.

Campbell, Joseph. *The Hero with a Thousand Faces.* 2nd ed. Bollingen Series 17. Princeton, NJ: Princeton University Press, 1968.

Fontenrose, Joseph. *Python: A Study of Delphic Myth and Its Origins.* Berkeley: University of California Press, 1980.

Gimbutas, Marija. *The Goddesses and Gods of Old Europe: 6500–3500, Myths and Cult Images.* Berkeley: University of California Press, 1982.

Grant, Michael, and Hazel, John. *Gods and Mortals in Classical Mythology: A Dictionary.* New York: Dorset Press, 1979.

Graves, Robert. *The Greek Myths.* 2 vols. New York: Penguin, 1979, 1982. (Originally published 1955.)

Guthrie, W. K. C. *The Greeks and Their Gods.* Boston: Beacon Press, 1950.

Hamilton, Edith. *Mythology.* Boston: Little, Brown, 1942.

Harrison, Jane Ellen. *Mythology.* New York: Harcourt Brace Jovanovich, 1963. (Originally published 1924.)

Hesiod. *Theogony.* Translated by Richard Lattimore. Ann Arbor: University of Michigan Press, 1959.

Hesiod. *Theogony.* Translated and introduced by Norman O. Brown. Indianapolis: Bobbs-Merrill, 1953.

Homer. *The Iliad of Homer.* Translated by Richard Lattimore. Chicago: University of Chicago Press, 1951.

Homer. *The Homeric Hymns.* Translated by Charles Boer. Irving, TX: Spring Publications, 1979.

Kerenyi, C. *The Heroes of the Greeks.* London: Thames & Hudson, 1959.

Kerenyi, C. *The Gods of the Greeks.* Translated by Norman Cameron. New York: Thames & Hudson, 1979. (Originally published 1951.)

Kerenyi, C. *Zeus and Hera: Archetypal Image of Father, Husband, and Wife.* Translated by Christopher Holme. Bollingen Series 65, vol 5. Princeton, NJ: Princeton University Press, 1975.

Kerenyi, Karl. *Apollo: The Wind, the Spirit and the God.* Translated by Jon Solomon. Dallas: Spring Publications, 1983.

Kerenyi, Karl. *Hermes: Guide of Souls.* Translated by Murray Stein. Zurich: Spring Publications, 1976.

Mayerson, Philip. *Classical Mythology in Literature, Music, and Art.* New York: Wiley, 1979.

Otto, Walter F. *Dionysus: Myth and Cult.* Translated and introduced by Robert B. Palmer. Bloomington: Indiana University Press, 1965.

Otto, Walter F. *The Homeric Gods.* New York: Thames & Hudson, 1979. (Originally published 1954.)

Stassinopoulos, Arianna (text), and Roloff Beny (photographs). *The Gods of Greece.* New York: Abrams, 1983.

Tripp, Edward. *The Meridian Handbook of Classical Mythology.* (Originally published as *Crowell's Handbook of Classical Mythology.*) New York: New American Library, 1970.

Walker, Barbara. *The Woman's Encyclopedia of Myths and Secrets.* San Franciso: Harper & Row, 1983.

Zimmerman, J. E. *Dictionary of Classical Mythology.* New York: Bantam Books, 1978. (Originally published 1964.)

2. ARCHETYPAL PSYCHOLOGY (JUNGIAN ANALYTICAL PSYCHOLOGY)

Bolen, Jean Shinoda. *Goddesses in Everywoman: A New Psychology of Women.* San Francisco: Harper & Row, 1984.

Colman, Arthur, and Colman, Libby. *Earth Father/Sky Father: The Changing Concept of Fathering.* New York: Spectrum Book, Prentice-Hall, 1981.

Henderson, Joseph L. "Archetype: Father." *International Encyclopedia of Psychiatry, Psychology, Psychoanalysis, and Neurology,* 1977.

Hillman, James. "Dionysos in Jung's Writings. In James Hillman, ed., *Facing the Gods.* Irving, TX: Spring Publications, 1980.

Hillman, James, ed. *Facing the Gods.* Irving, TX: Spring Publications, 1980.

Hillman, James, ed. *Fathers and Mothers: Five Papers on the Archetypal Background of Family Psychology.* New York: Spring Publications, 1973.

Hillman, James. "Puer Wounds and Ulysses' Scar." In James Hillman, ed., *Puer Papers.* Irving, TX: Spring Publications, 1979.

Hillman, James, ed. *Puer Papers.* Irving, TX: Spring Publications, 1979.

Johnson, Robert A. *He: Understanding Masculine Psychology.* New York: Harper & Row, 1977.

Jung, C. G. All references to Jung's *Collective Works* (abbreviated *CW*) are taken from *Collected Works of C. G. Jung,* edited by Sir Herbert Read, Michael Fordham, and Gerald Adler; translated by R. F. C. Hull; executive editor, William McGuire. Bollingen Series 20. Princeton, NJ: Princeton University Press.

Jung, C. G. "The Significance of the Father in the Destiny of the Individual." *CW,* vol. 4 (1970), pp. 301–323.

Jung, C. G. "Archetypes of the Collective Unconscious." *CW*, vol. 9, part 1 (1968), pp. 3–41.

Jung, C. G. "The Concept of the Collective Unconscious." *CW*, vol. 9, part 1 (1968), pp. 42–53.

Jung, C. G. "On the Psychology of the Trickster Figure." *CW*, vol. 9, part 1 (1968), pp. 255–272.

Jung, C. G. "Psychology and Alchemy." *CW*, vol. 12 (1968)

Jung, C. G. *Memories, Dreams, Reflections.* Recorded and edited by Aniela Jaffe, translated from the German by Richard and Clara Winston. New York: Pantheon Books, 1961.

Kerenyi, C. *Eleusis: Archetypal Image of Mother and Daughter.* Translated from the German by Ralph Manheim. New York: Schocken Books, 1977.

Kerenyi, C. "Zeus and Hera: Archetypal Image of Father, Husband, and Wife." Translated from the German by Christopher Holme. Bollingen Series LXV, vol. 5: *Archetypal Images in Greek Religion.* Princeton, NJ: Princeton University Press, 1975.

Lopez-Pedraza, Rafael. *Hermes and His Children.* Zurich: Spring Publications, 1977.

Monick, Eugene. *Phallos: Sacred Image of the Masculine.* Toronto: Inner City Books, 1987.

Moore, Tom. "Artemis and the Puer." In James Hillman, ed. *Puer Papers.* Irving, TX: Spring Publications, 1979.

Neumann, Erich. *The Origins and History of Consciousness.* Bollingen Series XLII. New York: Pantheon, 1954. (Originally published 1949.)

Perera, Sylvia Brinton. *The Scapegoat Complex.* Toronto: Inner City Books, 1986.

Samuels, Andrew, ed. *The Father: Contemporary Jungian Perspectives.* New York: New York University Press, 1985.

Sheldrake, Rupert. "Mind, Memory and Archetype: Morphic Resonance and the Collective Unconscious." *Psychological Perspectives* Vol 18: No. 1 (1987) pp. 9–25.

Sheldrake, Rupert. "Society, Spirit & Ritual: Morphic Resonance and the Collective Unconscious." *Psychological Perspectives* Vol. 18: No 2. (1987): pp. 320–331.

Stein, Murray. "Hephaistos: A Pattern of Introversion." In James Hillman, ed., *Facing the Gods.* Irving, TX: Spring Publications, 1980.

Stein, Murray. "Hera: Bound and Unbound." In *Spring 1977.* Zurich: Spring Publications, 1977, pp. 105–119.

Stein, Murray *In Midlife: A Jungian Perspective.* Dallas: Spring Publications, 1983.

Von Franz, Marie Louise. *Puer Eternus.* Zurich: Spring Publications, 1970.

3. PSYCHOLOGY OF MEN (OTHER THAN JUNGIAN)

Freud, Sigmund. The Standard Edition of the Complete Psychological Works. Translated from the German under the editorship of James Strachey.

Vol. 3: *Early Psycho-Analytic Publications* (1961). Vol. 17: *An Infantile Neurosis and Other Works* (1955).

Levinson, Daniel. *The Seasons of a Man's Life.* New York: Ballantine Books, 1978.

Maccoby, Michael. *The Gamesman: The New Corporate Leaders.* New York: Simon & Schuster, 1976.

McGill, Michael E. *The McGill Report on Male Intimacy.* New York: Harper & Row, Perennial Library, 1986.

Tiger, Lionel. *Men in Groups.* New York: Vintage Books, Random House, 1970.

Vaillant, George E. *Adaptation to Life.* Boston: Little, Brown, 1977.

Whyte, Jr., William H. *The Organization Man.* Garden City, NJ: Doubleday Anchor Books, 1957.

4. RELEVANT GENERAL PSYCHOLOGY, THEOLOGY, RELIGION

Dinnerstein, Dorothy. *The Mermaid and the Minotaur: Sexual Arrangements and Human Malaise.* New York: Harper Colophon Books, 1977.

Eisler, Riane. *The Chalice and the Blade.* San Francisco: Harper & Row, 1987.

Gilligan, Carol. *In a Different Voice: Psychological Theory and Women's Development.* Cambridge, MA: Harvard University Press, 1982.

The Holy Bible, Revised Standard Version (RSV). New York: Nelson, 1953.

Keen, Sam. *The Passionate Life: Stages of Loving.* San Francisco: Harper & Row, 1983.

Lukoff, David, and Everest, Howard C. "The Diagnosis of Mystical Experiences with Psychotic Features." *Journal of Transpersonal Psychology* 17, No. 2 (1985).

Masson, Jeffrey Moussaieff. *The Assault on Truth: Freud's Suppression of the Seduction Theory.* New York: Farrar, Straus & Giroux, 1984.

May, Rollo. *Courage to Create.* New York: Bantam Books, 1975.

Miller, Alice. *Prisoners of Childhood: The Drama of the Gifted Child and the Search for the True Self.* Translated by Ruth Ward. New York: Basic Books, 1981.

Miller, Alice. *For Your Own Good: Hidden Cruelty in Child-Rearing and the Roots of Violence.* Translated by Hildegarde and Hunter Hannum. New York: Farrar, Straus & Giroux, 1983.

Miller, Alice. *Thou Shalt Not Be Aware: Society's Betrayal of the Child.* Translated by Hildegarde and Hunter Hannum. New York: New American Library, 1986.

Miller, Jean Baker. "Domination-Subordination" In *Toward a New Psychology of Women.* Boston: Beacon Press, 1976, pp. 3–12.

The Nag Hammadi Library. Edited by James Robinson. Translated by members of the Coptic Gnostic Library Project of the Institute for Antiquity and Christianity. San Francisco: Harper & Row, 1978.

Needleman, Jacob. *The Way of the Physician.* San Francisco: Harper & Row, 1985.

Pagels, Elaine. *The Gnostic Gospels.* New York: Random House, 1979.

Sheldrake, Rupert. *A New Science of Life: The Hypothesis of Formative Causation.* Los Angeles: Tarcher, 1981.

Slater, Philip. *The Glory of Hera.* Boston: Beacon Press, 1968.

Stone, Merlin. *When God Was a Woman.* New York: Harcourt Brace Jovanovich, 1976.

Index